Design
Anthropological
Futures

Design Anthropological Futures

Edited by
Rachel Charlotte Smith, Kasper Tang Vangkilde,
Mette Gislev Kjærsgaard, Ton Otto, Joachim
Halse and Thomas Binder

Bloomsbury Academic
An imprint of Bloomsbury Publishing Plc

B L O O M S B U R Y
LONDON · OXFORD · NEW YORK · NEW DELHI · SYDNEY

Bloomsbury Academic

An imprint of Bloomsbury Publishing Plc

50 Bedford Square	1385 Broadway
London	New York
WC1B 3DP	NY 10018
UK	USA

www.bloomsbury.com

BLOOMSBURY and the Diana logo are trademarks of Bloomsbury Publishing Plc

First published 2016

British Library Cataloguing-in-Publication Data
A catalogue record for this book is available from the British Library.

ISBN:	HB:	978-1-4742-8062-4
	PB:	978-1-4742-8060-0
	ePDF:	978-1-4742-8064-8
	ePub:	978-1-4742-8063-1

Library of Congress Cataloging-in-Publication Data
Names: Smith, Rachel Charlotte, editor.
Title: Design anthropological futures : exploring emergence, intervention and formation / edited by Rachel Charlotte Smith, Ton Otto, Kasper Tang Vangkilde, Joachim Halse, Thomas Binder, and Mette Gislev Kjaersgaard.
Description: London ; New York : Bloomsbury Academic, an imprint of Bloomsbury Publishing, Plc, [2016] | Includes index.
Identifiers: LCCN 2016004386| ISBN 9781474280600 (pbk.) | ISBN 9781474280624 (hardback) | ISBN 9781474280648 (ePDF) | ISBN 9781474280631 (ePub)
Subjects: LCSH: Design--Anthropological aspects.
Classification: LCC NK1520 .D4544 2016 | DDC 745.4--dc23 LC record available at https://lccn.loc.gov/2016004386

Cover design by Romain Gorisse, Valeria Granillo, Sofie Mietke-Rasmussen, Sarah Nielsen and Stine Nygaard

Typeset by Fakenham Prepress Solutions, Fakenham, Norfolk NR21 8NN
Printed and bound in India

Contents

List of Figures

Contributors

Zoy Anastassakis is Associate Professor at the State University of Rio de Janeiro in the Superior School of Industrial Design (Esdi/UERJ), where she coordinates the Design and Anthropology Lab (LaDA). Anastassakis's research explores possible combinations between modes of knowledge production in design and anthropology and the implications for dealing with public issues.

Mike Anusas is a teaching fellow in the Department of Design, Manufacture and Engineering Management at the University of Strathclyde and a research associate in the 'Knowing From the Inside' project in the Department of Anthropology at the University of Aberdeen. His work focuses on practices of design and making and how these influence perceptions of matter, energy and ecology.

Thomas Binder is Professor of Co-Design at the Royal Danish Academy of Fine Arts, School of Design. He is co-director of the research centre, CODE, engaging open design collaborations and participatory design in the context of design anthropology, interaction design and social innovation. His research includes contributions to methods and tools for experimental design research and open innovation processes. Binder is co-founder of the international Research Network for Design Anthropology.

Laurens Boer is Assistant Professor in Interaction Design at the IT University of Copenhagen. He studied industrial design at the Eindhoven University of Technology and holds a PhD from the University of Southern Denmark, where he constructed 'provotypes' as platforms for situated critical reflection in participatory projects. Currently he explores critical and speculative approaches to designing computational materials.

Laura Boffi is an interaction and service designer. She focuses on how people create their own culture around the context they inhabit, often by appropriating in a spontaneous way the material and technology artefacts that surround them. She holds an MA in design from Design Academy Eindhoven and is a graduate of the Interaction Design Programme at CIID, the Copenhagen Institute of Interaction Design.

Anaïs Bloch is a designer, design lecturer, and researcher with experience leading design projects and socio-cultural research. She works as a designer and anthropologist in the heritage sector and the education sector. She holds a degree in product design at the University of Art and Design ECAL in Lausanne, and an MA in anthropology from University College London. Her current work focuses on design thinking, social practices and digital technologies.

Isabel Bredenbröker is a PhD candidate at the Institute for European Ethnology, Humboldt University Berlin. She holds an MA in comparative literature from Freie Universität Berlin and an MA in material and visual culture from University College London. Her research focuses on aspects of material culture in relation to economic exchange, value creation, housing and design. Isabel works in the contemporary art field.

Melissa L. Caldwell is Professor of Anthropology at the University of California, Santa Cruz, and Editor of *Gastronomica*: *The Journal of Critical Food Studies.* Her ethnographic research in Russia, publications and teaching have focused on the everyday politics and practices of material culture and social justice in state socialist and post-socialist societies.

Nazli Cila is a design researcher at the Applied University of Amsterdam in the School of Digital Media and Creative Industries. She holds a PhD in industrial design from Delft University of Technology. Her research combines data-driven design and design anthropology, with the goal of understanding people better and offering design solutions for wellbeing through the use of sensor data, participatory sensing, and citizen science.

Brendon Clark is Studio Director and Senior Researcher at Interactive Institute Swedish ICT and Adjunct Senior Lecturer of Design Anthropology at Umeå Institute of Design. His research focuses on knowledge (re)production practices in technology and service design processes in the public and private sectors. He co-led the DAIM project (Design Anthropological Innovation Model) and is developing a contextualized language-learning agenda, Language as Participation.

Alison J. Clarke, Professor of Design History and Theory and Director of the Victor J. Papanek Foundation at the University of Applied Arts Vienna, considers the intersections of design and social anthropology. Her publications include *Design Anthropology*: *Object Culture in the 21st Century* and a forthcoming MIT book project on the historical origins of design anthropology in 1960s/70s design activism.

Carl DiSalvo is Associate Professor in the School of Literature, Media, and Communication at the Georgia Institute of Technology, where he directs the Public

Design Workshop. He is the author of *Adversarial Design* (2012). DiSalvo's experimental design work has been exhibited and supported by the ZKM, Science Gallery Dublin, and the Walker Arts Center.

Adam Drazin is Lecturer in the Department of Anthropology at University College London, where he coordinates the MA in Materials, Anthropology and Design. His work focuses on two key areas: the material culture of professional design work, and consumption and care in the Romanian home. He is co-editor, with Susanne Küchler, of *The Social Life of Materials*: *Studies in Materials and Society* (2015).

Elisa Giaccardi is Professor and Chair of Interactive Media Design at Delft University of Technology, where she leads the Connected Everyday Lab. From her pioneering work in meta-design environments, to participatory technology and Internet of Things infrastructuring, her research reflects an ongoing concern with design as a shared process of cultivation and management of opportunity spaces.

Joachim Halse is Associate Professor at the Royal Danish Academy of Fine Arts, directing the MA programme in Co-Design and co-director of the research centre CODE. His work enables new forms of civic participation in future-making. Halse's main contributions to design anthropology include his PhD thesis (2008), the book *Rehearsing the Future* (2010), and the co-founding of the international Research Network for Design Anthropology.

Rachel Harkness is Research Fellow in the Department of Anthropology at the University of Aberdeen, Scotland. She is part of 'Knowing From the Inside', a project exploring the shared territories of art, anthropology, architecture and design. Harkness' work with people involved in eco-construction projects in the US and the UK centres upon issues of building, environment, materials and politics.

Mette Gislev Kjærsgaard is Associate Professor of Design Anthropology at the University of Southern Denmark. She has worked with design anthropology in industrial and academic contexts for more than fifteen years. Her research focuses on relations between anthropology and design at the intersection between the social and the material, production and use. She is co-founder of the international Research Network for Design Anthropology.

Robert Knowles is an artist, anthropologist and engineering risk management professional. As an artist he has exhibited and participated in projects in London, New York, Beijing, Dhaka, Montreal and Milan with the collaborative group Knowles Eddy Knowles. His anthropological work has focused on the 'risk imagination' of engineers as they collectively come to grips with complex infrastructural installations.

Tau Ulv Lenskjold is a postdoc at the University of Southern Denmark, Department of Design and Communication, and holds a PhD in interaction design. His research follows two avenues: the first investigating how speculative design practices engage with political and societal issues, the second concerning a post–anthropocentric rearticulation of design by means of experimental and interventionist modes of investigation.

Kristina Lindström is a postdoc at Umeå Institute of Design, Umeå University. With Åsa Ståhl she conducted a collaborative, practice-based PhD across inter-action design and media and communication studies on how hands-on making can facilitate collaborative co-articulations of emergent issues of living with mundane technologies. Her current research deals with public engagement, with a focus on hybrid matters.

George E. Marcus is Chancellor's Professor of Anthropology and founding director of the Center for Ethnography, both at University of California, Irvine. His work centres on the role of collaborations in transforming classic ethnographic research, the influence of design thinking and methods in the production of experiments alongside fieldwork, and the invention of alternative forms of analytic–descriptive 'results' of research.

Ramia Mazé is Professor of New Frontiers in Design at Aalto University, Finland. She specializes in critical and participatory approaches to design. Previously Mazé worked in Sweden at Konstfack College of Arts Crafts and Design, at KTH Royal Institute of Technology, at Designfakulteten, and at the Interactive Institute. A designer by training, she has a PhD in interaction design.

Sissel Olander is a postdoc at the Royal Danish Academy's School of Design. She holds a PhD in co-design and design anthropology. Her research explores partici-patory processes as experimental forms of knowing and making that tie together the empirical with the speculative. Currently, Olander works with Copenhagen libraries to explore everyday prototypical practices, representational procedures and larger societal issues.

Ton Otto is Head of the Ethnographic Collections at Moesgaard Museum, Aarhus, and Professor of Anthropology at Aarhus University, Denmark, and at James Cook University, Australia. Based on long-term ethnographic field research in Papua New Guinea he has published widely on issues of social and cultural change and the epistemology and methodology of ethnographic research, including visual, museum and design anthropology. Otto is co-founder of the international Research Network for Design Anthropology.

Morten Hulvej Rod is Associate Professor and Research Programme Director at the National Institute of Public Health, University of Southern Denmark. His research is located at the intersection between public health and anthropology. He has conducted fieldwork with public-sector professionals and has published on organizational, ethical and political issues related to public health policies and interventions.

Rachel Charlotte Smith is Assistant Professor of Design Anthropology at the Centre for Participatory Information Technology (PIT), Aarhus University. Her research focuses on relations between culture, design and technology, specifically on social change through emerging technologies and participatory design. Smith is co-founder of the international Research Network for Design Anthropology and co-editor of *Design Anthropology*: *Theory and Practice* (2013).

Chris Speed is Chair of Design Informatics at the University of Edinburgh, where his research focuses upon the network society, digital art and technology, and the Internet of Things. He is co-director of the Design Informatics Research Centre, which is home to researchers working across the fields of interaction design, temporal design, anthropology, software engineering and cryptocurrencies.

Åsa Ståhl is a postdoc in design at Umeå Institute of Design, Umeå University. She explores hybrid matters in public engagement events, building on her work with Kristina Lindström in their joint, practice-led PhD across interaction design and media and communication studies on making in relation to collaborative co-articulations of emergent issues of living with mundane technologies.

Barbara Szaniecki is Associate Professor at the State University of Rio de Janeiro, Superior School of Industrial Design (Esdi/UERJ), and researcher at Design and Anthropology Lab (LaDA). Based on experience in graphic design and micro activism from Universidade Nômade, her research emphasizes the relationship between visual expression and socio-political concepts, as well as critical creative practices.

Kasper Tang Vangkilde is Associate Professor of Anthropology at Aarhus University. His research interests are within business, organizational and design anthropology, with particular emphasis on processes of creativity, branding, management and organization. He is coordinator of the MA programme 'Innovation, Organization and Work' in Anthropology at Aarhus University and a co-founder of the international Research Network for Design Anthropology.

Acknowledgements

Seen from one perspective, this book is the material culmination of the international Research Network for Design Anthropology, generously funded over a two-year period by the Danish Council for Independent Research (grant number 1319-0017). Established in collaboration between the Royal Danish Academy of Fine Arts, Aarhus University and the University of Southern Denmark, the network objective has been to gather researchers from Denmark and internationally to identify potentials and challenges in the field of design anthropology. The network has explored important emerging modes of knowledge production and engagement at the intersection between design and anthropology, yet with constructive implications for both disciplines. To this end we convened three open seminars, focusing on Ethnographies of the Possible, Interventionist Speculation, and Collaborative Formation of Issues, as well as a closing conference on Design Anthropological Futures, to which we have met an overwhelming interest from around the world. If nothing else, this testifies to the growing interest in, and significance of, design anthropology as a distinct field of research and practice.

In this book we present sixteen chapters which constitute a selection of carefully developed contributions from the seminars and the conference. As editors, we would have liked to include all the papers and contributions – more than one hundred contributions – as we were thrilled by the perspectives and engagements that they represent. We are deeply grateful to each and every participant for their contribution and support and, not least, for the exceptionally good atmosphere at these events. In addition, we wish to thank the Danish Design Centre for hosting the opening conference reception, Brendon Clark, Sara Reinholtz and Nicholas Torretta of the Interactive Institute Swedish ICT for curating a number of interactive exhibitions as part of the conference, Moesgaard Museum for hosting one of the seminars, and the student volunteers and administrative personnel for assisting us whenever needed. In preparing this book, we have benefited from the assistance of Marie-Louise Christensen, who has done an excellent job in formatting the manuscript. Most of all, we sincerely thank each of the authors included in this book, without whose dedicated efforts and collaborative engagement the ambitions for this book could not have been realized. In this sense, the network may surely be said to have come to fruition in this book.

Yet from another perspective, nothing could be wider of the mark than to see this book as an end point. As will be clear in the chapters that follow, it is a key point that while a designed thing – such as, for instance, a book on design anthropology – may often pretend to stage a certain closure, representing a product at the end of a process, it is in fact always in the making, continuously about to disclose itself for what it is. That goes for this book as well. It is our intention and our wish that this book will essentially open up rather than close down our conceptions and explorations of design anthropological futures, thus initiating new thoughts, questions and encounters to be pursued in the years to come. While the book explores futures from a design anthropological perspective, it also creates new platforms and opportunities for the futures of design anthropology itself. This is the spirit in which we hope this book will be read and discussed in the near and emerging future …

New Year 2016
Rachel Charlotte Smith, Kasper Tang Vangkilde, Mette Gislev Kjærsgaard, Ton Otto, Joachim Halse and Thomas Binder

1 Introduction: Design Anthropological Futures

METTE GISLEV KJÆRSGAARD, JOACHIM HALSE,
RACHEL CHARLOTTE SMITH, KASPER TANG VANGKILDE,
THOMAS BINDER AND TON OTTO

The future is here. Or so it has often been proclaimed by futurologists, scientists and engineers, as the fruits of science labs and cutting-edge technological gadgets are showcased, promising to make our lives more productive and more enjoyable. The public facade of design shows grand visions of future possibilities, yet every imperfect Now is also the concrete instantiation of what was once a vision of a bright future. Envisioned futures, as Bell and Dourish (2007) remind us, tend to differ radically from how they eventually unfold in the situatedness of people's lives. The future is not an empty space awaiting projected visions from an incomplete present; neither is it a predefined destination that we can simply foresee and arrive at in due time (Yelavich and Adams 2014; Mazé, this volume). Rather than seeing the future as a separate space or time, design anthropologists in this book engage with the future as a *multiplicity* of ideas, critiques and potentialities that are embedded in the narratives, objects and practices of our daily lives. In this sense, multiple, often conflicting, futures are *always already here* as part of a continuously unfolding present and past.

Design Anthropological Futures explores futures and future-making from a design anthropological perspective. Here futures are not understood as striking visions created and implemented by scientists or designers, but rather as collaborative explorations of situated possibilities, formations and actions at the intersection of design and everyday life. The term *futures* relates both to the theoretical and practical engagement of design anthropology with futures and future-making as a subject – futures *in* design anthropology – and to the exploration of possible future directions for the discipline itself through such engagements – futures *of* design anthropology. Through various design anthropological investigations at specific sites – from care homes to corporate organizations, eco-homes to museums, Rio de Janeiro to Italy – this book critically addresses a number of dominant perspectives on, and approaches to, futures, including implied assumptions of *singularity*, *linearity*, *locality* and *novelty*. In the following we briefly elaborate on these themes and propose alternative perspectives for a design anthropological approach to futures.

First, 'The future' is often referred to in the singular, using the definite article to imply that there is only one version. Assuming eventual *singularity* of 'the future', futurologists, for example, tend to look at patterns of historical continuation and change, seeking to determine the probability of distinct future events. Although the established likelihood of a particular future does not rule out the realization of alternatives, it does foreground and authorize one dominant version of the future over alternative, subaltern ones (Mazé, this volume; Drazin, this volume). This idea of a singular future has political implications. As pointed out by Watts, 'telling stories of the future is always a social, material, and political practice. It always has effects; it is always non-innocent' (2008: 188). 'The future' is not only socio-politically positioned and negotiated, it is also culturally diverse and geographically dispersed (Appadurai 2013). Acknowledging that there is no single, neutral and shared future for all, contributors to this book discuss 'futures', in the plural form, as *multiple* and *heterogeneous* versions brought within experiential reach and shaped through uncertainty, experimentation, collaboration and contestation at specific sites of design anthropological engagement. Their concern is with the situated making of particular futures at specific sites, and how they might constitute possible alternatives to dominant perspectives on 'the future'.

Second, particular perception of time, as being linearly structured in past, present and future, permeates dominant approaches to 'the future'. Teleological ideas of the future as progress, for example, presenting 'the future' as an outcome that follows sequentially from past and present, is underpinned by such ideas of *linearity*. Seeing linearity as a particular, historical and cultural approach to time, futures and future-making (Grosz 1999; Jameson 2005; Mazé, this volume), the approaches presented in this book take other points of departure. Some focus on *emergence* and the *mutual constitution* of past, present and future, through practices of design and everyday life. Others engage with futures as imaginary 'others' outside the ordinary and the contemporary – what Rabinow refers to as 'the untimely' (Faubion, Marcus and Rabinow 2008) – from where we might question the taken-for-granted, and speculate about alternatives (Mazé, this volume). Foucault's *History of the Present*, (1995) showed how analyses of the past may be a powerful means of critical engagement with the present. With *Marking Time: On the Anthropology of the Contemporary*, Rabinow (2007) made a similar, but complementary move, by extending the analytical gaze to encompass the near future, still with the aim of critical engagement with the present. Such non-linear understandings of time and causality generally render the present contingent, and imply that things could be different. In this light, the relationship between the here-and-now and the there-and-then is constantly played out and reproduced through practice (Halse 2008: 22). With this book we seek to continue the development of conceptual and practical tools for inquiry into contemporary phenomena that are emergent and under-determined, and where pasts, presents and futures are closely linked and mutually constituted. One way of doing this is to engage in design anthropological speculations about how things could *actually* – not just in principle – be different.

Third, questions of *locality* and the politics of claiming a privileged space for inventing the future are critically addressed. Entrepreneurial startups, corporate innovation labs, even whole areas such as Silicon Valley are often seen as privileged centres of innovation; similarly, science, engineering and design labs are described as privileged spaces for inventing 'the new'. From an anthropological perspective, Lucy Suchman (2011) has critically questioned this localized optimism and hubris associated with design, arguing instead for the acknowledgement of design as just one among many figures and practices of transformation. From a design anthropological perspective, future-making is not the exclusive territory of the privileged few, but *dispersed* and *circulated* as a part of the social (re)production of daily life (Ehn, Nilsson and Topgaard 2014; Ingold 2012; Simon 1996). As science-fiction writer William Gibson once said of the inequalities of access to advanced technologies, 'the future is already here – it's just not very evenly distributed' (Gibson 1999). The approaches presented in this volume are acutely attuned to political issues, socio-economic differences and their effects on future-making practices in *situated contexts*. Challenging political, methodological and epistemological conventions, they relocate capacities for innovation and creativity among ordinary people in their everyday settings – even among animals and among things – in order to explore, practically and theoretically, how futures *are*, or *could be*, conceived and made.

Finally, even the basic assumption of *novelty* is in question in design anthropological approaches to futures. From science and technology studies, we learn that every new invention has its genealogy; it is composed of something more or less old (Pickering 1995), and made in ongoing everyday practices and places (Watts 2008: 187). Anthropologists also critically address ideas of novelty, arguing instead for dynamic and creative processes of social and cultural reproduction (Ingold 2012; Liep 2001). Ingold and Hallam (2008), for example, showed how the perception of 'the new' should not simply be taken for granted, but is underlain by a specific distribution and attribution of creative agency, along with a particular linear perception of the passage of time. Likewise, there is nothing entirely new in the design anthropological accounts in this book, only series of *continuous transformations* and reconfigurations, grounded in extended forms of the here-and-now. Yet from time to time we find ourselves in real-world encounters filled with the sense that everything has just changed, moments so laden with possibility or threat that afterwards nothing seems to be the same (e.g. see Binder, this volume; Rabinow et al. 2008).

Taken together, these tensions and perspectives fuel this volume, as design anthropologists engage critically, collaboratively and materially with futures from a position between the speculative and the mundane, between design and everyday life, between pasts, presents and futures. Building on previous developments in design anthropology (Clarke 2011; Gunn and Donovan 2012; Gunn, Otto and Smith 2013; Milev 2013; Smith and Kjærsgaard 2015), *Design Anthropological Futures* moves beyond disciplinary boundaries, to explore design anthropology as a fundamentally transdisciplinary field. In this effort, the contributors do not simply combine, but rework established methods and theories of design and anthropology, allowing new approaches and methodological entanglements to come into view. In some cases, historicity becomes a key to reconfiguring futuring, the everyday serves as a lab for experimentation, intervention becomes a path of speculative inquiry, and the environment emerges as a philosophical agent. In other cases, cultural imaginaries are challenged by fictions and prototypes, design objects are used to enter conversation *dispositifs*, and non-humans actively raise new social questions.

Together, the chapters provide rich empirical cases and theoretical reflections on design anthropological practices of future-making. In particular, they advance the use of transdisciplinary approaches and concepts while exploring the special relation between theory and practice that characterizes the distinct style of knowing in design anthropology (Otto and Smith 2013). Bringing together young experimental designers and anthropologists, and leading theoreticians engaged between the fields of design and anthropology, the book highlights four key themes that articulate emerging futures for design anthropology as a distinct transdisciplinary field of research. These themes structure the four major sections of the book: *Ethnographies of the Possible; Interventionist Speculations; Collaborative Formation of Issues;* and *Engaging Things*.

Ethnographies of the Possible

An often-mentioned difference between design and anthropology is their respective temporal orientations (Hunt 2011; Otto and Smith 2013). Whereas design, as the effort to create new things and solutions, is by definition concerned with the future, anthropology has traditionally been concerned with the analysis of past and present realities. In design anthropology, however, an orientation towards future social transformation is central to shaping the field. This raises epistemological and methodological concerns about how we conceive of what *is*, or *might be*, possible, and how we approach and handle the inherent complexities of emergent futures. What might an ethnography of the possible look like?

As they explore the possible, design anthropologists address differing temporalities, materialities and politics of future-making and their inherent relations to pasts and presents. According to Mead (2002 [1932]), all existence is situated in the present, which is always in a state of emergence. In the act of giving shape to the future, 'we evoke a past that makes this future possible' (Otto and Smith 2013: 17). This does not leave the future open to singular or arbitrary projections, but emphasizes the temporal entanglement of times and spaces, on the basis of which we may imagine and create possible futures. As Ramia Mazé (Chapter 3, this volume) argues, the future is never empty, but 'will be occupied by built environments, structures, policies and lifestyles, which we daily (re)produce by habit or with intent in design'. When we explore 'how things might be different' (Anusas and Harkness, this volume; Mazé, this volume), we thus engage in different ontologies and politics both *in* the present and *of* the possible.

A focus on 'ethnographies of the possible' draws attention to the peculiar and transformative spaces entangled in particular pasts, presents and futures – spaces that are highly contested in practice, yet relatively unexplored in theoretical term. (Smith and Otto, this volume; Mazé, this volume; Halse 2013; Kjærsgaard 2011). Design anthropologists engage in reflective and critical *positioning* within these spaces, in order to challenge assumptions and elicit alternative opportunities for the future. Their explorations of 'the possible' move beyond linear processes of artefact design and planning, towards more imaginative and speculative processes of co-producing knowledge with diverse stakeholders. Some core questions addressed in this section are: what characterizes the practices and spaces of the possible? How do the processes through which imaginative practices are conceived and materialized unfold? And what are the epistemological and methodological implications of conducting ethnography in a partly fictional space that resists full articulation?

A design anthropological approach has consequences for the ways in which knowledge is produced so as to open up the space of the possible. For anthropologists, this involves defining and inventing the ethnographic field, as well as acting situationally to co-produce various cultural agendas for the future that are not conventionally a part of anthropological research. This raises central epistemological questions concerning the nature and creation of such transformative knowledge. Rachel Charlotte Smith and Ton Otto (Chapter 2, this volume) work towards maturing a grounded theoretical approach to scaffolding possible futures. Focusing on *emergence* and *intervention* as central concepts and orientations for design anthropology, they argue that these concepts may be seen as complementary in a dialectical movement of exploration and knowledge production. Using an interactive exhibition as a research experiment, the authors demonstrate how emerging digital cultures were used as a basis for experimentation, first through a collaborative design process, and subsequently in an exhibition space involving public audiences. Viewing such processes as transformative sites of research and design may allow for the co-creation of ethnographies of the possible in various domains, such as digital cultural heritage or energy consumption (Mazé, this volume).

A design anthropological approach may be used to rethink design in terms of time and futures. Reflecting upon her own design research projects on the everyday use of energy, Ramia Mazé (Chapter 3, this volume) discusses how futurity may take on different representational expressions (forms) and embody different socio-economic models (politics). Mazé uses 'concept', 'critical' and 'persuasive' design practices as lenses for examining, more critically, the forms and the politics of design futures/ fictions through interventions in the field. Through such examples it is clear how discussions of ethnographies of the possible are central not only to rethinking the forms and politics of the future, but to critical consideration of 'ontological politics' in processes of preferring and enacting one reality over another (Law 2004).

Approaching the future from an extended temporal perspective may help us to conceive of the possible in terms of emergent cultural forms that encompass multiple perspectives on the present. Mike Anusas and Rachel Harkness (Chapter 4, this volume) describe different *presents in the making,* in and through which various

ime, materials and ecology are reflected in processes of design and
idering two cases, one from a UK design studio and another involving
elf-built eco-homes in the United States, the authors demonstrate how
esses of making reveal differing perceptions of time: what they call
close-presents and *far-reaching presents*. Such 'presents in the making' are constitutive of different types of sociality of making. The authors argue that they comprise
perceptions of time and engagement with materials that may be used in forging a
more socially aware and ecologically conscious approach to design anthropology.

Examining the historical dimension of the interrelatedness of design and anthropology, Alison J. Clarke (Chapter 5, this volume) demonstrates how an interest in
the space of the possible emerged as early as the late 1960s and early 1970s in
response to growing criticism of design and design research. In this period, the shift
from historical rationalism and industrial productivity (Mendini 2013) to embracing
anthropological discourses of social, contextual and political matters opened up
new ways of imagining a transitional future. Unlike the industrial, user-centred focus
of ethnography in design, these were activist reactions to global politics (including
the Vietnam war) actively negotiating alternative visions for the future. The visionary
responses were visible, for example, in dispersed activist movements among design
radicals in Italy and Scandinavia, and also in Papanek's 1971 influential book, *Design
for the Real World*. The early activists add to the history of design anthropology and
show its varied contributions to imagining and conceptualizing ethnographies of the
possible. They remind us that design anthropology is not exclusively captured within
the more recent focus on participatory, and human-centred, approaches to research
and design.

Throughout this section of the book the need to explore the epistemologies of
a design anthropological approach is clearly represented. The extended temporal,
political and socio-material frames both alter and create new opportunities for design
anthropological research and knowledge-production of possible futures.

Interventionist Speculations

Design practice is centred on intervention, and has a historically established focus
on creating change. But anthropology, too, essentially and increasingly, intervenes
in the worlds and lives of the people being studied (Hastrup 2003; Smith 2013). In
both design anthropology and constructive design research, intervention is increasingly employed as an action research method, allowing new forms of experience,
awareness and dialogue to emerge (Ericson and Mazé 2011; Koskinen et al.
2011). In this book, the term 'interventionist speculations' is used to draw together
and spotlight inventive methodologies that embrace open-ended speculation and
concrete proposals for change as modes of inquiry. When we speculate about
something, we engage in a form of reasoning that is based on inconclusive evidence.
This section of the book is marked by contemplation of issues that are unsettled and
thus issues that it is not possible, or even desirable, to know fully. Can the particular

staging of possibilities be seen as a new mode of ethnographic inquiry into people's concerns, aspirations and imaginative horizons?

In a number of cases, design intervention figures as a research method and as an occasion for knowledge production. Joachim Halse and Laura Boffi (Chapter 6, this volume) lay out what happens when conventional outcomes of design processes – namely material, visual and bodily articulations of new possibilities – are used to raise new questions, and to prompt reflection among participants. The specific speculations of this chapter are of an existential character, as Halse and Boffi speculate about how communication tools might support relationships at the end of life in a hospice setting in Rome. They argue that particular stagings of dialogues around evocative probes, props, and prompts may be seen as an empirical inquiry into what matters to people.

Interventionist and experimental forms of ethnography are also advanced as George Marcus (Chapter 7, this volume) weaves and reframes concepts and concerns from anthropology, design and art practices in the performance installation '214 Square Feet'. Marcus illustrates how varying degrees of awareness of inequality among the privileged were used to engage publics in imaginary scenarios of homelessness among poor working families in Los Angeles. Concepts and theories come into being in the field, and circulate as *prototypes* among diverse publics before they find their way into print at the hands of academic specialists. Marcus argues that these prototypes of thinking, through productive encounters, operate as *research in the world*.

As field sites are prioritized, not only as the primary base of ethnographic knowledge, but as sites of participatory experimentation, they may also become productive dialogic encounters. This is one of the concerns of Zoy Anastassakis and Barbara Szaniecki (Chapter 8, this volume). Anastassakis and Szaniecki take their point of departure in the intense urban transformation of downtown Rio de Janeiro, Brazil, where the football World Cup (2014) and the Olympic games (2016) have prompted large-scale projects of urban 'requalification'. The authors promote speculative interactions about emerging questions and alternative ways of imagining in this urban environment. Anastassakis and Szaniecki speculate about how impoverished communities might enter into a dialogue about development plans for mega-events in Rio de Janeiro. Methodologically, they propose the concept of *conversation dispositifs* for creating dialogues in and with the city and its inhabitants, about the collective imagining of alternative possibilities (Gunn and Donovan 2012; Hunt 2011) for the city.

When speculation is combined with participatory design and the social sciences, a new mode of exploration can emerge – a kind of cooperative inquiry through which matters of concern are collectively articulated and made available for experience and analysis. Drawing on recent projects involving food, farming and drones, Carl DiSalvo (Chapter 9, this volume), describes the practice of speculative design as cooperative inquiry. DiSalvo and his colleagues speculate on how new surveillance technologies such as camera drones, typically associated with industrial agriculture, may potentially subvert urban fruit spotting and picking in Atlanta. The author explores how this practice and this inquiry push speculative design to balance the spectacular with the ordinary. This endeavour also challenges us, as researchers, to develop new forms of design representation, enactment and critique.

As delightful as it may be to let the mind wander into imaginative thought-constructions and what-if scenarios, speculative thinking is fraught with the temptation to lose sight of concrete limitations and constraints, or to gloss over very real controversies and conflicting viewpoints. Such para-empirical positioning is generally not compatible with the critical and constructive approaches that have driven the recent development in design anthropology. To qualify speculative thinking about wishful potentials, all the authors in this section share a methodological commitment to embody, materialize and actualize the issues under speculation, in order to make them experientially available as productive empirical encounters for more public scrutiny and experimentation. Thereby, designers, researchers and the emerging micro-publics can employ their various analytical and empirical sensibilities to play with modes of reality.

The interventions presented here are concerned with grounding speculation in the specificities of lived experience. With their differing cases and viewpoints, the authors show great methodological inventiveness in their deployment of material, visual, emotional, and functional articulation of their respective issues. The particular experimental method-constructs include situationally improvised video scenarios built around props and prototypes (Halse and Boffi, this volume); productive encounters, contraptions, and prototypes of thinking (Marcus, this volume); sketching for engagement and conversation dispositifs (Anastassakis and Szaniecki, this volume); and the use of irony and paradox as motivation to investigate and experiment (DiSalvo, this volume). Together, these constitute an array of theoretical and practical constructs for probing emergent realities.

Throughout the four chapters we see glimpses of deep care for the issues in question: from the dignity of meaningful interactions at the end of life, and the politics of uneven access to participation in urban development, to the awareness of inequality among the privileged, and the leveraging of technologies from industrial agriculture to urban foraging. These are not innocent accounts; they actively forge new alliances, while challenging others. Taken together, this section provides conceptual and practical exemplars of interventionist speculation as a promising line of design anthropological inquiry, committed to both crafting expressions of opportunity, and to attending to empiricist specificities of their implications.

Collaborative Formation of Issues

While the romantic trope of creativity and design locates transformative capacities within the individual human being, even representing them as a sort of emissary of the divine (Negus and Pickering 2004: 3–4), it follows from our conception of futures as embedded in our presents that creativity and design, along with innovation and art, are inherently *social* processes – if only because these processes must resonate with people's experiences and perceptions if they are to 'move the world' (Liep 2001: 1). In his classic, *Art Worlds* (1982), Becker emphasizes this inherent sociality by focusing on 'the cooperative networks through which art happens'. As he elaborates, '[t]he work always shows signs of that cooperation' (ibid.: 1). While this focus on collaboration has gained prominence in the field of design as user-centred design, participatory design, co-design, and democratic design have become influential (Ehn, Nilsson and Topgaard 2014; Simonsen and Robertson 2013); it also goes to the heart of the field of anthropology, as anthropologists are immersed in concrete contexts of joint activity, learning other ways of perceiving the world by being and studying *with* people, not merely by gaining knowledge *about* them (Gatt and Ingold 2013; Ingold 2008).

In design anthropology, collaboration and participation among a variety of stakeholders, most notably users, citizens, and professional experts, have become points of convergence between the two disciplines – not least because of ethnographers' ability to mobilize and engage 'ordinary people' in professional design processes (Blomberg, Burrell and Guest 2003; Blomberg and Karasti 2012). In fact, following Gatt and Ingold (2013), Otto and Smith argue that a possible new criterion of success could be 'how design anthropologists are able to correspond and collaborate with people as co-creators of desirable futures' (2013: 13). This suggestion puts 'collaborative formation of issues' centre stage, urging us to explore how such collaboration may unfold. What role, for instance, does the socio-material setup play in how publics gather around an issue? What kinds of framing, scaffolding, and politics are involved? And how do we make the collaborative formation of issues available for scrutiny, not after the fact, but while it is taking place?

One central issue is the very foundation upon which collaborative relations operate: that is, the underlying perceptions and agendas brought to the table by each participant. Collaborative processes are frequently emphasized because of their potential to activate the participants' different skills and knowledge (e.g. see Ehn 1993; Kensing and Blomberg 1998), not to mention, to allow them to 'speak for themselves'. But Kasper Tang Vangkilde and Morten Hulvej Rod (Chapter 10, this volume) explore whether this foundation for collaboration might take a different, more ethnographically focused form. Rethinking the idea of *para-ethnography* (Holmes and Marcus 2006; 2008), they experiment with designing a concept of management development in which the managers and employees involved are purposely instructed in basic ethnographic methods, and then encouraged to conduct (para-) ethnographic observations *on* and *by* themselves. Moving beyond mere participation to instilling an ethnographic sensibility in the stakeholders, Vangkilde and Rod reconceptualize the relations and processes of collaboration in design anthropological future-making.

The collaborative endeavours described in this section of the book bring about the much-debated question of the role of the design anthropologist. While current discussions of this question present a variety of roles – from contributing 'a corpus of field techniques for collecting and organizing data' (Dourish 2006: 543) to consti-tuting 'a critical holistic and material engagement' (Kjærsgaard and Otto 2012: 179) – they also often search for the 'right' way of being a design anthropologist. Clearly, collaborative issue-formation does challenge the conventional roles of designer and anthropologist. But as Brendon Clark and Melissa L. Caldwell (Chapter 11, this volume) demonstrate, different design anthropological roles may serve different purposes in different situations. Based on their own collaboration across the industry–academia divide, Clark and Caldwell describe how each of them had distinct roles in their joint work in 'innovation labs' for a global food corporation, Clark being the co-creation lead, Caldwell, the academically based consultant. Importantly, their design anthropological contribution emerged in the dynamic between those roles, as the nature of the collaboration blurred the distinction between applied and academic research; above all, because of a shared commitment to ethnographic research as improvisational and emergent.

Underlying collaborative engagements is the ever-present issue of the politics of collaboration. This is not just a question of whose voices are heard but, more generally, of the particular assumptions framing the collaborative engagement. It is nearly unthinkable to be *against* collaboration, which shows how collaboration itself has become an ideological construct, and perhaps is even at risk of becoming a new tyranny (see Cooke and Kothari 2001). Although such broad issues are not addressed in detail here, Kristina Lindström and Åsa Ståhl (Chapter 12, this volume) engage with the 'politics of inviting' by proposing a shift in what design anthropolo-gists invite to, and when. While it is a common practice to invite stakeholders to participate in designing artefacts and solutions to be used in the future, Lindström and Ståhl argue for the value of inviting to co-articulations of *issues* that emerge in the ongoing use of, and engagement with technologies. In such 'designerly public engagements', people are not invited to solve problems or represent issues of living with technologies; rather, these issues *emerge* as distinct compositions of the dynamic between the invitations, the participants, the researchers, and the materials. Thus, the politics of inviting essentially frame (but do not determine) the collaborative formation of issues.

Finally, collaborative processes do not merely bring together different stake-holders, but are also entangled in different temporalities. While it may be discussed whether Papanek was right in his claim that '[a]ll that we do, almost all the time, is design' (1984: 3), it is evident that design work always happens in the wake of previous design, as Adam Drazin, Robert Knowles, Isabel Bredenbröker, and Anais Bloch point out (Chapter 13, this volume). This raises the question of how a pre-designed world is reworked to create both continuity and change, which is explored by Drazin et al. in their discussion of an installation exhibited at the Bauhaus in Dessau. Focusing on cleaning and archiving, they argue that futures do not belong exclusively to designers, as the 'heritage of the future' at the Bauhaus is collabora-tively created by different stakeholders who negotiate what is dirt, what is heritage, and what is something else. The authors suggest that design anthropological work should help a design-interested audience to see how their own approach to futures is essentially entangled in such past materializations of visions for the future.

Overall, the focus on collaborative issue-formation explores how the inherent sociality – or collaborative nature – of design anthropological future-making may unfold in various ways, influenced by specific relations, roles, politics, materialities and temporalities.

Engaging Things

In the coming together of design and anthropology, a major point of convergence is the embodied and material engagement with 'things' in social and collaborative encounters. Within anthropology, the recent 'material turn' has placed particular emphasis on the agency of objects, the affordances of materials, and the interplay between humans and non-humans. As a result, we have seen an increased interest in 'things' and the making of things as objects of, and for, anthropological research (Ingold 2013; Henare et al. 2007; Miller 2005). Within design and design research, the growing sensitivity to processes of collaborative making has raised questions about what is accomplished in design practices, and about the status of the material artefacts that these practices produce. Binder et al. (2011) have proposed that design collaborations should be treated as socio-material assemblies of humans and artefacts. They suggest the notion of 'design things' to capture what is accomplished in design as these assemblies form and evolve as a gathering around matters of concern. What constitutes a thing, and how things participate and become concretely engaged in practices of design anthropology, is unfolded in this section of the book. The theme, 'Engaging Things' refers to both the practical engagement *of* things as *tools* for collaboration, exploration and experimentation in design and research practices and to the engagement *in* and the fascination *with* things as *objects* of design anthropological inquiries.

How speculative objects may be engaged in productive friction in real-world settings to challenge and influence future-making practices – practically, politically, and epistemologically – is explored by Mette Kjærsgaard and Laurens Boer (Chapter 14, this volume). Here, the authors outline potentials for the development of a more critical form of design anthropology in parallel with a more engaged and situated approach to speculative design. Based on empirical examples of critical-design engagements with practices of urban development in Denmark, the authors suggest an approach based on situated and critical material engagement (Boer, Donovan and Buur 2013; Kjærsgaard 2011) that brings together speculative and mundane practices of future-making, in the field as well as in the design studio. Such an approach extends design anthropology (beyond ethnography) towards a more critical material engagement with the possible, while moving speculative design beyond the critical object itself (Koskinen et al. 2011). This (also) allows things and objects to take on new forms and agency in exploratory research activities.

As Elisa Giaccardi, Chris Speed, Nazli Cila, and Melissa L. Caldwell (Chapter 15, this volume) demonstrate, things may intentionally become tools for critically exploring, conceptualizing and influencing future-making practices, through what the authors describe as a 'thing perspective'. Drawing on a project – ThinkTank – deploying an Internet of Things related to household items and appliances, the authors demonstrate how a combination of field studies, object instrumentation, and machine learning may enable design anthropologists to listen to what *things* have to say about their use, reuse and deviant repurposing. Here, intelligent cameras attached to coffee cups, kettles and refrigerators operate as autographers, which, through automatic image capture invoke everyday temporalities in which non-humans create shared futures with humans (Bleecker 2009; Giaccardi and Fischer 2008). The authors discuss the potential of seeing things as co-ethnographers, opening up experimental approaches, articulating design spaces and potential futures based on non-human perspectives. This is not simply about seeing *more,* but about seeing *differently* through 'things'. Here, things serve as critical prisms through which we might engage in design anthropological issues from a non-anthropocentric perspective.

The interest in the non-anthropocentric is a further point of convergence between design research and contemporary anthropology (Callon 2004; Kohn 2013; Tsing 2015), which Tau Ulv Lenskjold and Sissel Olander (Chapter 16, this volume) also address. Challenging the inherent privileging of the human-centred perspectives of design and anthropology, Lenskjold and Olander explore *interspecies relations* between elderly residents of a care home and wild birds in the surrounding area. Inspired by the 'ontological turn' (Holbraad 2009) and constructive design research (Koskinen et al. 2011), they engage speculative design objects in what the authors call a material-experimental practice. Arguing for a re-calibration of the relationship between design and anthropology, they suggest a more deliberately experimental form of design anthropology that embraces the ontological engagement of its own practice. Along the same lines, they propose that constructive practices, and what the authors call *material speculations,* must be understood as full-blown modes of inquiry in their own right. Such arguments reposition the engagement with things. From being something, which can be anthropologically reflected upon, things become sites through which we may experimentally attend to human, as well as other-than-human, encounters.

The role of things in experimental, collaborative and imaginary design encounters is also addressed in the final chapter. Here, the emphasis is less on the thing itself, and more on the way that issues and people are brought together in performative and collaborative engagements with things. In this chapter, Thomas Binder (Chapter 17, this volume) retraces what he calls *moments of encountering the possible:* that is, moments where imagination and experimentation suddenly come together in new forms of reflection on the future. Drawing on work with a design laboratory approach to participatory design (e.g. Binder et al. 2011; Lanzara 1991; Ehn 1988), he demonstrates how moments of encountering the possible grow out of the staged design anthropological encounter as a mutual experience of becoming, between knowledge, agency, and material issues – of 'thinging' (Binder et al. 2011; Latour and Weibel 2005) entering emerging landscapes through 'the things we do'. The author argues that such moments are engagement with things, which come into being through the collaborative encounter. For this reason, they cannot be planned or controlled, and, rather than being moments of reflection, 'breakdown', or accomplishing a goal, they are moments of flow and becoming, moments that bring different worlds within reach.

Together, the chapters in this final section of the book explore how things and the making of them become engaged in matters of social, material, political, or epistemological concern. The 'things' encountered in these chapters are somewhat out of the ordinary, designed to create friction, provoke debate, elicit insights, spark reflection, materialize understandings, and explore alternatives through engagement in and with specific sites of research. They are also, to some extent, critical objects, as they directly or indirectly challenge the status quo by facilitating other types of encounters, conversations, and imaginaries, and by giving a voice to people, things, and animals otherwise marginalized by design and research projects.

*

What stands out in the four sections and themes described above is a renewed curiosity about our ways of living as being contingent, constructed, and transformable. Together they show how material, theoretical, and methodological experiments can open new spaces for insight and social change. Most of all, they demonstrate how future-making is part of everyday, emergent, collaborative, and political practices of shaping and defining possibilities.

Through specific encounters, we sense the methodological and epistemological challenges and potentials of contemporary design anthropology, and glimpse the contours of possible futures for this transdisciplinary approach to knowledge production and change.

Futures are now. Let us engage.

References

Appadurai, A. (2013), *The Future as Cultural Fact*, London: Verso.

Becker, H. S. (1982), *Art Worlds*, Berkeley and Los Angeles: University of California Press.

Bell, G. and Dourish, P. (2007), 'Yesterday's Tomorrows: Notes on Ubiquitous Computing's Dominant Vision', *Personal and Ubiquitous Computing*, 11 (2): 133–43.

Binder, T., De Michelis, G., Ehn, P., Jacucci, G., Linde, P. and Wagner, I. (2011), *Design Things*, Cambridge, MA: MIT Press.

Bleecker, J. (2009), *Design Fiction*, San Francisco: Near Future Laboratory.

Blomberg, J., Burrell, M. and Guest, G. (2003), 'An Ethnographic Approach to Design', in J. A. Jacko and A. Sears (eds.), *The Human–Computer Interaction Handbook*:

Fundamentals, Evolving Technologies and Emerging Applications, 964–86, Mahwah, NJ: Lawrence Erlbaum Associates.

Blomberg, J. and Karasti, H. (2012), 'Positioning Ethnography within Participatory Design', in J. Simonsen and T. Robertson (eds.), *Routledge International Handbook of Participatory Design*, 86–116, London: Routledge.

Boer, L., Donovan, J. and Buur, J. (2013), 'Challenging Industry Conceptions with Provotypes', *CoDesign, International Journal of CoCreation in Design and the Arts*, 9 (2): 73–89.

Callon, M. (2004), 'The Role of Hybrid Communities and Socio-technical Arrangements in the Participatory Design Unities', *Journal of the Center for Information Studies*, 5 (3): 3–10.

Clarke, A. J. (2011), *Design Anthropology – Object Culture in the 21st Century*, Vienna and New York: Springer.

Cooke, B. and Kothari, U. (2001), *Participation: The New Tyranny?* London: Zed Books.

Dourish, P. (2006), 'Implications for Design', in *Proceedings of the SIGCHI Conference on Human Factors in Computing Systems*, 541–50, New York: ACM Press.

Ehn, P. (1988), *Work-Oriented Design of Computer Artifacts*, Stockholm: Arbetslivscentrum.

Ehn, P. (1993), 'Scandinavian Design: On Participation and Skill', in D. Schuler and A. Namioka (eds.), *Participatory Design*: *Principles and Practices*, Hillsdale, NJ: Lawrence Erlbaum Associates.

Ehn, P., Nilsson, E. M. and Topgaard, R. (eds.) (2014), *Making Futures: Marginal Notes on Innovation*, *Design, and Democracy*, Cambridge, MA: MIT Press.

Ericson, M. and Mazé, R. (eds.) (2011), *Design Act*: *Socially and Politically Engaged Design Today*: *Critical Roles and Emerging Tactics*, Berlin: Sternberg/Iaspis.

Faubion, J., Marcus, G. and Rabinow, P. (2008), *Designs for an Anthropology of the Contemporary*, Durham, NC: Duke University Press.

Foucault, M. (1995), *Discipline & Punish*: *The Birth of the Prison*, New York: Vintage Books.

Gatt, C. and Ingold, T. (2013), 'From Description to Correspondence: Anthropology in Real Time', in W. Gunn, T. Otto and R. C. Smith (eds.), *Design Anthropology: Theory and Practice*, 139–58, London and New York: Bloomsbury.

Giaccardi, E. and Fischer, G. (2008), 'Creativity and Evolution: A Metadesign Perspective', *Digital Creativity*, 19 (1): 19–32.

Gibson, W. (1999), 'The Science in Science Fiction', radio programme, *Talk of the Nation*, NPR, 30 November 1999.

Grosz, E. (ed.) (1999), *Becomings: Explorations in Time, Memory and Futures*, Ithaca, NY: Cornell University Press.

Gunn, W. and Donovan, J. (eds.) (2012), *Design and Anthropology*, Farnham: Ashgate.

Gunn, W., Otto, T. and Smith, R. C. (eds.) (2013), *Design Anthropology*: *Theory and Practice*, London and New York: Bloomsbury.

Halse, J. (2008), *Design Anthropology: Borderland Experiments with Participation*, PhD dissertation, IT University of Copenhagen.

Halse, J. (2013), 'Ethnographies of the Possible', in W. Gunn, T. Otto and R. C. Smith (eds.), *Design Anthropology*: *Theory and Practice*, 180–96, London and New York: Bloomsbury.

Hastrup, K. (2003), *Ind i Verden*: *En Grundbog i Antropologisk Metode*, Copenhagen: Gyldendal.

Henare, A., Holbraad, M. and Wastell, S. (2007), 'Thinking Through Things', in *Thinking Through Things. Theorising Artefacts Ethnographically*, 1–31, London and New York: Routledge.

Holbraad, M. (2009), 'Ontology, Ethnography, Archaeology: An Afterword on the Ontography of Things', *Cambridge Archaeological Journal*, 19 (3): 431–41.

Holmes, D. R. and Marcus, G. E. (2006), 'Fast Capitalism: Para-Ethnography and the Rise of the Symbolic Analyst', in M. S. Fisher and G. Downey (eds.), *Frontiers of Capital*: *Ethnographic Reflections on the New Economy*, 33–57, Durham, NC: Duke University Press.

Holmes, D. R. and Marcus, G. E. (2008), 'Collaboration Today and the Re-Imagination of the Classic Scene of Fieldwork Encounter', *Collaborative Anthropologies*, 1: 81–101.

Hunt, J. (2011), 'Prototyping the Social: Temporality and Speculative Futures at the Intersection of Design and Culture', in A. J. Clarke (ed.), *Design Anthropology*: *Object Culture in the 21st Century*, 33–44, Vienna and New York: Springer.

Ingold, T. (2008), 'Anthropology is *Not* Ethnography', in *Proceedings of the British Academy*, 154: 69–92.

Ingold, T. (2012), 'Toward an Ecology of Materials', *Annual Review of Anthropology*, 41: 427–42.

Ingold, T. (2013), *Making: Anthropology, Archaeology, Art and Architecture*, London: Routledge.

Ingold, T. and Hallam, E. (eds.) (2008), *Creativity and Cultural Improvisation*, London: Bloomsbury.

Jameson, F. (2005), *Archaeologies of the Future*, London: Verso.

Kensing, F. and Blomberg, J. (1998), 'Participatory Design: Issues and Concerns', *Computer Supported Cooperative Work*, 7 (3): 167–85.

Kjærsgaard, M. (2011), *Between the Actual and the Potential: The Challenges of Design Anthropology*, PhD dissertation, Faculty of Arts, Aarhus University.

Kjærsgaard, M. and Otto, T. (2012), 'Anthropological Fieldwork and Designing Potentials', in W. Gunn and J. Donovan (eds.), *Design and Anthropology*, 177–91, Farnham: Ashgate.

Kohn, E. (2013), *How Forests Think*: *Toward an Anthropology Beyond the Human*, Jackson, CA: University of California Press.

Koskinen, I., Zimmerman, J., Binder, T., Redstrom, J. and Wensveen, S. (2011), *Design Research Through Practice*: *From the Lab, Field, and Showroom*, Waltham, MA: Morgan Kaufmann/Elsevier.

Lanzara, G. F. (1991), 'Shifting Stories. Learning from a Reflective Experiment in a Design Process', in D. A. Schön (ed.), *The Reflective Turn: Case Studies in and on Educational Practice*, 285–320, New York: Teachers College Press.

Latour, B. and Weibel, P. (eds.) (2005), *Making Things Public: Atmospheres of Democracy*, Cambridge, MA: MIT Press.

Law, J. (2004), *After Method: Mess in Social Science Research*, London and New York: Routledge.

Liep, J. (2001). *Locating Cultural Creativity*, London: Pluto Press.

Mead, G. H. (2002 [1932]), *The Philosophy of the Present*, Amherst, NY: Prometheus Books.

Mendini, A. (2013), 'The Role of Radical Magazines', in A. Coles and C. Rossi (eds.), *The Italian Avant-Garde 1968–1976*, 7–22, Berlin: Sternberg Press.

Milev, Y. (2013), *A Transdisciplinary Handbook of Design Anthropology*, Bern: Peter Lang Verlag.

Miller, D. (ed.) (2005), *Materiality*, Durham, NC: Duke University Press.

Negus, K. and Pickering, M. (2004), *Creativity, Communication, and Cultural Value*, London, Thousand Oaks, CA and New Delhi: Sage Publications.

Otto, T. and Smith, R. C. (2013), 'Design Anthropology: A Distinct Style of Knowing', in W. Gunn, T. Otto and R. C. Smith (eds.), *Design Anthropology: Theory and Practice*, 1–29, London and New York: Bloomsbury.

Papanek, V. (1984), *Design for the Real World: Human Ecology and Social Change*. 2nd edition, Chicago: Academy Chicago Publishers.

Pickering, A. (1995), *The Mangle of Practice: Time, Agency, and Science*, Chicago: University of Chicago Press.

Rabinow, P. (2007), *Marking Time: On the Anthropology of the Contemporary*, Princeton, NJ: Princeton University Press.

Rabinow, P. and Marcus, G. E. with Faubion, J. and Rees, T. (2008), *Designs for an Anthropology of the Contemporary*, Durham, NC: Duke University Press.

Simon, H. (1996), *The Sciences of the Artificial*, Cambridge, MA: MIT Press.

Simonsen, J. and Robertson, T. (eds.) (2013), *Routledge International Handbook of Participatory Design*, London and New York: Routledge.

Smith, R. C. (2013), *Designing Digital Cultural Futures: Design Anthropological Sites of Transformation*, PhD dissertation, Faculty of Arts, Aarhus University.

Smith, R. C. and Kjærsgaard, M. (2015), 'Design Anthropology in Participatory Design', *Interaction Design and Architecture(s) Journal*, 26: 73–80.

Suchman, L. (2011), 'Anthropological Relocations and the Limits of Design', *Annual Review of Anthropology,* 40: 1–18.

Tsing, A. L. (2015), *The Mushroom at the End of the World: On the Possibility of Life in Capitalist Ruins*, Princeton, NJ: Princeton University Press.

Watts, L. (2008), 'The Future is Boring: Stories from the Landscapes of the Mobile Telecoms Industry', *The 21st Century Society: Journal of the Academy of Social Sciences*, 3 (2): 187–98.

Yelavich, S. and Adams, B. (eds.) (2014), *Design as Future-Making,* London: Bloomsbury.

Section I
Ethnographies of the Possible

2 Cultures of the Future: Emergence and Intervention in Design Anthropology

RACHEL CHARLOTTE SMITH AND TON OTTO

Possible Futures

The research field of design anthropology is emerging between the fields of anthropology and design research. The potential that it offers lies in the transdisciplinary orientation towards possible futures; but its methodology and epistemology are still largely unexplored. We argue in this chapter that we need to pay more attention to the ways in which design anthropologists engage with the complex challenges of emergent cultural forms, and with exploring directions for possible futures.

The theoretical positioning of design anthropology creates interesting convergences between approaches of social anthropology and of design research. One of these convergences occurs between the democratic visions and critical design ideas moulded by participatory design and speculative design (Mazé, this volume; DiSalvo, this volume; Simonsen and Robertsen 2013) and the contextualized cultural imaginaries that arise in anthropological engagements with the future (Anusas and Harkness, this volume; Halse 2013; Kjærsgaard and Otto 2012). In the field of design anthropology, we argue, such agendas for change, modes of engagement and critical reflection become deeply entangled. Participatory design research focuses on 'drawing things together' (Binder et al. 2011) through situated activities and iterative transformation; an anthropological approach provides critical distance and contextualizes these socio-material and political processes (Smith and Kjærsgaard 2015). The design anthropological result is the creation of transformative sites of research and knowledge production through which we may attempt to address aspects of the contemporary condition (Blomberg and Karasti 2013; Light 2015).

In Otto and Smith (2013), we argue for design anthropology as a *distinct way of knowing*, one which incorporates both analysis and intervention in the process of constructing knowledge. This approach involves defining and inventing the ethnographic field, and even to an extent the ethnographic subject(s), as well as acting situationally to produce various cultural agendas through the research and design process. While such developments are based on long-standing connections between anthropology and design (Clarke, this volume; Otto and Smith 2013), they move beyond a conventional empirical focus on ethnography *for* purposes of design and represent a move towards dynamic processes that intervene in existing and emerging social realities with the aim of identifying and scaffolding potential change. Smith (2013) argues that such future-oriented processes of inquiry and exploration aiming at cultural production and transformation, rather than just developing alternative perspectives or opportunities, constitute an *interventionist* design anthropological approach. These ways of knowing are based on a distinctive approach to emergence and intervention, framed within design and anthropology. Here the conditions for possible futures are imagined and negotiated, but also actively co-constructed in relation to given contexts, through processes of *designing cultures* and *making futures* (Smith 2013; Ehn et al. 2014).

In this chapter we explore some central epistemological questions concerning this kind of knowledge – transformative knowledge, created *in* and *through* action and engagement rather than by observation and reflection alone – to explore and to provoke intentional change. We focus on *emergence* and *intervention* as central concepts for design anthropology, and argue that these concepts are intrinsically connected in a dialectical movement of exploration, knowledge production and transformation. Our aim is to explore the possibilities of an anthropology that engages with emergent cultural practices as a way of producing knowledge that is part of, and itself constitutes, transformative practices (Suchman 2011). In doing this we intervene in the cultural patterns and prospects of the emerging future, rather than focusing on the ethnographic realities of the past present, which is normally in focus. The concepts of emergence and intervention can help us to develop a grounded theoretical approach to knowing through situated interventionist practices, addressing issues such as: How do we develop design anthropological interventions that open up perspectives on the emergent future? How can design anthropological ways of knowing through action and intervention be ethnographically significant, valid and effective?

We use the case of *Digital Natives* to discuss the concepts of emergence and intervention and the role of the anthropologist in design anthropology. *Digital Natives* was a research and exhibition experiment exploring possible futures of cultural heritage communication in a digital era. The project was created through a collaborative process over eight months involving anthropologists, interaction designers, museum curators and a group of young people aged 15–19, who were involved in co-designing an interactive exhibition based on their own everyday practices and engagements with digital technologies (see e.g. Smith 2013; Smith and Iversen 2014). We describe below how forms of emergence and intervention were central both to the framing and the outcome of the design anthropological process and the knowledge it produced. First, we elaborate on the concept of *emergence* and its central importance to developing a theoretically grounded design anthropological approach.

Exploring the Emergent

The question of emergent cultural and social realities poses a major challenge to anthropology today. As Rabinow (2008: 3) states, anthropology has predominantly focused on how society or culture reproduces itself through institutions, symbolic work, power relations, etc. But there are also phenomena that are emergent: 'That is to say, phenomena that can only be partially explained or comprehended by previous modes of analysis or existing practices. Such phenomena, it follows, require a distinctive mode of approach, an array of appropriate concepts, and almost certainly different modes of representation' (ibid.: 4). In a discussion with George Marcus on designs for an anthropology of the contemporary (Rabinow et al. 2008: 64), Rabinow addresses the same issue: 'The task is to invent concepts to make visible what is emerging. This needs a critical distance from the present, and this distance, at least in part, is achieved through the proper use of analytical tools.'

But what are these tools and what, in fact, do we understand by the emergent? At a fundamental level, one can argue that social reality is always in a state of emergence. This view has been developed by the pragmatist philosopher Mead (2002 [1932]). According to Mead, the present is the true *locus of reality*: all existence is situated in the present. It is the central characteristic of the present that it is continuously moving, evolving from a past present and continuing into a new one: in short, the present is always in a state of emergence. Mead does not propose to deny the reality of the past and the future, but he emphasizes that past and future are not independent entities, but accessible only as dimensions of the present. He argues: 'Given an emergent event, its relations to antecedent processes become conditions or causes. Such a situation is a present. It marks out and in a sense selects what has made its peculiarity possible. It creates with its uniqueness a past and a future' (ibid., 52; cf. Otto 2013: 66; Otto and Smith 2013: 17).

From Mead's perspective, emergence is a fundamental quality of social reality. But this quality is only poorly reflected in our research methodologies. As mentioned, anthropology has paid more attention to *what is* than to what *might be,* and has had a greater interest in how societies are reproduced than how they are transformed. But if we accept Mead's perspective on the present, reproduction too should be seen as a modality of the emergent. As Mazé (this volume) argues, the emerging future is never empty; it is already populated, by built environments, things and skills and, we would add, by social institutions and cultural categories, that impact on the space of the possible. Narrowing down the emergence of new social and cultural forms as one particular modality of the continuously emerging present, the central question remains how we can explore and identify these new emerging forms through a design anthropological approach. According to Rabinow, such a form of anthropological practice is to be characterized by what he calls *a mode of virtual untimeliness*:

> The difference between a mode of potentiality and what Deleuze has called a mode of virtuality consists in the fact that potentiality actualizes a state, a quality,

or a form that is already inherent or resident in the being, thing, or process under consideration. The mode of virtuality does not directly partake of this metaphysical world. It operates adjacent to it, moving alongside potentialities and actualities so that these can be taken up and refracted in another form. In another mode. That is to say, the virtual as opposed to the potential is a mode replete with real things and processes but redirected, removed from their habitual courses (Rabinow 2008: 49–50).

Both Rabinow and Marcus appear to be seeking a mode of virtuality, adjacency and critical distance through the development of critical concepts in the *process* of ethnographic fieldwork, which are somehow out of sync with the reality being studied. According to Marcus this happens through the 'modulation of tempos' (Rabinow et al. 2008: 74), a term that can refer both to the slowness of the ethnographic process (Marcus 2013) and the recursiveness of contemporary collaborative and experimental forms of fieldwork (Marcus, this volume). Rabinow, supported by Marcus, highlights the 'untimeliness' of ethnography, which marks a 'critical distance from the present that seeks to establish a relationship to the present different from reigning opinion' (Rabinow et al. 2008: 59). While we are fully sympathetic to the diverse ways in which the play with temporalities enables and defines ethnographic fieldwork, including slowing down and creating critical distance (see also Otto 2013; Dalsgaard and Nielsen 2013; Otto 2016), here we explore a slightly different mode of virtual untimeliness that can reveal the emergent in a design anthropological context. What we suggest is that design anthropological interventions might function to condense or accelerate time in order to explore and understand the emergent and the potential futures and imaginations it may hold or, in other words, to make virtual experiments on the emergent.

This happened through the creation of the interactive exhibition, *Digital Natives*, with a group of young people who, during the limited time of the experiment, explored emerging everyday digital cultural forms and potentials of digital cultural heritage in a Western, Danish, context. As an exhibition, our intervention was virtual and adjacent to the emerging cultural forms we wished to investigate and experiment with, in order to develop alternative imaginations of cultural heritage in an increasingly digital era. What the exhibition showed is that our virtual experiment demonstrated a (real) potential – openings and reflections of a possible future actualized in the intervention of the exhibition and the collaborative process preceding it. We describe below how we worked with emergence and intervention to co-create possibilities for future cultural heritage in a digital age.

Transforming Emergent Digital Cultures

The aim of the *Digital Natives* exhibition experiment was to explore ways for museums to engage audiences in experiences of cultural heritage in the digital era. The research project aimed to generate knowledge of possible convergences between anthropology and participatory design by means of processes of research through design. The project was initiated as a collaboration involving a research environment for interaction design and development of advanced technologies, a large cultural heritage museum and an academic department of social anthropology. As the design *anthropologist* in charge of the project, Smith defined and laid out the conditions for the research and the exploratory framing of the project, in ways that challenged both existing approaches to curation in museums and the role of anthropologists and designers in design processes.[1] Rather than focus on developing new forms of digital communication based upon existing – material and temporal – conceptions of cultural heritage and curation *inside* the museum, the *Digital Natives* project took its point of departure in young audiences and their everyday digital cultures *outside* the museum. This reframed the object of research from technology-enhanced heritage communication to exploring 'the digital' as an emergent cultural and social phenomenon.

Contrary to influential assumptions and the myths of tech-savvy youth (Prensky 2001; Palfrey and Gasser 2008), the project's ethnographic approach and design activities revealed a more fragmented image, closely embedded in the particularities of the teenagers' everyday practices (Ito et al. 2010). The teenagers did not view themselves as 'digital natives' with particular practices or traditions, and did not identify immediately with the concept. Both their everyday practices and their involvement in the design process revealed strong aspects of attraction to, as well as critique of their use of, the technologies surrounding them. Through field research in their own environments, and collaborative explorations of the digital

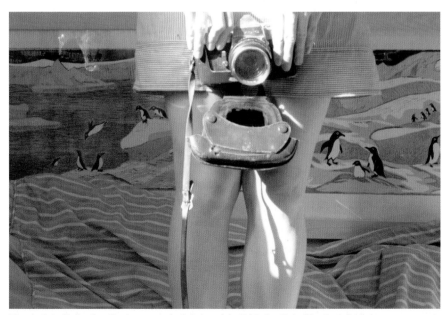

Figure 2.1 Reflecting the teenagers' digital worlds © Metha Rais-Nordentoft

which led to a mock-up exhibition for engaging with the interaction designers, these relations were explored, negotiated and experimented with. The particular framing of the collaboration at this stage was critical and exploratory, with the intention of addressing and moving beyond the shared myths and assumptions of new digital generations (prevalent also among the curators and interaction designers involved) through exploring the situated particularities of seven young Danish people (see Figure 2.1).

The teenagers selected for the project represented diverse forms of everyday engagement with the digital – from engaging in the cultural production of artistic film and photography, through political and cultural activism, to the shaping of identity through fashion blogs, gaming, or engagement via social media platforms. The technologies were often backgrounded and tacit for the teenagers themselves, both as a means of everyday engagement and as a lack of reflection and language concerning their influence on everyday practices. Apart from two male teenagers with a dedicated interest in technology that extended beyond the interfaces of computers, mobile phones and gaming devices, the youngsters tended to have targeted or specific means of use that depended on their interests and social identities. A girl interested in fine arts had a passionate relationship to her iMac devices and was a keen user of Facebook, but kept a clear separation between her social (everyday) use of Facebook and her private passion for film and aesthetics in her way of storing and organizing her data, time and interests. A fashion-interested male invested much time researching and collecting images and materials for his fashion blog, in order to invent and project that identity creatively. Two females cherished their out-dated computer and mobile phones, the physical materiality of analogue video recordings and the experience of handling pages in a book, while keenly using the digital as opportunities for developing their visual and aesthetic interests, and their social connections. The reflections upon such different digital practices and values and their complex relations to socio-material everyday concerns were allowed to emerge and take new shapes through the process.

Rather than merely develop insights into the teenagers' 'digital worlds', the aim was actively to explore and co-create imaginations and expressions of these worlds. Through their collaborative engagements with each other, the design anthropologist and a curator, the teenagers became aware of their positions as digital subjects in and of contemporary society. They explored these subject positions through directed discussions of digital objects and habits, sketches and development of material concepts. This allowed the teenagers to externalize interests and ideas, and functioned as a way of inviting the designers into their reflections. Ethnographic research (observations and semi-structured interviews) into the teenagers' everyday contexts was conducted in parallel and provided insights and details of their situated digital cultures. The traditional properties of cultural heritage exhibitions were backgrounded. Rather, a list of principles was created for the project, directing a common focus *away* from the museum, the 'individual' experience, 'formal' heritage, the 'static' and confined exhibition space, towards a dialogic and open-ended conception of the exhibition as a 'processual' and 'hybrid' experience, that centrally 'engaged' the audience and took point of departure in continually emerging cultural practices (Smith and Iversen 2014). By creating such an exploratory framework, the designers and curators were prompted to engage actively with the youngsters' everyday lives and interests, as well as technological artefacts or curatorial concepts in processes (usually) controlled by themselves.

Through continuous design anthropological framings of the collaboration, using the insights and materials from these encounters to navigate the process, we co-created our own ethnographic field. We explored – challenged and disrupted – both the emerging digital practices of youth cultures and interactive technologies at the forefront of technological 'innovation', as well as the boundaries of user participation and audience engagement experienced by the design researchers and curators. As a result, the *emergent* digital practices functioned both as object and subject of the research and design process. This extended scope allowed us to use the transient character of the present as ethnographic material for re-imagining potential futures of digital heritage. The situated framing intentionally reversed not only the traditional temporal (past) and material (object) focus of cultural heritage, and the focus on technological concepts and artefacts of designers, but also the myths surrounding the practices of emerging technologies, while opening up fields of possibility in the design project (see Figure 2.2).

Figure 2.2 Transforming digital cultures through the design process © Rachel Charlotte Smith

Scaffolding Futures Through Intervention

Design researchers and anthropologists are increasingly addressing the complex relations between culture, technology and design (Dourish and Bell 2011; Balsamo 2011; Drazin 2013). Central to such contributions is that design is not merely a site of technological production, but an important process of cultural production and reproduction as well. Culture is not simply a state of the present from which novel technological artefacts are projected. As Balsamo (2011: 11), following Bourdieu (1984), argues, culture is both a resource for, and an outcome of, the process of designing. From this perspective, technologies become not simply digital objects to be designed, but assemblages of people, materialities, practices and possibilities that can be experimented with in different ways. As Balsamo states, however, 'To transform them requires the employment of a framework that can identify the complex interactions among all these elements' (ibid.: 31).

As seen in the context of *Digital Natives* and described by Dourish and Bell (2011), mythologies are often agents in determining how digital futures are imagined and produced in the context of technological innovation. As the authors argue, myths in fields of ubiquitous computing drive forward certain ideas of technological development 'in much the same way that myths provide human cultures with ways of understanding the world and celebrating their values' (2011: 4). It is in understanding how *framing of* and *intervening in* these cultural imaginations and conceptions have material effects that design anthropology can play an important part in cultural production and reproduction.

Design interventions are commonplace in participatory design research and practice, often supported by a range of tools and frameworks (for, e.g. exploration, ideation, prototyping) that allow for material and collaborative engagements with the objects and subjects of design (Simonsen and Robertsen 2013; Binder et al. 2011; Koskinen et al. 2011). But the interconnectedness of digital and socio-material issues increases the complexities and messiness of everyday cultural production, in which these processes of intervention are embedded. Anthropologists have been highly ambivalent about engaging in such practices of design(ed) intervention beyond critical reflection (Hunt 2011). Mostly, they have carried out small disruptive experiments or social interventions in the field, or among researchers themselves, with the aim of eliciting new perceptions on existing realities (Leach 2010; Fortun 2012; Willerslev, Marcus and Meinert forthcoming).

In a design anthropological context, intervention goes beyond critical commentaries or (self)awareness. It can be seen as a form of transdisciplinary fieldwork, using intervention to scaffold potential transformation. This involves the application of anthropological theory in extending the object(s) of design beyond an *interest* in social change, so as to act in complex and dynamic roles as researchers, facilitators, and co-designers of possible futures (Smith 2013; Halse and Boffi, this volume). This reflexive extension of the research field from both anthropology and design is particular for a design anthropological approach, in the sense that it engages in this reframing of the 'field' or 'design space' from the perspective of both disciplines. Binder et al. (2011) make an important shift in the concept of the *design space,* moving from a confined space in which professionals design and create particular objects and products to spaces created by the iterative movements and transformative representations of the various stakeholders involved in the collaboration. This paves the way for a perspective on the design space as extended and decentred – intervening and experimenting with social, digital and material contexts in/through a virtual mode – a space in which the coming together of certain potential and virtual futures *emerges.* Such developments represent a shift from predictability in the design practice and taxonomical understandings of culture towards the *enabling* and *becoming* of potential futures and of situated future making (Binder et al. 2011; Ehn et al. 2014) that can be negotiated and performed through socio-material processes of design anthropological intervention. The contexts that characterize these interventions are neither 'wild' nor 'exterior' to the design process and space. They are entangled situations and contexts of fieldwork and design.

The ethnographic inquiry does not cease with the design intervention. Rather, these experimental forms of contemporary anthropological research generate new ways of constructing the objects and sites of fieldwork themselves. The design anthropological approach consists of improvisatory and recursive movements in which the emergent present moves the ethnographic inquiry forward, while at the same time forming an imaginary basis from which mutual and speculative concepts can be developed in the field (Marcus 2012). Thus rather than through empirical data and analysis alone, the interventions produce theory through its reverse, as Marcus (this volume) argues: theory here is understood as a primary and dialogic form of data and thought 'located in the sites and situations of fieldwork'.

Accordingly, our perspective is that central to a design anthropological approach is a focus on the dynamic processes of cultural production and reproduction, and that these are explored *while emerging* (as modes of potentiality) through performative processes of intervention and experimentation (in a virtual mode). Such encounters are scaffolded based on a sensitivity to the wider (political, ethical, material, etc.) contexts that matter, and formed by particular intentions and concerns that are experimentally put into play (Koskinen et al. 2011). Rather than targeted, specific artefacts or outcomes, the design anthropological contexts and processes of intervention are often open-ended, focused on emergent issues of knowledge production through collaborative and material engagements.

Exhibition as Virtual Experiment Through Intervention

The *Digital Natives* experiment may be seen as inherently a move from situated explorations of digital culture extending far beyond the museum, towards a process of intervention and virtual experimentation on the emergent. The myths about new generations that had to be engaged in particular ways through, e.g. common uses of social media or technological applications in the museum (Parry 2010) prompted us to set up a virtual experiment, using the concept of digital natives to tease out the potentiality and heterogeneity of an emerging cultural form (towards future forms of digital cultural heritage). Thus the anthropologists' intervention and framing created an untimely and virtual mode of investigation. *Untimely* because it used a category of identification – Digital Natives – that was not part of the emerging culture being studied, and *virtual* because the exhibition was a cultural form that was adjacent to, rather than part of, the emerging realities.

At the micro-level, each research and design activity in the project had to be considered, anticipated, planned, disrupted, reflected, and acted upon. The complexity of the process, centrally involving twenty to thirty stakeholders, meant that the participants' views on what was developing were always situated and incomplete. Moreover, the heterogeneous perspectives of different participants, and the scaffolding of dialogues, became a central dynamic to the process of intervention. The teenagers' digital lives were a principal focus point and a field of exploration for the teenagers and the anthropologists. The interactive technologies and participatory conceptions of audience engagement were emphasized by the interaction designers. However, the teenagers had little or no experience with interactive technologies and often found the interaction designers' attention to modes and means of interacting with an unknown audience too abstract and of little interest to their own concerns.

The design anthropological strategy was to generate a dialogic process of engagement in which the teenagers and the designers worked collaboratively in groups towards generating new perspectives and imaginations by developing a series of interactive installations (Smith and Iversen 2014). Through the process, we oscillated between large collective design workshops and work within more limited groups, allowing the multiplicity of concerns and agendas between and across different stakeholders to emerge, but also to give direction to one another throughout the process. Within the groups, Smith functioned as the mediator between the designers' professional interests and the youngsters' personal perspectives. Beyond the groups, her role was to shape and give direction to the exhibition and research process.

Establishing these *third spaces* (Muller 2002) was a way to explore and create alternative expressions between the digital lives of the teenagers and the research interests of the interaction designers. This method revealed, for example, *how* the digital in the teenagers' worlds was enmeshed in complex ways with situated relations with peers and interests in film, fashion, political work, etc., in which the technology merely fashioned the means or modes of expression. It showed how the designers saw themselves as akin to (the myths of) digital natives due to their expertise with advanced technologies, which affected their decisions in the design process when shaping the digital prototypes. These aspects were externalized through the collaborative and material engagements, and constituted an ethnographic site and material for the anthropologist and participants to work with towards a common output.

The strategy of dialogue and circulation was at points contested by the participants, as it insisted on alternative modes of transdisciplinary engagement. But it created an open-ended framework in which new perspectives were iteratively co-developed, often in unanticipated ways. In one group, two girls and two inter-action designers both took charge of the process in order to pursue their interests in what was to be a common concept: the girls emphasized that their own production of an artistic film was to be merely represented for the audience, while the designers' interests aimed to use the visual outputs as data material in a larger framework for interacting with the audience. Negotiations between the two positions, push-button or subtle interaction, contextualized representations through digital technology and abstract concepts of engagement, were contentious. Smith's role here was to continuously engage in dialogues to find openings between these positionings that would allow for alternative visions to emerge. As the two girls expressed it, in a critical situation coming out of a workshop with the designers:

> 'I just can't believe it! What was *that*?' one girl bursts out before the heavy front doors of their design partners' building closed behind them. The two girls quickly light up two cigarettes and stand back against the brick wall, with their heads facing the sky. 'The designers were meant to help us realize our idea, but they just keep pulling it apart. I don't know what the fuck they're doing?'

The concrete challenge as we invested effort in taking these mutual epistemological and cultural positionings of the participants seriously was to scrutinize assump-tions and perspectives about the digital (as, e.g. merely a means of representation), as well as perceptions about people's 'desires' to participate (through particular modes of interaction). The nature of the process meant that Smith's role was to insist on dialogic engagement, and constantly to respond to the unfolding events to intervene and give direction (Nelson and Stolterman 2012). Joint workshops were set up to enact the different prototypes being developed in the project – first in the vicinity of the advanced technology premises, later in the empty exhibition space. Through these events the exhibition gradually emerged as a common concept and third space among the participants, and unexpected feedback was given to each of the five digital installations. For example, the installation 'Portraits' (see Figure 3), presented by the two girls and interaction designers above in a time of confusion over the direction of their work, was positively received precisely for its aesthetic and subtle form of interaction, more poetic and imaginative than other installations. Their large-screen projection of a girl and her passion for reading books could be engaged with through hidden means of bodily movements in front of the screen.

Based on the prior one-to-one discussions with the girls and the designer, such encounters provided alternative perspectives that were included in further discus-sions with the group about the possibilities for their installation. These dialogues and the continued material explorations provided the basis for co-articulations common concerns: what modes of interaction did the coding of technology afford, which colours and effects could represent particular moods in the teenagers' lives, how were the filmed and mixed fragments to become 'engageable' by the audience, and how could the missing narrative create new reflections on what

Figure 2.3 Developing the 'Portraits' installation © Rachel Charlotte Smith

'the digital' meant to young generations? Such issues shifted the focus from specific design solutions towards the scaffolding of dialogues, thus providing rich contexts for engagement through which perceptions of the possible could be developed. It was through these continuous dialogic micro-acts – of *relational expertise* (Dindler and Iversen 2014) and of establishing *points of discourse* (Rabinow 2008; Kjærsgaard 2011) within the design process – that untimely connections and imaginations between digital cultures, advanced interactive technologies and future cultural heritage were shaped. As a result of the two teenagers' perspectives, particular visual aesthetics and emotional expressions from the teenagers' lives were foregrounded, while the rational use of technology was backgrounded in the Portraits installation. The designers on the other hand insisted on the deliberate fragmentation of linear film, and developed new modes of interacting with the specific content at hand. Within the framework of dialogic engagement, such constraints provided collaborative spaces for new common concepts to emerge.

Cultures of the Future

Designing a possible future through decentred processes of inquiry and experimentation in this sense entails envisioning a possible past, extending the temporal horizon both forward and backward (Otto 2016). In the *Digital Natives* project, we

Figure 2.4 Audiences at the 'Digital Sea' installation © Rachel Charlotte Smith

argue, it was through staging and scaffolding a concrete intervention – in a virtual mode – that particular futures and pasts were defined and experimented with in the act of co-creating the exhibition.

The final exhibition comprised five interactive installations that used advanced digital technologies, creating diverse forms of engagement for the audience. The dialogic process leading up to the exhibition was continued into the exhibition, now framed within the hybrid environment of the museum space (see Smith 2013; Iversen and Smith 2012). Here the exhibition emerged as *another* manifestation of the virtual landscape created during the design process. The different installations contained curated fragments of produced audio and digital depositories from the teenagers' everyday lives, with which audiences could engage physically and socially through floor projections, advanced tracking and tactile interactions.

The installation 'Digital Sea' (see Figure 2.4) was a visually striking floor projection allowing visitors to explore digital materials from online media and mobile platforms – Facebook updates, private photos, text messages, etc. – by standing and stepping onto the floating images. The installation created the central ecology for the exhibition, drawing in materials from all seven teenagers' lives, and connecting them to the other installations, thereby creating a kaleidoscope of perspectives on the contemporary digital. In this way the exhibition prompted the inquiry to continue, opening new cultural reflections, rather than communicating formalized knowledge. As a present concern, these experiences and imaginations emerged out of the collaborative third space of the design process and continued into the third space of the exhibition, in which a public audience became co-creators of experiences and cultural imaginations.

Stepping, dancing or jumping onto the floating images, these physical and social modes of interaction allowed people to explore and co-create unique meanings of the exhibition *in situ.* A woman in her forties commented, '… it's incredibly visual and it's an experience to tread on something to get it enlarged. (…) Had this been a painting on a wall, it would just be hanging there, as part of the wall. Here you can walk around and create your own small paintings, on the floor.' The exploratory nature of the exhibition, created a frame that people could position themselves within. For many this was an empowering way of experiencing the exhibition through their own engagement, which prompted alternative reflections and experiences of technology. A woman in her thirties experienced 'being caught in' by the technology, which was a rare sensation for her. '… I get some impressions that I'm *completely surprised* about getting through the media. (…) I really can't imagine how you would do that. It's precisely that the technology gets something more drawn in. That it gets the human drawn in. I think that's the essence of it: the sense that there is a *human presence* there'. Such experiences illustrated that some intentions of the dialogic collaborations in the design anthropological process had emerged as part of the exhibition's special character.

In the exhibition, Smith deliberately foregrounded the teenagers' role and their physical presence as informal hosts. The direct engagement between the teenagers and an active audience, from school classes to teenage friends, older visitors, and the press, allowed cultural meanings of being digital to be actively exchanged and negotiated. This was done while showing people how to interact in the exhibition, listening to other people's reflections about their own relations to technology while engaging with the installations, or being asked reflective questions about how the ideas and concepts had emerged through the design process. The interaction changed the teenagers' role from that of being participants in the design process to being subjects and agents in the exhibition. Through this process, the youngsters came to realize themselves as a group or category: they temporarily *became* the Digital Natives, thus appropriating an agentive identity potentially representative of an emergent digital culture (Otto 2016). Simultaneously, the dialogic nature of the interactive installations transformed the audience from being receivers of formal knowledge to engaged subjects using their situated positionings inside the hybrid space to generate experiences and cultural narratives from the digital world(s) at hand.

Following Mead's and Rabinow's perspectives, the virtual mode of the exhibition was realized through the dialogic engagements between people, technologies and materialities in the present. This created a special form of emergence through the active engagement of the audiences themselves. The exhibition in this sense was envisaged (not as a design outcome but) as the coming together of fragmented elements, using the digital as a *dynamic cultural material* for engagement and reflection. This prompted new experiences through dialogic engagements with the installations and other audiences, connecting them with reflections about people's own use of technology, in the past and present, as well as the future. Hence, the exhibition and the knowledge it generated was no less real, or authentic, than other representations of digital culture. But as a virtual site of engagement and transformation, the exhibition created a distinct, 'untimely' and adjacent way of knowing about possible futures in and of the museum.

Emergence and Intervention in Design Anthropology

Intervening in social realities with the aim of scaffolding possible change, we argue, prompts anthropologists actively to engage in processes of emergence, dialogue and co-design. This kind of future making, of actively co-creating aspects of culture and technology, is central to the type of interventionist design anthropological approach we have sketched out. The design *anthropological* contribution in our case was partly to draw in people, contexts and relations, connected to situated and emergent digital cultures, and actively to become part of these worlds and imaginations so as to frame and facilitate dialogic encounters, resulting in collaborative experiments in a virtual mode. These experiments, adjacent to, and partly out of sync with, the actual, make way for various co-articulations of the potential. In other words, they create ethnographies of the possible.

In the *Digital Natives* project, the anthropological framing of the design process and exhibition was a way of exploring aspects of an emergent digital culture, and of creating connections between these emergent characteristics and conceptions of digital cultural heritage in a broader societal context. The exhibition at once created a temporary manifestation of digital culture and was a co-created research process for experimenting with alternative futures. Anthropological encounters like these are not mere sites of cultural and material inquiry; they become sites of virtual experimentation with cultural transformation. As such, they are dialectic and transitive processes, shaped within and between technology, people and culture, thus producing and transforming cultural experiences and conceptions.

A design anthropological focus on *emergence* and *intervention* may provide an approach to creating, in a virtual mode, assemblages of connections, materialities and potentialities that allow us actively to give shape to possible futures in the present. Working with the emergent quality of social life, rather than leading to systematic understandings and stable cultural 'wholes', these transitive processes generate their ethnographic significance as contextualized relationships 'to a known and carefully conceived incompleteness' (Marcus 2012: 28). It is through these situated movements and positionings of emegence and internation that alternative futures can emerge, creating the distinct style of knowing through design anthropological practice and engagement.

Note

1   The Digital Natives project ran over a period of one year between 2010 and 2011, during which Smith acted as design anthropologist responsible for the design and execution of the project, while Otto was the principal supervisor as well as leader of the comparative project on 'Innovation in Cultural Heritage Communication', funded by the Danish Agency for Science, Technology and Innovation, grant number 645–08–0120. The Digital Natives project was also part of the Center for Digital Urban Living, funded by the Danish Council for Strategic Research, grant number 2128-07-0011.

References

Balsamo, A. (2011), *Designing Culture*: *The Technological Imagination at Work*, Durham, NC and London: Duke University Press.
Binder, T., De Michelis, G., Ehn, P., Jacucci, G., Linde, P. and Wagner, I. (2011), *Design Things*, Cambridge, MA: MIT Press.
Blomberg, J. and Karasti, H. (2013), 'Positioning Ethnography within Participatory Design', in J. Simonsen and T. Robertson (eds.), *Routledge International Handbook of Participatory Design*, 86–116, New York: Routledge.
Bourdieu, P. (1984), *Distinction: A Social Critique of the Judgement of Taste*. Cambridge, MA: Harvard University Press.
Dalsgaard, S. and Nielsen, M. (2013), 'Introduction: Time and the Field', *Social Analysis*, 57 (1): 1–19.

Dindler, C. and Iversen, O. S. (2014), 'Relational Expertise in Participatory Design', in *Proceedings of the Participatory Design Conference*, 1: 41–50, New York: ACM Press.

Dourish, P. and Bell, G. (2011), *Divining a Digital Future*: *Mess and Mythology in Ubiquitous Computing*. Cambridge, MA: MIT Press.

Drazin, A. (2013), 'The Social Life of Concepts in Design Anthropology', in W. Gunn, T. Otto and R. C. Smith, (eds.), *Design Anthropology*: *Theory and Practice*, 33–50, London and New York: Bloomsbury.

Ehn, P., Nilsson, E. and Topgaard, R. (eds.) (2014), *Making Futures: Marginal Notes on Innovation, Design, and Democracy*. Cambridge, MA: MIT Press.

Fortun, K. (2012), 'Ethnography in Late Industrialism', *Current Anthropology*, 27 (3): 446–64.

Halse, J. (2013), 'Ethnographies of the Possible', in W. Gunn, T. Otto and R. C. Smith, (eds.), *Design Anthropology*: *Theory and Practice,* 180–96, London and New York: Bloomsbury.

Hunt, J. (2011), 'Prototyping the Social: Temporality and Speculative Futures at the Intersection of Design and Culture', in A. J. Clarke (ed.), *Design Anthropology. Object Culture in the 21st Century*, 33–44, Vienna and New York: Springer.

Ito, M., Baumer, S., Bittanti, M., Boyd, D., Cody, R., Herr-Stephenson, B., Horst, H. A., Lange, P. G., Mahendran, D., Martínez, K. Z., Pascoe, C. J., Perkel, D., Robinson, L., Sims, C., Tripp, L., with contributions by Antin, J., Finn, M., Law, A., Manion, A., Mitnick, S., Schlossberg, D. and Yardi, S. (2010), *Hanging Out, Messing Around, Geeking Out: Kids Living and Learning with New Media,* Cambridge, MA: MIT Press.

Iversen, O. S. and Smith, R. C. (2012), 'Connecting to Everyday Practices: Experiences from the Digital Natives Exhibition', in E. Giaccardi (ed.), *Heritage and Social Media*: *Understanding Heritage in a Participatory Culture,* 126–44, London and New York: Routledge.

Kjærsgaard, M. (2011), *Between the Actual and the Potential*: *The Challenges of Design Anthropology,* PhD dissertation, Faculty of Arts, Aarhus University.

Kjærsgaard, M. and Otto, T. (2012), 'Anthropological Fieldwork and Designing Potentials', in W. Gunn and G. Donovan, (eds.), *Design and Anthropology. Anthropological Studies of Creativity and Perception*, 177–91, Farnham: Ashgate.

Koskinen, I., Zimmerman, J., Binder, T., Redström, J. and Wensveen, S. (2011), *Design Research Through Practice: From the Lab, Field and Showroom*, Waltham, MA: Morgan Kaufmann/Elsevier.

Leach, J. (2010), 'Intervening with the Social? Ethnographic Practice and Tarde's Image of Relations Between Subjects', in M. Candea (ed.), *The Social After Gabriel Tarde*, 191–207, Abingdon: Routledge.

Light, A. (2015), 'Troubling Futures: Can Participatory Design Research Provide a Constitutive Anthropology for the 21st Century?', *Interaction Design and Architecture(s) Journal*, 26: 81–94.

Marcus, G. E. (2012), 'The Legacies of Writing Culture and the Near Future of the Ethnographic Form: A Sketch', *Cultural Anthropology,* 27 (3): 427–45.

Marcus, G. E. (2013), 'Afterword: Ethnography between the Virtue of Patience and the Anxiety of Belatedness Once Coevalness is Embraced', *Social Analysis*, 57 (1): 143–55.

Mead, G. H. (2002 [1932]), *The Philosophy of the Present,* Amherst, NY: Prometheus Books.

Muller, M. J. (2002), 'Participatory Design: The Third Space in HCI', in J. A. Jacko and A. Sears (eds.), *The Human Computer Interaction Handbook*, 1051–68. Mahwah, NJ: Lawrence Erlbaum Associates.

Nelson, H. G. and Stolterman, E. (2012), *The Design Way: Intentional Change in an Unpredictable World,* Cambridge, MA: MIT Press.

Otto, T. (2013), 'Times of the Other. The Temporalities of Ethnographic Fieldwork', *Social Analysis*, 57 (1): 64–79.

Otto, T. (2016), 'History in and for Design', *Journal of Design History* 29 (1): 58–70.

Otto, T. and Smith, R. C. (2013), 'Design Anthropology: A Distinct Style of Knowing', in W. Gunn, T. Otto and R. C. Smith (eds.), *Design Anthropology*: *Theory and Practice*, 1–29, London and New York: Bloomsbury.

Palfrey, J. and Gasser, U. (2008), *Born Digital*: *Understanding the First Generation of Digital Natives,* New York: Basic Books.

Parry, R. (ed.) (2010), *Museums in a Digital Age*, New York: Routledge.

Prensky, M. (2001), 'Digital Natives, Digital Immigrants', *On the Horizon*, 9 (5): 1–6.

Rabinow, P. (2008), *Marking Time*: *On the Anthropology of the Contemporary,* Princeton, NJ and Oxford: Princeton University Press.

Rabinow, P. and Marcus, G. E. with Faubion, J. D. and Rees, T. (2008), *Designs for an Anthropology of the Contemporary*, Durham, NC: Duke University Press.

Simonsen, J. and Robertson, T. (eds.) (2013), *Routledge International Handbook of Participatory Design*, London and New York: Routledge.

Smith, R. C. (2013), *Designing Digital Cultural Futures: Design Anthropological Sites of Transformation*, PhD dissertation, Faculty of Arts, Aarhus University.

Smith, R. C. and Iversen, O. S. (2014), 'Participatory Heritage Innovation: Designing Dialogic Sites of Engagement', *Digital Creativity*, 25 (4): 254–68.

Smith, R. C. and Kjærsgaard, M. (2015), 'Design Anthropology in Participatory Design', *Interaction Design and Architecture(s) Journal*, 26: 73–80.

Suchman, L. (2011), 'Anthropological Relocations and the Limits of Design', *Annual Review of Anthropology,* 40: 1–18.

Willerslev, R., Marcus, G. and Meinert, L. (forthcoming), 'Introduction: Obstruction as a Method in Anthropological Research', *Ethnos: Journal of Anthropology*.

3   Design and the Future: Temporal Politics of 'Making a Difference'

RAMIA MAZÉ

Futurity

It is difficult to know what the future holds. The future is by no means empty – it will be occupied by built environments, infrastructures and things that we have designed. It will bear the consequences of our histories, structures, policies and lifestyles, which we daily (re)produce by habit or with intent in design. The future is already loaded with our fantasies, aspirations and fears, persuasively designed visions and cultural imaginaries. Designed things, lifestyles and imaginaries, or 'stuff-image-skill' (Scott, Bakker and Quist 2012), endure, proliferate and occupy the future. By (re)producing things, lifestyles and imaginaries, design takes part in giving form to what will be in the future.

This is sometimes made explicit in design. The future, time, memory and change were themes in *acceptera*, for example, the first manifesto of Swedish Modern design (Åhrén et al. 2008 [1931]). *Acceptera* evoked, in text, image and proposed designs, a modern, or future, 'A-Europe', 'The society we are building for' and 'B-Europe', or 'Sweden-then', fragmented spatially, temporally and socially. Some values, customs, peoples and cultures were portrayed as regressive and stuck in past centuries. It was a manifesto for a specific kind of development, in a predetermined direction, an arrow of time leading to a particular, singular and common future. The politics of this designed future are also explicit in this example – *acceptera* was published by the Social Democratic party, and it has had powerful and lasting effects on the ideological and socio-material construction of the Swedish welfare state (Mattsson and Wallenstein 2010).

Design can be understood as a powerful practice that takes part in giving form to the future, or, as *acceptera* exemplifies, a possible or preferred future. Thus, the future, or futurity, in design may expose relevant issues for design research and design anthropology concerned with 'the possible'.

Futurity is at stake in many design arguments and practices. Assumptions about the direction of time, progression and progress seem to underlie popular design rhetorics concerning 'the new', 'transformation' and 'innovation', for example. Directed action toward preferred futures may even be understood as fundamental to some conceptions of design – for example in the classic formulation by Herbert Simon: 'Everyone designs who devises courses of action aimed at changing existing situations into preferred ones' (1996: 130) thereby 'addressing differences between the desired and the present' (1996: 141). Particular ideas or ideals of the future are mobilized by socially- and politically-engaged designers (e.g. Ericson and Mazé 2011) or by 'redirective designers' addressing 'defuturing' phenomena such as climate change (Fry 2010). Possible or preferred futures are explicitly addressed in 'concept', 'critical' and 'persuasive' design practices discussed further below.

Discussions of the future may raise questions such as what can be known about the future, and how. In design research, such epistemological questioning can become preoccupied with the nature and scope of knowledge and recourse to more established ways of relating to such questions from the natural and social sciences. Indeed, if we reason, as above, that the future is not empty and, further, that we can know something about what has come before, then we can know something about what the future holds by studying the past and the present.

But futurity also raises other questions. We can query, for example, an ontology of time structured in the three categories of past, present and future. Indeed, this tripartite ontology can itself be queried as a historically- and culturally-specific assumption, and alternatives can be explored (e.g. Grosz 1999; Inayatullah 1990; Jameson 2005). Within a tripartite ontology, still further questions can be raised in terms of relations and differences between the temporal categories. Contemporary philosopher Elizabeth Grosz, for example, poses a potential of futurity that is given precisely by the ontological assumption that the future is different. It is, categorically, not the past nor the present. Exploring notions of 'the possible' in Henri Bergson's philosophy, she queries the future as other than a 'preformed version of the real' (Grosz 2001: 12). From this perspective, futurity can be a conceptual modality through which it is possible to ask: *How can things be different?*

The future as different is a political as well as a philosophical question. Grosz also queries 'the supervalence of the future' (Grosz 1999: 7), or how the future can have agency and wield power over the present. It is this question that is central to the field of futures studies or research, originally developed in the context of policy planning, which can be understood as engaging the future to inform, understand and/or control the present (Wangel 2012). Futures researcher Sohail Inayatullah articulates: 'every planning effort involves philosophical assumptions as to what is considered immutable and what is negotiable; the significant and the trivial. Thus, every effort to plan the future is submerged in an overarching politics of the real' (1990: 116). The future exposes basic philosophical questions about our assumptions and world-views. That things can be different also raises political questions about what can, or should, change and what difference that makes.

As design takes part in giving form to the future, to possible or preferred futures, we need more and critical ways of relating to issues of futurity. Asking *How can things be different?* raises philosophical and political questions. These are questions for design as we aspire and/or claim to 'make a difference' and go about 'changing existing situations into preferred ones' (Simon 1996), 'making things better' (to borrow the motto of Philips Design, Baxter 1996) or 'Massive Change' (as Bruce

Mau proposes, Mau and Leonard 2004). But the future is not merely something that might be known and thus be available for us to determine (or design), a destination that might merely be defined and reached with the right methods. Although the future is not empty, it is open, and this makes all the difference.

In this chapter, I reflect upon issues of futurity for design. I briefly characterize 'concept', 'critical' and 'persuasive' design practices, because they explicitly take on the future by formulating visions, speculating on alternatives and steering toward particular ideals. While important in my own work as a practice-based design researcher, these practices expose issues that I problematize here in terms of futurity. I have (re)positioned my own work over the years, and, increasingly, in relation to futures studies and philosophies of time, as illustrated here through a description of the project 'Switch! Energy Futures'. Suggesting that futurity can be a philosophical and political modality for 'seeing and acting' differently in and through design, I frame two proposals to invite further work in design research and design anthropology.

Design and the Future

The future – indeed, temporality – has only entered substantially into design discourses and practices relatively recently. Design, and other disciplines such as architecture, geography and geology, have long been materially and spatially preoccupied (Grosz 1999). Over the last half-century, however, there has been a shift to design 'beyond the object' with the diffusion of post-industrial technologies (Thackara 1988) and the innate 'temporal form' of (inter)active materials, products, environments and systems (Mazé 2007).

Today, temporal rhetorics of 'change', 'transformation', 'innovation' and 'the new' pervade design. However, other temporal phenomena such as 'chance', 'indeterminacy' and the 'untimely' seem less welcome (Grosz 2004, cf. Rabinow 2008). This implies certain assumptions, ideals, priorities – and political dimensions – in making a difference between what is real now and what is, or is not, desirable or negotiable for the future. Indeed, the 'arrow of time' in *acceptera* was directed not to any possible future but to a specific and preferred future reality with explicit political intent. Recalling Inayatullah, we may query how this and other examples of design may 're-inscribe the power politics of the present instead of the openness or alternative possibilities of the future' (1990: 134). To elaborate further, I point at 'concept design', 'critical design' and 'persuasive design', in which the future is explicitly at stake.

Concept, Critical and Persuasive Design

Notions of concept design, critical design and persuasive design vary widely. These are not fixed or well-established categories in design discourse, since examples are not easily or exclusively identified and terminologies are highly contingent (Mazé 2007), and since positions are continually renegotiated and reframed, for example in relation to more recent tendencies in speculative design and design futures. Here, I evoke these as tropes through which to discuss ways in which design may aspire or claim to project, challenge and steer the future, often without articulating or addressing political dimensions.

Concept design flourishes in trade shows and world exhibitions, for example in the form of prototypes of the 'ideal home', 'future city', 'concept car' and 'The World of Tomorrow' (e.g. Rydell and Schiavo 2010). In a similar vein, Philips Electronics' *Vision of the Future* and other industrial and strategic design programmes fuse forecasting, sociology and high-tech research in concept designs (Baxter 1996). Concept designs have become central to business strategies, building shared values and commitments, expanding and marketing the 'corporate imagination' within a company, an industrial sector or a target group. Foresight may be essential for industries that depend on a twenty-year lifespan (Gabrielli and Zoels 2003), however such genres go well beyond technical questions of lifespan. Concept design induces desire and (re)produces cultural imaginaries for particular industrial futures.

Allied with art, critical industrial and interaction design[1] produces artefacts that debate futures. Resisting the 'dreams of industry', practices such as Dunne and Raby (e.g. Dunne and Raby 2001, cf. Antonelli 2008) borrow strategies of defamiliarization and estrangement from modernist aesthetics to provoke debate about current norms, 'alternative nows' or 'speculative futures'. Critical designs are intended as 'material theses', physical rather than written critiques, of established models of production and consumption (Seago and Dunne 1999, cf. Mazé and Redström 2009). Designs are crafted, placed and photographed carefully, often in exclusive settings such as art museums, coffee table books and lifestyle or culture inserts in the media. While opposing traditional models of design industry, such designs nevertheless seem to assume and prefer a particular socio-economic niche.

Persuasive design for behavioural change aims to redirect norms. In the area of sustainability, for example, ideals, consequences or futures around electricity and water consumption are monitored and visualized in forms intended to educate, persuade, incentivize or even coerce change in perceptions and 'good' behaviour (Verbeek and Slob 2006, cf. Klanten, Ehmann and Bohle 2012). Designed to 'fit' people's bodies and sensory capacities, or cognitive and emotional ergonomics, such approaches steer behavioural change in more or less explicit and conscious ways. Persuasive designs induce self-discipline, regulating, affirming and governing particular behaviours in forms intended to be internalized and reinforced in an ongoing manner in everyday life and social practices (Mazé 2013). While perhaps not always aware or reflexive about the ideologies and policies (re)produced, persuasive designs oppose present conditions and propose quite particular alternatives and futures.

Some Political Dimensions

Concept, critical and persuasive design point at various ways of approaching the future, which I characterize here in slightly over-generalized terms and tropes in order to articulate potential political dimensions. By 'the political', I do not refer to party politics or state sovereignty but, rather, philosophical and analytical uses of the term in the social and political sciences. In this sense, I argue that the future, or futures, that are imagined, materialized and intervened by design, represent different perspectives, preferences and, indeed, different realities. This can be understood in relation to what anthropologist and philosopher Annemarie Mol calls the 'ontological politics' of (re)producing, choosing between and multiplying different realities (Mol 1999).

The choices made in concept, critical and persuasive design are far from neutral. Concept design, for example, identifies and selects particular trends and values to extrapolate and amplify in imagined 'ideal' futures of the home, car or city. There are endless socio-economic and techno-material possibilities, and choices are made about which may or may not be identified, reproduced or changed (see Wangel 2012 for a discussion of possible versus preferred or normative futures studies). Choices are normative – they are made from and for particular positions, in relation to specific conditions, contexts and worldviews. Critical designers can be politically blind to how their work is situated and to its political consequences (Prado 2014). Elaborating and multiplying possible futures is an exercise of power, even if position or preference is not articulated or if neutrality is claimed. Not acknowledging or recognizing underlying norms entails that assumptions and alternatives can remain unavailable to others, thus limiting their possibilities for (re)positioning or choosing otherwise.

Relating to futures through design is therefore a political act. Here I should distinguish between issues of morals and ethics – and 'the political'. There are important moral dimensions involved in judgements of what is 'good' or 'better', but there are also profound political dimensions to ontologies and the privileging or subordination of other ways of perceiving, organizing and ordering the world (see Mouffe 2005 for a discussion of the political versus post-political morality e.g. of Latour). For example, persuasive design explicitly establishes moral registers ('good' i.e. as sustainable consumption). It also – politically – (re)orders realities and lifeworlds through materially and spatio-temporally embodied designs that determine what and how others are able to think, react and act differently.

That design is political is perhaps not surprising given accounts of design, architecture and technology as instruments of power, discipline and oppression (Fry 2011; Dovey 1999; Barry 2001; Ericson and Mazé 2011). Design can be understood as a profoundly political act, whether we are reflexive or intentional about this or not. We give form to what and how a particular reality (or future) may be confronted with others (Keshavarz and Mazé 2013). As designers, we may not only reflect critically on the question *How things might be different?*, but open up possibilities for thinking and doing otherwise, including handing over the question to others (as a political act).

Switch! Energy Futures – A Design Example

I have been (re)positioning my work in relation to concept, critical and persuasive design within practice-based design research programmes for several years. An example is the Switch! programme (Mazé 2013b), in which we explored and developed approaches to changing perceptions, behaviours – and futures – of electricity consumption within six experimental projects. For example, 'Green Memes' are concept designs that visualize electricity consumption within corporate settings, the 'Symbiots' photographic series reverses human-centred design paradigms and social norms in order to facilitate debate, and a 'Telltale' prototype was placed into homes to probe effects upon perceptions and energy-related behaviors.

Within Switch! 'Energy Futures', more specifically, we drew on futures studies to open up new ways of identifying and imagining possible futures of energy production and consumption. We attempted new combinations of futures methods such as environmental scanning, scenario building, role-play, fore- and backcasting with those more familiar in design, such as qualitative interviews and personas, visualization and prototyping, interventions and participatory events (see Figure 3.1). This methodological mix supported us in moving beyond typically incremental approaches to sustainability in user-centred design, which often privilege the current needs of proximate stakeholders within near-future proposals. Our approach implicated familiar and everyday situations, participating stakeholders and existing contexts, but also explored larger-scale and longer-term dimensions. For example, enacting three different scenarios from the standpoints of the diverse personae (based on qualitative interviews and political segments), engaged power and (infra)structural dynamics, socio-economic and ideological distances, conflicts as well as transitions.

Energy Futures generated five '(super)fictive realities' or 'superfictions', which were articulated through collections of highly-considered and -crafted artefacts and media (e.g. 'conceptual modelling'), including mock-ups and working prototypes, family snapshots and journalistic photos, Wikipedia and YouTube media. Rather than one-liners (which is typical of many visionary images in concept and critical design), these blur between sci-fi and oral history, personal anecdote and reportage, to develop qualities that are nuanced and complex as well as strangely familiar, difficult and socio-psychologically conflicting as well as humorous.

Each 'superfiction' materializes tropes that can be traced within contemporary sustainable development and scenarios of energy futures. For example, while one evokes a technological silver bullet and win-win solution (Figure 3.2.15), a typically 'eco-modernist' trope, others raise issues of eco-disobedience and socio-spatial inequity. One focuses on potentially new cultural forms and communal solidarity (Figures 3.2.10–13), while others suggest increased individuation, austerity and separatism (Figure 3.2.14). While the content varies, along with implied costs, benefits, exclusions and beneficiaries, each is carefully crafted from a first-person standpoint in order to humanize possible experiences, worldviews and realities that are, nonetheless, very different. Since we were interested in opening up, rather than resolving or closing the future, each superfiction is crafted individually and in relation to one another such that further qualities emerge in juxtaposition.

Energy Futures involved the staging of an exhibition that invited – and required – participation in interpreting and making sense of these strangely familiar and potentially difficult realities, through which visitors examined their assumptions, discussed alternatives and declared their own position(s).

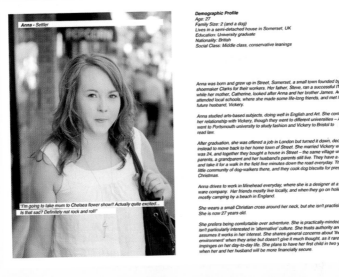

Demographic Profile
Age: 27
Family Size: 2 (and a dog)
Lives in a semi-detached house in Somerset, UK
Education: University graduate
Nationality: British
Social Class: Middle class, conservative leanings

Anna was born and grew up in Street, Somerset, a small town founded by the shoemaker Clarks for their workers. Her father, Steve, ran a successful IT business while her mother, Catherine, looked after Anna and her brother James. Anna attended local schools, where she made some life-long friends, and met her future husband, Vickery.

Anna studied arts-based subjects, doing well in English and Art. She continued her relationship with Vickery, though they went to different universities – Anna went to Portsmouth university to study fashion and Vickery to Bristol to read law.

After graduation, she was offered a job in London but turned it down, deciding instead to move back to her home town of Street. She married Vickery when she was 24, and together they bought a house in Street – the same village where her parents, a grandparent and her husband's parents still live. They have a dog and take it for a walk in the field five minutes down the road everyday. There is a little community of dog-walkers there, and they cook dog biscuits for presents at Christmas.

Anna drives to work in Minehead everyday, where she is a designer at a leather-ware company. Her friends mostly live locally, and when they go on holiday, it's mostly camping by a beach in England.

She wears a small Christian cross around her neck, but she isn't practising. She is now 27 years old.

She prefers being comfortable over adventure. She is practically-minded, and isn't particularly interested in 'alternative' culture. She trusts authority and assumes it works in her interest. She shares general concerns about 'the environment' when they arise but doesn't give it much thought, as it rarely impinges on her day-to-day life. She plans to have her first child in two years, when her and her husband will be more financially secure.

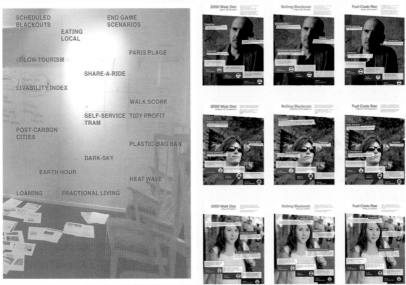

Figure 3.1 Sampling from our methods documentation © Interactive Institute Switch! Energy Futures team: Ramia Mazé, Aude Messager, Thomas Thwaites, Basar Önal

Problematics of the Future as Present

The future is at stake, as I have briefly traced here across concept, critical and persuasive design and in my own work, including critical dimensions as we engage with (re)producing and/or confronting 'politics of the real' (Inayatullah 1990).

In discussions of concept, critical and persuasive design as well as Switch! Energy Futures, however, attention often seems to shift to other issues, such as what can be known about the future, and how. Discussions can get stuck, for example, around epistemological dilemmas concerning what can be known, the limits of knowledge, issues of uncertainty and indeterminability, and the use of design as methods or instruments to know, test and determine future phenomena. Often we end up circling around issues of knowledge and method in the natural and social sciences or instrumentalizations of pathways toward a particular place or time called 'the future'. Such issues have generated a range of responses within my own work and related communities of design research, including (re)connections with and across the social sciences and futures studies.

The basic epistemological dilemma is also discussed by futures researchers, since knowledge in futures studies lacks the empirical basis of other disciplines (or deals with ontological uncertainties, Svenfelt 2010; Wangel 2012). For futures researcher Jerome Glenn, this means that a core question of futures studies is 'What

Figure 3.2.1–5 'Socket Bombing is direct action performed as a protest against excessive electricity consumption. It involves purposefully causing a short circuit in a building's electrical mains or light sockets. Consisting only of cheap and rewired electrical hardware and timers, socket bombs are typically planted to target supermarkets, chain stores and corporations. Incidents have been reported in London, Paris, Istanbul and Stockholm. One group managed to cut the power to the majority of shops in Kista Galleria in Sweden on the 6th of September 2008.' (Mazé, Messager, Thwaites and Önal 2013: 28)

Figure 3.2.7–8 'And now for the Power Forecast. This afternoon, we'll see some bright sun of about 80W per square meter for around 3 hours, so it'll be a great time to get those appliances working. Things get a bit dimmer towards the weekend with only about 46W per square meter penetrating the clouds, so plan for a quieter Sunday. If you've got the big family lunch planned, you'll have to use dirty power, I'm afraid, as there also won't be much wind.' (Mazé, Messager, Thwaites and Önal 2013: 31)

Figure 3.2.10–13 'Today, we celebrate our penance. Today we mustn't use power. We know we're not perfect, but we keep on trying. So we wrap our needy objects to resist temptation! And we gather outside and together turn the sky red!' (Mazé, Messager, Thwaites and Önal 2013: 36)

Figure 3.2.14 'Before, we were living in a kind of fast-forward dream world – our senses constantly assaulted by all the usual so-called 'modern conveniences' – everything wanted our attention. We didn't know it, but we just didn't have time to think. Then, the power went out for a week, and we found we preferred it. So we decided to move to a Blackout Zone that has electricity for only one hour in the evening. Now, we get more sleep, we spend more time together, we're calmer – it saved our family life!' (Mazé, Messager, Thwaites and Önal 2013: 32)

Figure 3.2.15 'At last! Energy Independence and Great Looks from just one mildly invasive procedure!' (Mazé, Messager, Thwaites and Önal 2013: 35)

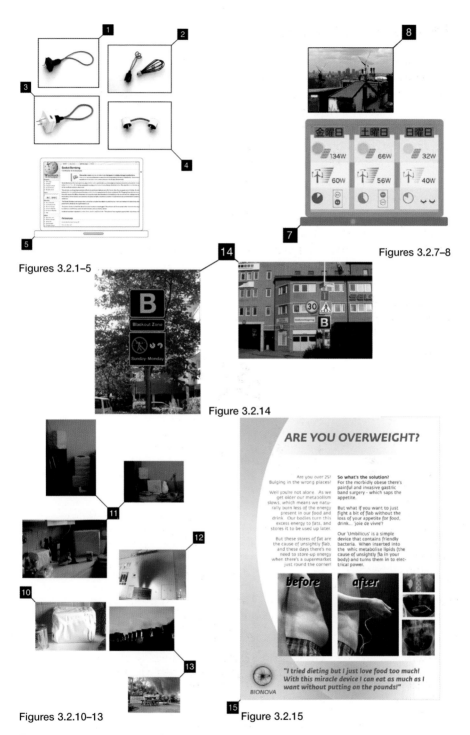

Figures 3.2.1–5

Figures 3.2.7–8

Figure 3.2.14

Figures 3.2.10–13

Figure 3.2.15

Figure 3.2 Five 'superfictions' © Interactive Institute Switch! Energy Futures team: Ramia Mazé, Aude Messager, Thomas Thwaites, Basar Önal

difference does it make?' rather than 'How well do you know it?' (Glenn and Gordon 2003: 8). One way to address this core question is to examine the future as different from a given current situation. For example, a possible or preferred future can be developed, intervened and studied – not only in terms of the knowledge it is based on but in terms of how it can affect the present. For example, its capacity to 'expand mental horizons', 'enhance anticipatory consciousness' and 'stimulate change in the present' (Glenn and Gordon 2003) can be studied using existing or extended methods from the social sciences and design.

In design research, and transdisciplinary intersections among disciplines (e.g. Vergragt 2010; Quist 2007), related questions and methodological extensions have emerged. In my own work, and with colleagues specializing in futures studies, planning and design, we are exploring how concept, critical and persuasive designs can be developed, intervened and studied in a similar way. For example, designs may be deployed within interventions as 'probes' deployed in 'niches' (such as 'living labs') to explore, co-produce or steer towards desired futures that can be monitored and studied in the present through 'learning loops' (Wangel et al. 2012; de Jong and Mazé 2010). This epistemological shift and subsequent conceptual and methodological work has been important for disentangling some questions generated from and arising around our Switch! Energy Futures project.

In this disentangling, further questions were exposed that required other responses. Some of my questions resonate with philosophical and political critiques of predominant predictive-empirical and techno-deterministic varieties of futures studies and searches for alternatives. There are limits to predictive-empirical approaches, for example, in which the future is typically imagined as empty, a particular place or time into which possible and preferred images (whether fiscal, scientific or cultural) are treated as distinct realities that may be reached through linear transition pathways. In such approaches, the question of 'difference' can become merely an instrumental question of technique and method. Critiques and alternatives have spurred the development of 'prospective-action research', 'cultural-interpretive' and 'critical-postmodern' futures studies (Gidley et al. 2009; Inayatullah 1990). These discussions in futures studies parallel my search for developing further philosophical and political inquiries into futurity.

Figure 3.3 'Energy Futures' exhibition event. The doors open at 18:00. The space is empty and bare, there are no hosts, those who arrive may wonder whether this is, in fact, an opening at all. But visitors, including designers, architects, educators, engineers and historians, begin to gather, meet and serve themselves drinks … Over the course of an hour, the contents of a closed case have taken over the gallery space, an exhibition unpacked and arranged as a narrative of instructions and fictions unfolds. Amongst themselves, the visitors have had to collaborate to unfold and make sense of these. Emerging along the way were a variety of intimate stories and personal opinions, as well as political issues and professional points of view © Interactive Institute Switch! Energy Futures team: Ramia Mazé, Aude Messager, Thomas Thwaites, Basar Önal

Temporal Politics of 'Seeing and Acting' in and through Design

As designers more substantially engage with the future, we also need to engage more fundamentally with ideas and politics of futurity. Contemporary philosophers concerned with temporality and futurity argue that dominant scientific modes or forms of knowing cannot grasp critical aspects of the future, the new, or becoming different, which are better addressed through other epistemologies and philosophies. Grosz articulates: 'If dominant modes of knowledge (causal, statistical) are incapable of envisioning the absolutely new, maybe other modes of knowing, other forms of thinking, need to be proposed' (1999: 21). Art and architectural theorist John Rajchman (1999) calls for another 'art of seeing and acting' than those preoccupied with future causalities or determinisms, prophecy or prediction. Here, I probe some philosophical and political discourses of futurity, starting with two (among any number of possible) frames through which I can also reflect upon how design, including my own work, might offer possibilities for 'seeing and acting' differently.

Future as Outside?

An ontological structure for time that posits 'the future' as a place or time apart makes possible our dominant conceptions of history and modernity. It also allows us to posit the future as an outside. The future can be a place or time that affords a perspective, the possibility of looking at ourselves, inside and immersed in the present, from a distance (Grosz 2001). From there, then, we can examine and compare with the here and now. This kind of critical distance is used by Inayatullah to analyse how practices within his field of futures studies 're-inscribe the power politics of the present instead of the openness or alternative possibilities of the future' (1990: 134). From this perspective, concept, critical and persuasive designs might be studied or produced in terms of how an envisioned technology, product or environment could entail different ways of living and organizing a society and/or industry.

Reflecting back on my own work, this perspective could entail a reconsideration of how 'strangely familiar' Energy Futures might or should be crafted. I can look more closely at the choices, aesthetics and placement of imagery, graphics, texts and typography – how do they replicate or reference current and particular lived experiences or material cultures, how may these be crafted to reveal differences between a current situation and a future scenario, within a future scenario or between scenarios? I could query the extent to which societal issues and structures are evident and problematized within or across Energy Futures. Only a few years afterwards, the logics and aesthetics of one superfiction may not be critically distant enough from Transition Town phenomena (Figures 3.2.7–8), while the fully functioning Socket Bombs (Figures 3.2.1–5) still provoke debate about socio-economic structures and effect altered positions in debates.

Seeing and acting towards the future as outside must also be problematized. This ontological structure of time is specific to modern Western societies and there are many other ways of understanding and relating to time (Jameson 2005; Harding 2009). Further, positing the future as 'a place or time' like the present and the past can imply that the future can be fully known, determined and occupied – such assumptions already dominate predictive-empirical and techno-deterministic varieties of futures studies. As a critical modality, a perspective on the future as outside requires that differences and consequences be identified and articulated, between a present and future or between possible futures. What is in- and outside need to be put in relation to one another – for example, the positions and conditions from which particular concept, critical and persuasive designs are crafted may need to be declared in order that others can 'see and act' also in relation to underlying norms, morals and politics.

Future as Agency?

In contemporary philosophy, the concept of difference engenders a critical modality, in which relations between and among things may be queried and alternatives constructed. Perhaps because it is difficult to know what the future holds, the future has a hold over us. As Grosz recounts, the unavailability of the future to knowledge is what propels us forward; in Hermann Minkowski's philosophy, the future is a mysterious and majestic horizon 'without which we could not continue to live' (in Grosz 1999: 21). Inherently full of surprises, 'newness', unknowns and the 'untimely', the future is a fundamentally active force, it has agency. From this perspective the future does not only surrender to our sciences, control and occupations. To the extent that the future holds surprises, unknowables and, importantly, others or 'future people' who will have the capacity to change us, to reframe our present and rewrite history, the future has a 'decolonizing' power.

For design, this requires us to rethink our own 'will to power' over the future. Our designed 'stuff-image-skill' gives form to the future in many ways – rather than inhibiting us from designing, the agency of the future means that things will always turn out differently from the way we intend them. That we cannot entirely know or control the future does not mean that our concept, critical and persuasive designs should proliferate any old 'vision of the future' or (unsustainable) behaviour. It does not give us license to leave behind questions of norms, morals and politics. A danger, as sociologist Ruth Levitas suggests (2007), is that if our utopias (or future designs) are only the expression of our desires, we risk a perpetual present mode of living with alienation. We need to be even more selective and explicit about our positionality and how our (design) practices open or foreclose other(s) agency, the possibilities for others to 'see and act' in relation and otherwise.

Reflecting on Energy Futures from this perspective, I could further examine how the project's and my positionality, conditions and worldviews in the here and now are expressed in the logics and aesthetics of representations and performances. We could reflect upon the selection, practices, material cultures and voices of others within the environmental scanning, qualitative interviews, personae and role-play, superfictions and participatory event. Taking this further would require a reconfiguration of my practice to engage more extensively and carefully beyond the here and now of proximate contexts and participants. Considering political scientist Wendy Brown's (1995) 'world-based' (rather than identity-based) political arguments, I can consider the socio-material implications of a shift from 'who I am' to 'what I want for us' and the necessity of more inclusive recognition and participation without the 'indignity of speaking for others' (Rajchman 1999).

Politics of Future-Making in Design and Design Anthropology

To take on the question *How can things be different?* in design and to claim that design can 'make a difference', I inquire here into issues of futurity. The future is not empty – it is already occupied by stuff, images and skills that design takes part in (re)producing. Design activities, such as those amended as 'concept', 'critical' and 'persuasive' outlined here, orient explicitly toward the future or, rather, possible and preferred futures. A more profound problematization of futurity is required given inevitable impacts on the future, deriving from explicit intentionality toward the future and increasing hegemony of values of 'newness' and 'innovation' in design (and research in general, e.g. Wakeford 2014). Historical examples such as *acceptera* demonstrate profound philosophical and political impacts of design, however today we must seek further examples and beware of nostalgia for the lost Modern horizon of consensus, solidarity and singularity (Rajchman 1999).

I have unfolded various approaches to futurity. Since the future is not empty, we can come to know something about the future by studying the past and the present, drawing on historical and social sciences approaches. At the epistemological and methodological limits of these, further approaches within futures studies address the question 'What difference does it make?' Intersections between approaches draw on sociology, psychology or pedagogy to probe into how visions of different possible or preferred futures can affect change in the present. These kinds of questions and intersections have shaped a range of interdisciplinary research practices, including my own, explored through design-practice-based research collaborations and examples within the Switch! programme.

For design anthropology, such intersections (and examples) expose important potentials. Signalling a more general 'social' shift in design and a 'designerly' turn in the social sciences, intersections among disciplines are generating a range of mixed approaches including more interventionist, propositional and 'inventive' qualitative research methods (e.g. Lury and Wakeford 2012). In particular, design anthropology has emphasized collaboration and co-creation (Gunn, Otto and Smith 2013), through which emerge a potentially new 'style of knowing' (Otto and Smith 2013). Tim Ingold (2013) argues for an anthropology not *of* but *with* design, art and architecture and emphasizes *making* as a way of creating knowledge. Eeva Berglund (2015) elaborates some specifically *future-making* potentials of design anthropology.

From my perspective in design, these disciplinary intersections are crucial responses to the particular epistemological dilemmas of futurity (and, indeed, of design as a specifically temporal form-giving practice, e.g. Mazé 2007).

Still, political questions of futurity linger and the need to further query 'difference'. Political as well as philosophical dimensions concerning the future are exposed in 'concept', 'critical' and 'persuasive' design. As in futures studies, 'an overarching politics of the real' is revealed in design acts of identifying, preferring, imagining and steering toward particular (out of all possible) futures. It was the political dimensions of futurity that we attempted to explore in Switch! Energy Futures – the politics of different futures, and design (future-making) as a political act.

Through making Energy Futures, we also explored ways of 'seeing and acting' in relation to different futures. Through the process (with mixed design and futures methods) and through articulation (in aesthetic and narrative forms), we came to know something about the politics of different worldviews, priorities, competing and conflicting realities. Thus conceiving of the future 'as outside', for example, could be understood as an attempt to deliberately distance the future, to encounter very different realities, experiences and others. In the process (as well as in the participatory event), we encountered futures 'as agency', and the fine line between future possibilities as too different and alienating versus too desirable and as something to appropriate. While exploring the future – which is not empty – we have been struggling with ways of seeing and acting that do not fully determine or colonize the future (or the present), to leave things open for others and, indeed, for difference.

As I have been problematizing futurity in this paper, I have pointed at some (re)connections between design and the social sciences. Potentialities of design anthropology are being forged in addressing common questions – for example, to investigate 'What difference does it make?' as well as new or alternative 'styles of knowing' such as alternative ways of 'seeing and acting' in relation to the future. These are important intersections and foundations of design and anthropology in relation to futurity, which are, in process and in substance, 'in the making'. I resist the entanglement of design and design anthropology in predictive-empirical and techno-deterministic perspectives on futurity. Framing, instead, philosophical and political questions, I argue for a further turn to post-structuralist, participatory and critical futures studies, feminist and post-colonial discussions of temporal politics. The future – not empty but open – should not be merely a design rhetoric, a scientific 'no man's land' or a place/time for occupation by policy, planning and design. Instead we should engage profoundly, and together, in our ideas and politics of future-making.

Acknowledgements

Switch! was a collaborative and interdisciplinary design research programme at the Interactive Institute that I led in 2008–10, funded primarily by the Swedish Energy Agency. The Switch! Energy Futures team was Aude Messager, Thomas Thwaites, Basar Önal and myself. All artefacts, imagery and photography are from Switch!

Energy Futures documented in Figures 3.1, 3.2.1–15 and 3.3 and are by the Switch! Energy Futures team. Figure 3.1 displays documentation as pages from the Switch! book (Mazé 2013b) for which the graphic design was by Martin Frostner and Lisa Olausson at Medium.

Writing this paper was made possible through the project *Utopia Now Here* which was based at Konstfack University College of Arts, Crafts and sponsored by grants from Architecture in Effect, a strong research environment funded by the Swedish Research Council Formas at the School of Architecture of KTH Royal Institute of Technology and from Konstfack's Artistic Development fund. I am grateful for the helpful peer reviews from contributors to and editors of this book.

Note

1   While much of my work expands and develops notions of critical practice across contemporary (and some historical) design, architecture and craft (e.g. Mazé 2007, Ericson and Mazé, 2011), here I refer to a narrower niche of practice within industrial and interaction design.

References

Åhrén, U., Asplund, G., Gahn, W., Markelius, S., Paulsson G. and Sundahl E. (2008 [1931]), 'Acceptera', reprinted in L. Creagh, H. Kåberg and B. Miller Lane (eds.), *Modern Swedish Design*, 140–347, New York: Museum of Modern Art.

Antonelli, P. (ed.) (2008), *Design and the Elastic Mind*, New York: Museum of Modern Art.

Barry, A. (2001), *Political Machines*, London: Athlone Press.

Baxter, A. (ed.) (1996), *Vision of the Future*, Bliaricum, NL: V+K Publishing.

Berglund, E. (2015), 'Doing Things Differently is Always Theory and Practice', in Digital *Proceedings of the Design Anthropological Futures Conference*, Copenhagen, dK, unpaginated.

Brown, W. (1995), *States of Injury*, Princeton, NJ: Princeton University Press.

Dovey, K. (1999), *Framing Places: Mediating Power in Built Form*, New York: Routledge.

Dunne, A. and Raby, F. (2001), *Design Noir: The Secret Life of Electronic Objects*, Basel: Birkhäuser/August Media.

Ericson, M. and Mazé, R. (eds.) (2011), *DESIGN ACT Socially and Politically Engaged Design Today – Critical Roles and Emerging Tactics*, Berlin: Sternberg Press/Iaspis.

Fry, T. (2010), *Design as Politics*, New York: Bloomsbury.

Gabrielli, S. and Zoels, J. C. (2003), 'Creating Imaginable Futures', in digital *Proceedings of Designing User Experiences*, New York, unpaginated.

Gidley, J., Fien, J., Smith, J. A., Thomsen, D. and Smith, T. (2009), 'Participatory Futures Methods', in *Environmental Policy and Governance,* 19 (6): 427–40.

Glenn, J. C. and Gordon, T. J. (eds.) (2003), *Futures Research Methodology* 2, Washington DC: AC/UNU Millennium.

Grosz, E. (ed.) (1999), *Becomings: Explorations in Time, Memory and Futures*, Ithaca, NY: Cornell University Press.

Grosz, E. (2001), *Architecture from the Outside*, Cambridge, MA: MIT Press.

Grosz, E. (2004), *The Nick of Time: Politics, Evolution and the Untimely*, Durham, NC: Duke University Press.

Gunn, W., Otto, T. and Smith, R. C. (eds.) (2013), *Design Anthropology: Theory and Practice*, London and New York: Bloomsbury.

Harding, S. (2009), *Modernities, Sciences, and Democracy*, New York: Springer.

Inayatullah, S. (1990), 'Deconstructing and Reconstructing the Future: Predictive, Cultural and Critical Epistemologies', *Futures* 22 (2): 115–41.

Ingold, T. (2013), *Making: Anthropology, Archaeology, Art and Architecture*, London: Routledge.

Jameson, F. (2005), *Archaeologies of the Future*, London: Verso.

Jong, A. de and Mazé, R. (2010), 'Cultures of Sustainability: "Ways of Doing" Cooking', in digital *Proceedings of the ERSCP-EMSU Conference*, Delft, The Netherlands, unpaginated.

Keshavarz, M. and Mazé, R. (2013), 'Design and Dissensus: Framing and Staging Participation in Design Research', *Design Philosophy Papers,* 11 (1): 7–29.

Klanten, R., Ehmann, S. and Bohle, S. (eds.) (2012), *Cause and Effect: Visualizing Sustainability*, Berlin: Gestalten.

Levitas, R. (2007), 'The Imaginary Reconstitution of Society', in T. Moylan and R. Baccolini (eds.), *Utopia Method Vision: The Use Value of Social Dreaming*, 47–68, Bern: Peter Lang.

Lury, C. and Wakeford, N. (eds.) (2012), *Inventive Methods; The Happening of the Social*, New York: Routledge.

Mattsson, H. and Wallenstein, S. O. (2010), *Swedish Modernism: Architecture, Consumption and the Welfare State*, London: Black Dog.

Mau, B. and Leonard, J. (2004), *Massive Change*, London: Phaidon.

Mazé, R. (2007), *Occupying Time: Design, Technology and the Form of Interaction*, Stockholm: Axl Books.

Mazé, R. (2013a), 'Who is Sustainable? Querying the Politics of Sustainable Design Practices', in M. Plöjel, R. Mazé, L. Olausson, J. Redström and C. Zetterlund (eds.), *Share This Book: Critical Perspectives and Dialogues about Design and Sustainability*, 83–122, Stockholm: Axl Books.

Mazé, R. (ed.) (2013b), *SWITCH! Design and Everyday Energy Ecologies*, Stockholm: Interactive Institute Swedish ICT.

Mazé, R., Messager, A., Thwaites, T. and Önal, B. (2013), 'Energy Futures', in R. Mazé (ed.), *SWITCH! Design and Everyday Energy Ecologies*, 6–44, Stockholm: Interactive Institute Swedish ICT.

Mazé, R. and Redström, J. (2009), 'Difficult Forms: Critical Practices of Design and Research', *Research Design Journal,* 1 (1): 28–39.

Mol, A. (1999), 'Ontological Politics', in J. Law and J. Hassard (eds.), *Actor Network Theory and After*, 74–89, Oxford: Blackwell and the Sociological Review.

Mouffe, C. (2005), *On the Political (Thinking in Action)*, New York: Routledge.

Otto, T. and Smith, R. C. (2013), 'Design Anthropology: A Distinct Style of Knowing', in W. Gunn, T. Otto and R. C. Smith (eds.), *Design Anthropology: Theory and Practice*, 1–29, London and New York: Bloomsbury.

Prado, L. (2014), 'Privilege and Oppression: Towards a Feminist Speculative Design', in *Proceedings of the Design Research Society DRS Conference*, 980–90.

Quist, J. (2007), *Backcasting for a Sustainable Future*, Delft: Eburon Academic Publishers.

Rabinow, P. (2008), *Marking Time: On the Anthropology of the Contemporary*, Princeton, NJ and Oxford: Princeton University Press.

Rajchman, J. (1999), 'Diagram and Diagnosis', in E. Grosz (ed.), *Becomings*, 42–54, Ithaca, NY: Cornell University Press.

Rydell, R. and Schiavo, L., (eds.) (2010), *Designing Tomorrow: America's World's Fairs of the 1930s*, New Haven, CT: Yale University Press.

Scott, K., Bakker, C. and Quist, J. (2012), 'Designing Change by Living Change', *Design Studies,* 33 (3): 279–97.

Seago, A. and Dunne, A. (1999), 'New Methodologies in Art and Design Research: The Object as Discourse', *Design Issues,* 15 (2): 11–17.

Simon, H. (1996), *The Sciences of the Artificial*, Cambridge, MA: MIT Press.

Svenfelt, Å. (2010), *Two Strategies for Dealing with Uncertainty in Social-Ecological Systems*, PhD dissertation, KTH Royal Institute of Technology, Sweden.

Thackara, J. (ed.) (1988), *Design after Modernism: Beyond the Object*, London: Thames and Hudson.

Verbeek, P-P. and Slob, A. (eds.) (2006), *User Behavior and Technology Development*, Berlin: Springer.

Vergragt, P. (2010), 'Sustainability Future Visions: Impacts and New Strategies', in *Proceedings of the LeNS Conference*, 134–42.

Wakeford, N. (2014), Unpublished opponent comments to the PhD dissertation of Kristina Lindström and Åsa Ståhl, Malmö University, Sweden.

Wangel, J. (2012), *Making Futures: On Targets, Measures and Governance in Backcasting and Planning*, PhD dissertation, KTH Royal Institute of Technology, Sweden.

Wangel, J., Mazé, R., Jong, A. de and Höjer, M. (2012), 'Backcasting and Design for Sustainable Social Practices', in digital *Proceedings of the Nordic Conference on Consumer Research*, unpaginated.

4 Different Presents in the Making

MIKE ANUSAS AND RACHEL HARKNESS

Positionings and Possibilities

This chapter seeks to challenge aspects of anthropology and design that curtail their potential to be significant agents of social, material and ecological change for the better. In doing so we also seek to open up the possibility for the anthropological imagination to play a greater role in the shaping of the world; we are critical of anthropology where the discipline tends not to build upon observations of the world and keeps itself at an arm's length from the practical formation of future environments and things. Addressing design, we critique practices that produce and proliferate material things largely ignorant of the extended dynamics of time, materials and ecology. Whilst we acknowledge that these versions of the disciplines are to some extent stereotypes and (therefore) do not reflect their full scope, we still make the case that there is need for a radical reformulation of how materials, time and ecology are considered in anthropologically informed processes of design and making.

We develop our argument through the discussion of periods of participant observation that we carried out within two distinct situations of making. The first case is concerned with everyday working life in a product design studio, where activities of making are situated within a commercial consulting context. Here we examine how day-to-day experiences of time become contracted and relations with materials and ecology become narrowed. The second case focuses upon the practice of self-building, whereby people construct their own eco-friendly homes. Here, the makers work with a more extended idea of time, one that correlates with a pronounced sensitivity to materials and ecology.

Considering these two cases together, we draw out an important analytical point: that the different situations or processes of making reveal *different senses of the present,* and, furthermore, that different processes of making may invoke or at least encourage different perceptions of time. We refer to this phenomenon as 'different presents in the making', whereby socialities of making, perceptions of time, involvements with materials and sensitivities to ecology become bound up together and co-productive of one another. Underlying our point here is the idea that the grander notions of 'future', 'society' and 'ecology', and the possibilities that they entail, are always grounded in the experiential qualities of the present.

Whilst we are critical of the example of mainstream design that we see in our first case, and largely supportive of the alternative presented in the latter, our point is not to set them in opposition to one another. Instead, we wish to highlight that, the alternative approach of the latter opens up possibilities for practices of design and anthropology which are attuned to more extended dynamics of time, materials and ecology. Furthermore, we position ourselves within a stream of recent design anthropology thinking that considers 'ethnographies of the possible' (Halse 2013), adding our voices to attempts to 'counter the simplified image of ethnographers documenting existing practices and designers inventing future practices' (ibid.: 184). We concur with Otto and Smith when they suggest that a key contribution to be made by design anthropology is 'to extend the temporal horizon both forward and backward' (2013: 4).

With others within this stream (Gunn, Otto and Smith 2013; Otto 2013; Smith and Otto, this volume) we proceed in part by turning to the idea of the present and by drawing upon the argument that the present is 'constitutive of both past and future' (Halse 2013: 184). In this vein, Joachim Halse suggests that 'that which is proto-typed during a design event can be understood as extending the boundaries of the present' (ibid.). In this chapter, we draw upon our fieldwork to highlight practices of design and making that both depend upon and generate extended (that is, histori-cally sensitive and future-oriented) senses of the present. These practices often seem to do this by offering for consideration critical-hopeful possible alternatives – alternatives that are often beyond the boundaries of the present as it is currently conceived.

In drawing upon our fieldwork we intend to yield a fine-grained understanding of the everyday (in regular anthropological fashion), whilst pursuing a hope that 'the future could be different' (Bezaitis and Robinson 2011: 185), and it is here, in such a combination, that we think there lies a sense of what it means to practise design anthropology. That is to say that we pursue our work committed to a detailed elucidation of social life, but rather than being inclined to impress such insights into an ethnography, the 'descriptive or documentary aims of which impose their own finalities' (Ingold 2014: 390), we wish instead to energize and empower anthropo-logical insight in an active expository stance on design 'that could help us to think through its history and possibilities in a more critical and generative way' (Suchman 2011: 3). This would be a stance that extends the imaginative potential of anthro-pology to 'join in correspondence with those with whom we learn or among whom we study, in a movement that goes forward rather than back in time' (Ingold 2014: 390). Hence, it is with a purposeful, critical and exigent address that we carry a design anthropology not so much towards a disciplinary exchange of methods or innovation in research and design, but more towards a position from which it can combine a concern with critically interpreting the world with the intent to *change* it for the better (Marx 2014 [1845]).

We also aim to further anthropological engagements with making beyond those with craft practices and towards a critical interest in 'professional technology design' (Suchman 2011: 1). However, while keenly following Suchman's critical perspective, we do not find our anthropological approach aligning with either of her binary positions of anthropology *as* (or for) design or anthropology *of* design. That is, we are with Suchman when she is cautious about the idea of design 'as a model for anthropology's future' (ibid.), but do not see the best alternative to this as being the adoption of an 'of' stance that ultimately sees design 'best positioned as a problematic object for an anthropology of the contemporary' (ibid.). For if anthropological engagement recourses to conventionally positioning design as an object *of* examination, then a significant opportunity to grasp the potentially enlightening collaborative future of design anthropology as an integrated field has been missed. Moreover, our fieldwork reveals that makers – whether in arts, crafts, design or technology – possess their own *self*-critical capacities, with many striving to work critically and ecologically in their practice. We would rather, then, join with these socially hopeful projects, and add our critical and constructive energies to the efforts of those designers and makers, who, like many people, attempt to find a course in life that contributes to social, political and ecological transformation.

Working beyond Suchman's *as* and *of* binary, we tend towards Ingold's (2011: 226) anthropology *with*. Here we work with anthropology as a line of enquiry that can *weave in with* the lives of others, rather than as a discipline that has to encounter a socially encapsulated other. This, we think, is a much more empowering and hopeful future orientation for anthropology and design than that offered by remaining in a relationship of 'critic' versus 'subject of criticism'. Of course, to carry out an anthropology that is genuinely *with* others involves its challenges. To do so takes time, in part to gain the trust of participants, and much work to identify how, as anthropologist, one can be practically useful to projects that are in-the-making. When the skills possessed by an anthropologist are less valuable to projects at hand, they can often end up more on the sidelines of making activity and thus find themselves acquiring more of an *of* position.[1] In our experience, being able to become closely involved in a *with* capacity involves the shared unfolding of a subtle, careful and developmental course of discovering how one's own personal and anthropological skills can best be brought to bear on the particular characteristics of a common project. By steering and following this course, we have found that the anthropologist can lend a particularly valuable contribution by encouraging makers to attend to the deeper complexities of their practice and helping to realize the unfolding of new possibilities – possibilities which might have otherwise gone unnoticed. Overall, however, our trajectory towards a design anthropology *with* exists as one of ongoing aspiration and work-in-progress.

Making in a Close-Present

Our first field case is concerned with everyday working life in a commercial product design studio located on an industrial estate adjacent to the centre of a large UK city. Here, between 2012 and 2013, Anusas engaged in participant observation for a period of eight months, working as a full-time product designer, assisting project planning, research, conceptual design and prototype making, within a team of approximately eight people. We draw on this case because it is representative of design studios that operate in an industrial context and carry out a diversity of projects with specific creative and technical requirements. This particular studio designs products for professional, consumer, medical and energy sectors and typically has numerous projects running in parallel with different demands on expertise and time. Its capacities of making are diverse in terms of the range of skills employed and the associated tools and materials used, and on any day it is typical to see the practitioners engaged with freehand drawing, computer modelling, calculations and prototype-making using manual and machine skills.

Observations within the studio revealed time experienced as a linear particularization, where positioned intervals of minutes, hours, days and weeks are used to express temporal positions and outlooks within projects. Rarely do concerns with time extend beyond the largest of these intervals, and while sometimes there is reflection upon the past, there is overwhelmingly an orientation towards a future, as part of a plan of action. This notion of time is thus concerned with instances of time as detailed entities which are *about to* occur or *will soon* occur, and as particular, positioned entities they emphatically bind social activity into temporal units associated with specific actions. We refer to this notion of time as a *close-present*,

Figure 4.1 A typical working environment of a UK product design studio. In this case the practitioners are concurrently engaged in conversation, computation and making © Mike Anusas

Figure 4.4 Left: The south face of a relatively newly built Earthship home, New Mexico, 2006. The north face is 'bermed', or banked-up, with earth from the site. Right: An Earthship builder 'mudding' a wall with adobe (earthen) plaster © Rachel Harkness

earth and other 'natural' materials such as sheep's wool insulation too, and these are used as if they are 'borrowed' by the builders from their wider environments: they are incorporated with the knowledge that they will cycle back into the wider environment without negative or gross impact upon it.

The building of Earthships happens in 'free' time of evenings, weekends and holidays and during the more conventional 'work' times of 9am to 5pm. Boundaries between work and play, between the private space of the home and public spaces of work or meeting, are thus blurred. The way that Earthship-dwellers build and live is not so strictly clock-bound as their on-grid neighbours; schedules of building lurch and race depending on the people at the building's core and their lives, and upon the light and temperature afforded by season and weather. Furthermore, because many of the materials used to build Earthships are free or of low cost, and because low-tech methods and one's own labour are central to the Earthship concept, once the builder has secured land they are generally able to reduce their participation in conventional wage labour for money. Earthship homes are also powered by renewable energy systems (inexpensive to run once installed) and supplied by water catchment and treatment systems that tap into, and tend to mimic, weather cycles that are much greater than them. This tends to mean that as the sun rises, shines and sets, the rain falls or the snow melts, as the wind blows or dies down, and as the plants (of the dirty-water filtration system) grow, the builders and their buildings are part of these cyclical occurrences. As a result, their sense of time, like the shifting of their dependencies, tends to shift into those of their renewable resources, their water systems and their gardens.

Crucially, the eco-builders of Earthships (as is common with people across the wider field of eco-design and making) make the *far-reaching present* real or manifest in

Figure 4.5 Images from Earthship homes in New Mexico, United States. Left: Mosaic elaboration of a light switch in an earthen-plaster and rammed-earth-tyre wall. Right: A curved glass bottle-brick bathroom wall in-the-making © Rachel Harkness

the materials that they use and the way they make things because of a shared environmental sensibility or awareness. Environmental sensibilities and awareness then also become embedded in the everyday material culture of Earthships. For example, Figure 4.5, above, shows how something as simple as a light switch is visually formed so that it can be apprehended not just as a discreet entity in and of itself, but also as a point of relation between the utility of light and wider solar ecologies.

Though not everyone holds this sensibility in the same way, or even to the same extent, it will tend to include an agreement that many of the ways that people live on the planet are destructive. The wealthy people of the energy-intensive mass-consumerist so-called developed countries in the West are seen to have perhaps the most damaging ways of living. These ways are destructive not only to the natural environment of plants, animals, air, soil and water around them, but also to other people and ultimately also to their own health and happiness. Earthship builders gain their education in eco-building in various ways. Sometimes they have gleaned it themselves from 'how to' eco-build books and socio-environmental literature such as Leopold's *Sand County Almanac* (1949) or Rachel Carson's *Silent Spring* (1965). Other times it will have been picked up from fellow builders as they volunteered or worked together on eco-builds, or sometimes they will have had more formal environmental or ecological schooling. Often their education is by a mix of all of these means. Whichever way they have learnt, they talk about pollution – the phenomenon that their re-use of rubbish helps to combat – as a temporally extended phenomenon. They are both cognizant and vocal about the fact that pollution lasts, often long after the polluters, and its impact (whether plastic in the sea or chemical pollution and atmospheric change) reaches further than its initial area of release. The majority of these people have learnt and taken to heart that what is done or made here and now can have long-lasting and far-reaching impact, good or bad. Therefore, they take the time to source materials in relation to their provenance and potential future use; they are conscious of the limited resources on our planet; they consider architectural components not just in terms of their formative qualities, but also in terms of their embodied energy and/or their carbon footprint. This all takes time and care – often much more time than if they just used the resources supplied by their local building suppliers. Recycling, re-using, reclaiming and repurposing are integral to the activities of building and lend a cyclical sensibility to the whole project, where even human excreta are re-envisioned as useful and plentiful resources.

The eco-builders of Earthships often express themselves as being 'empowered' to forge alternative futures through being equipped to critique histories and the status quo. They draw on ideas of living from other places and times as design influences and thus are able to imagine, and literally build, different ways of living. Gathering their influences from far and wide, they see themselves as situated within the wider world, not only their immediate locale. Examples of this attitude can be found in builders' referencing of the communal efforts involved in American barn-raising as a historical precedent for the way that the Earthship community help each other to build. Similarly, it can be seen in the way that the influences of, say, a style of North African architecture, might be visible in the design and construction of a person's New Mexican desert home. As the Earthship owner-dwellers build their homes, the building competence that they possess and the relative freedom they have to experiment with their own building, on their own land, allows them to create homes which are intentionally understood as on-going, open to change and adaptation. Homes are rarely finished here it seems, with additions and adaptations and ongoing, in-progress-whilst-living-in building often being the norm. These buildings are transformative projects, coupling action at the everyday level of the home with a social, environmental and global perspective, connecting the everyday moment with other times – past and future both.

The Possibilities Afforded by Embracing the Extended Dynamics of Time, Materials and Ecology

Both cases of making that we draw upon are (as with all practices of making) ecologically situated: taking place within a dynamic of materials, organisms and forces. However, the way in which a *consciousness* of ecology is present within each case is notably different, and this correlates with different relations with materials and time. We now elaborate on this link between the different sorts of present being experienced and the quality of people's material, social and ecological engagements.

In the first case of the design studio, the practitioners' growth of their ecological awareness is not the primary intention of their practice. Rather, they are subject to, or complicit in, an industry that is primarily concerned with the formation of material objects and with the aim of enhancing human social and technical capacities whilst generating economic growth. However, in moments of reflection outwith the immersion of work towards a deadline, these practitioners do often express ecological concerns.[4] Such concerns, when pursued, typically involve engagements with reading on the subject,[5] or interest in state eco-initiatives such as those concerning the development of 'circular economies'.[6] These inclinations signal an openness to the social and cultural aspects of ecology as well as an interest in rethinking the fundamental conventions of design process and the material structures of manufacturing economies. However, the extent to which these design studio practitioners can act upon ecological concerns is always subservient to the interests of the project and the client. As we have seen, working within a *close-present* affords little opportunity for deeper reflection concerning the origin or the future of the materials they work with. Despite the existence of ecological design thinking – such as Stewart Brand's notion of the 'long now' (2000) which pushes to make long-term thinking more common – there still seems to be little momentum towards a perspective in product design which might offer a more radical and temporally-mobile sense of the present. That is, much 'ecological' product design fits too easily into the conventional ontologies the designers have acquired through their standard routes of learning. Ecological design is therefore often presented as another add-on methodology to product design, subsumed into a temporally-contracted close-present commercial perspective.

In our second case, the eco-builders are building their own homes, over time and in a different type of present that is far reaching in its outlook. These eco-builder practitioners are seemingly very aware – in their own way – that 'matter matters' (Barad 2003). They choose materials carefully and place great value upon hands-on engagement with them, while in-the-making. They hold the materiality of their physical surroundings as being incredibly important to their own health and wellbeing and that of others (human and non-human both). In addition to a different model of labour and ownership of the means of production, the approach to making that the self-builders take is fundamentally *not* object-bound. Their approach is generally an anti-consumerist one that is at play with multiple and simultaneous material, spatial, political, ecological and temporal concerns in the midst of a fluid materiality. Here the builder works with these flows to remain sensitive to their Earthship dwelling and its relationship with nearby people and habitats, as well as with global-scale transformations and atmospheres. Though building 'off-grid' so-to-speak, these builders are the opposite of isolationist: they are celebrators of life's interdependences and flows. Working with them as a researcher, one cannot help but become aware of, and responsive to, these characteristics of life, living and making.

On the subject of materials Karen Barad has suggested that '… materiality is an active factor in processes of materialization. Nature is neither a passive surface awaiting the mark of culture nor the end product of cultural performances' (Barad 2003: 827). With thinkers such as Ingold (2012), who paints a picture of the world as a dynamic meshwork, and De Landa (1997), who has argued for a deeply material and non-linear understanding of time, Barad therefore cogently presents the idea that 'matter is not a fixed essence; rather, matter is substance in its intra-active becoming—not a thing but a doing' (2003: 828). These ideas are highly evocative of the Earthship-builders' approach to living and dwelling: they and their makings *become together* in a world in motion. Their homes materialize as part of the builders' movement within the world's fluxes over time and from place to place. Thus, to work with Earthship builders is to feel these contemporary anthropological ideas become vital, to be able to think through, and think-through-making, this interpretation in a lived reality.

To summarize, the different presents that we have encountered in our research are indicative and generative of different socio-material ecological relationships with/in the world. In the nascent interest in circular design economies or the more radical eco-self-build movements, what is key is the forging of a different, alternative path. In fact, it is the myriad forging of many alternatives. It is this spirit of possible alternatives, of acting in a socially- and ecologically-conscious way, and of critical material engagement as a designer-maker in/of the world, that we then consider as being the sphere for our own practice as design anthropologists. We are inspired to think that our practice, here at this design/anthropology intersection (Bezaitis and Robinson 2011: 185), could be similarly oriented towards hopeful, socially-aware and ecological transformation, that we too could extend our present, and reach, with others, for different material and more ecological futures.

So, we close with a proposition: that there be a move towards a hopeful, open and projective ecological design anthropology practice. We believe that the adoption of a far-reaching present in processes of design, analysis and making can usefully dislodge both linear ideas of progress and object-bound and temporally-limited conceptions of materiality. It can pave the way for an acknowledgement of the unbounded and energetic qualities of materials, and reveal an extended sense of temporality where materials are in flux, continually undergoing transformation. We see an opportunity here for widespread hopeful design throughout communities and societies and a design anthropology that has far-reaching and long-term thinking at its core. This would be a design anthropology that draws on a reflexive and diverse understanding of life's multiple temporalities, and that directs such insight towards the formulation of a more open, socially-just and environmentally-conscious material life, intent on continued reinterpretation and resisting foreclosure.

Acknowledgements

We would like to acknowledge the support of the European Research Council funded 'Knowing From the Inside' project (University of Aberdeen) and the international Research Network for Design Anthropology. We would also like to thank the editors, Ton Otto and Rachel Charlotte Smith, and our network colleagues, Adam Drazin and Ramia Mazé, for their peer reviewing and input. Finally, we are very grateful to those with whom we worked during our fieldworks.

Notes

1 Of course, this is valuable in and of itself in that it affords opportunity to reflect upon things from a different angle.

2 The use of this phrase to denote technology as an agent for reducing development time is reflected in its acronymization in the title of a leading UK technology trade show: 'TCT Show + Personalize' run by the Rapid News Communications Group.

3 Materials that – we might note – take time to collect and gather.

4 The level of this concern tended to vary between individuals: some would regard an ecological focus as a progression of design thinking and methodology; others would hold ecological concerns close to their hearts, speaking of strong ethical orientations and even personal dilemmas about the effect of their own professional work.

5 The practitioners here showed interest in McDonough and Braungart's (2002) case for industry to adopt a cyclical, rather than unidirectional, design and manufacturing process, and an enthusiasm for the way in which Chapman (2005) foregrounds issues of emotional material attachment in ecological design.

6 The conceptual framework of the 'Circular Economy' highlights the transformational properties and potential of materials through considering artefacts as 'roundputs', designed to be 'made and made again' as part of processes of continual cyclical production and material flow. Such frameworks, which essentially highlight that materials have both histories and futures, sit in notable contrast to conventional linear depictions of the design process where materials appear to arrive from a virgin, neutral origin and, after a life as a specific object or artefact, appear to have no future destination as they disappear into the hidden realms of 'waste'.

References

Barad, K. (2003), 'Posthumanist Performativity: Toward an Understanding of How Matter Comes to Matter', *Signs: Journal of Women in Culture and Society*, 28 (3): 801–31.

Bezaitis, M. and Robinson, R. (2011), 'Valuable to Values: How "User Research" Ought to Change', in A. Clarke (ed.), *Design Anthropology: Object Culture in the 21st Century*, 184–201, Vienna and New York: Springer.

Brand, S. (2000), *The Clock of the Long Now: Time and Responsibility: The Ideas Behind the World's Slowest Computer*, New York: Basic Books.

Carson, R. (1965), *Silent Spring*, Harmondsworth: Penguin, in association with Hamilton.

Chapman, J. (2005), *Emotionally Durable Design: Objects, Experiences and Empathy*, London: Earthscan.

De Landa, M. (1997), *A Thousand Years of Nonlinear History*, Brooklyn, NY: Zone Books.

Design Council (2015), 'What is the Double Diamond?' September, 2015, http://www.designcouncil.org.uk/news-opinion/design-process-what-double-diamond (accessed 5 January 2016).

Gunn, W., Otto, T. and Smith, R. C. (eds.) (2013), *Design Anthropology: Theory and Practice*. London and New York: Bloomsbury.

Halse, J. (2013), 'Ethnographies of the Possible', in W. Gunn, T. Otto and R. C. Smith (eds.), *Design Anthropology: Theory and Practice*, 180–96, London and New York: Bloomsbury.

Harkness, R. (2009), *Thinking Building Dwelling: Examining Earthships in Taos, New Mexico and Fife, Scotland*, PhD dissertation, University of Aberdeen.

Ingold, T. (2011), *Being Alive: Essays on Movement, Knowledge and Description*, Abingdon: Routledge.

Ingold, T. (2012), 'Toward an Ecology of Materials', *Annual Review of Anthropology*, 41: 427–42.

Ingold, T. (2014), 'That's Enough About Ethnography!', *HAU Journal of Ethnographic Theory*, 4 (1): 383–95.

Leopold, A. (1949), *A Sand County Almanac and Sketches Here and There*, New York: Oxford University Press.

Marx, K. (2014 [1845]), 'Theses on Feuerbach', reproduced on *The Marx/Engels Internet Archive*, August 2014, www.marxists.org/archive/marx/works/1845/theses/engels.htm (accessed 5 January 2016).

McDonough, W. and Braungart, M. (2002), *Cradle to Cradle: Remaking the Way We Make Things*, New York: North Point Press.

Otto, T. (2013), 'Times of the Other: The Temporalities of Ethnographic Fieldwork', *Social Analysis,* 57 (1): 64–79.

Otto, T. and Smith, R. C. (2013), 'Design Anthropology: A Distinct Style of Knowing', in W. Gunn, T. Otto and R. C. Smith (eds.), *Design Anthropology: Theory and Practice*, 1–29, London and New York: Bloomsbury.

Suchman, L. (2011), 'Anthropological Relocations and the Limits of Design', *Annual Review of Anthropology*, 40: 1–18.

Ulrich, K. T. and Eppinger, S. D. (2012), *Product Design and Development*, New York: McGraw-Hill.

5   The New Design Ethnographers 1968–1974: Towards a Critical Historiography of Design Anthropology

ALISON J. CLARKE

Through examining the historical dimensions of the interrelatedness of design and anthropology, and the ways in which 'the space of the possible' emerged in the late 1960s and early 1970s, this chapter addresses the growing critique of design research in general, and its almost complete disregard of historiography. It examines how design shifted from a practice anchored to 'historical rationalism and industrial productivity' (Mendini 2013) to one embracing anthropological discourse and method as a means of setting in motion new ways of imagining a transitional future that repositioned design at the forefront of negotiating the relationship between the past, present and future.

Understanding the Politics of Participation

Contemporary design has emerged as an endlessly expandable phenomenon: trans-disciplinary, multi-disciplinary, cross-disciplinary, collaborative, participatory, critical, discursive, speculative, transitional. Within these various manifestations, the notion of the 'social' has taken on a newly valorized currency. A recent UK creative industries report analysing shifts in design practices identified the area of 'social design' alone as having proliferated to such an extent in the last decade as to make a fully conclusive overview of its economic and research-impact unfeasible (Armstrong et al. 2014). This design boom is a strikingly recent phenomenon warranting urgent critical historicization. As Guy Julier has observed, when the Yellow Pages (UK commercial telephone listings) were launched in 1966 'there were just three design consultancies listed in central London' (2012: 312). Today, it would be near impossible to calculate the sheer scale, configuration and variety of stakeholders – users, citizens and professional experts – that make up the list of global design consultancies and related offshoot design activities.

The prising away of design from conventional linear models of conceptualization, production, materiality and concomitant constructs of future-making is a well-rehearsed 'post-thing' narrative of twenty-first century design; hailing from the broader post-Fordist shift of the 1970s and 1980s (Thackara 1988) and re-claimed more recently in contemporary 'transition' design education curricula (Irwin, Tonkinwise and Kossoff 2014). Within this shift one specific area that design anthropology and material culture studies has brought to the fore is an emphasis on the practice of design itself, rather than its objects and outcomes. Anthropologist Adam Drazin has argued further that 'design negotiate[s] subject–object relationships in everyday life, […] with particular social effects in the world' and so 'merits attention as a cultural field in itself' (Drazin 2013: 37). Design, according to Drazin, is not a 'politically or socially neutral space', rather design concepts themselves should be understood as 'phenomena that mediate what kinds of relationships individual people, citizens, consumers, and others have with governments, corporations, and international bodies' (Drazin 2013: 36).

In this description, Drazin also brings to mind the historiography of design history, a discipline emerging in the UK in the late 1970s in conjunction with the radicalism of the so-called 'new art history' as a response to the perceived lack of theoretical and empirical understanding of design's constituency within political economy and everyday life (Rees and Borzello 1986; Walker 1989). Along with the rise of visual culture analysis, which challenged the hierarchical paradigms of art history, design history merged with cultural studies concretizing in publications such as BLOCK magazine. Featuring key contemporary figures including feminist art historian Griselda Pollock and ersatz design historian Dick Hebdige (Hannah and Putnam 1996), BLOCK defined a new approach to popular culture, the politics of objects and the experiential validity of users, marking design as a serious object of political study (Bird et al. 1996). Conceptually tied to the ground-breaking Birmingham Centre for Contemporary Cultural Studies (CCCS), which heralded cultural studies as a new discipline embracing ethnographic methodology applied to contemporary life, BLOCK and its authors represented a broader shift towards social and cultural emphasis that would transform design education curricula from polytechnics to art schools.

A similarly radical shift has taken place in the twenty-first century as 'the social' is placed centre-stage in an explosion of generalized academic programmes; co-design, design research, design thinking and design cultures and their concomitant hybridized doctorates, now the staple of design education unhinged from the disciplinary straitjackets of a 'beaux-arts' art school model. Partly in response to the debates around sustainability and the 'Anthropocene', alternative design 'schools' based on experiential events and workshop-based activities are excising the Eurocentric modernist legacy from design and bringing to account its overly-simplistic problem-solving humanist agendas (Irwin, et al. 2015; Thackara 2015). New design initiatives have even extended backwards into secondary education, claiming 'to shape students into change agents', equipping them with an agility demanded by an increasingly 'complex world'.[1] The conceptual opening up of design beyond the 'man-made', as well as a growing scrutiny of its historical role in the inculcation of Western development agendas has undeniably lent design a newly honed contemporary relevance (Escobar 2011; Clarke 2016a).

Surely then this diffuse and expanded activity in design, the unerring emphasis on the social, participatory and co-created, provides a progressive and fecund backdrop to the future of a field loosely defined as design anthropology? Yet untethered from historiographical underpinning, this hyper-inflated design culture runs the risk of undermining itself; its pluralism and amorphous quality, as design critic Rick Poynor asserts, leading to the loss of design's capacity for dissent (Poynor 2014).

It would be no exaggeration to claim that the perceived 'post-thing' shift in design's social and economic relevance, at this point in the twenty-first century, is as fictionalized as the populist notion of the industrial design profession in the 1930s, famously culminating with Raymond Loewy's appearance on the front cover of *Time* magazine in 1949. Hailed as the saviour of the US economy, 'futuring' everyday life and boosting consumer spending through the application of streamlining to the entire spectrum of material culture, Loewy and contemporaries such as Bel Geddes promoted consumer-driven 'futurama' design visions at events such as the 1939 New York World's Fair (Rydell and Schiavo 2010).

While Loewy's single-handed transformation of a nation's corporate fortune is an over-simplistic cliché of design culture, it is useful to remember that this simplistic representation of design as a totem of 'futuring' is an integral part of a historio-graphy to which contemporary design anthropology belongs. Within later design criticism (from Reyner Banham to Tony Fry; compare Banham 1971 and Fry 1999) and purist European modernism, 'streamlining' came to represent the false promise of market-driven design, its outer casing seen as a metaphor for design's role in disguising the authentic inner workings of messy social life – a messiness that the 'real' design discourse popularized in Victor Papanek's *Design for the Real World: Human Ecology and Social Change* (1971) was built upon addressing in the late post-war period. It is perhaps at this juncture that the emergence of a type of design anthropology that we might recognize today first becomes visible.

The commonsensical notion of the designer as envisaging and 'making' the future is at once clichéd and pertinent. Yet this largely unexamined process of imagining, veiled in the rhetoric of intuition, still lies at the core of design practice's representation. As Jamer Hunt (2011) describes in his essay 'Prototyping the Social: Temporality and Speculative Futures at the Intersection of Design and Culture', the coming together of design and anthropology opens up a fertile tension between the non-projective analysis of ethnography and design. An ethnographer, observes Hunt, 'works in ever greater detail to ensure that she has got the present "just right"'. Design, on the other hand, 'is a practice of material and immaterial making, […] generative, speculative, transformational'. In contrast to the ethnographer, 'the designer uses the present – and uses it often imperfectly – as a provisional leaping off point for re-imagining possible futures' (Hunt 2011: 35).

It is worth remembering that at the core of the imaginary and the speculative within design, history has always played a major theoretical and conceptual part that this explosion in contemporary design now largely neglects, or actively denies through its lack of engagement with historiographical framing and its acritical approach to 'the social'.

Within the area of art practice, Hal Foster has similarly queried the effect of the diminishing critical role of history in the realm of the 'contemporary'. 'Perhaps it might not matter anymore if [art]work has a historical connection', comments Foster, '[Maybe] that is just no longer the point. But, if so, consider what is lost. Not so long ago art not only "made it new" but also made things count, or made the attempt to count' (Schneider and Hussain 2010).

Likewise, art historian Claire Bishop's searing critique of 'relational aesthetics' and the rise over the last decade of participatory art projects (conceived as counterpoint to the commodified, self-branded neo-liberal artist) highlights the loss of criticality that has evolved with 'the social turn' in practice: 'the urgency of this *social* task has led to a situation in which socially collaborative practices are all perceived to be equally important' (Bishop 2012: 12, emphasis in original). In an historiographic overview of participatory art practice, Bishop concludes that contemporary art has lost its critical capacity, with the collaborative and the social now 'perceived to offer an automatic counter-model of social unity, regardless of its actual politics'. Like Foster, she argues for the vital interweaving of historiography within practice, finding it almost entirely absent from current practice discourse.

As design shifts to an ever-expanded entity historiography takes on a vital prescience. 'Without [history]', Foster has argued, it is 'hard to determine what is at stake and of value' (Schneider and Hussain 2010). How can design anthropology avoid descending into an aggregate field of participatory methodologies loosely premised on an acritical notion of 'the social' that assumes some inherent and automatic agenda of innovation, just through the mere inclusion of participatory methodology? In exploring this question, I argue for the need to examine precisely the historical roots, circumstances and discourses of alternative design movements that emerged in protest against Western power structures in their modernist manifestations, from development policies to urban planning, from consumerism to elitist design education.

Anthropological Futures: Italian Design Radicals meet US Populism

In 1974, the agenda-setting design journal *Casabella* spelled out an explicit shift in editorial stance. Distancing itself from what it described as the 'historical rationalism and industrial productivity' of the Hochschule für Gestaltung Ulm that had dominated design discourse and form-making over the previous decade, the cutting-edge Italian journal pointed instead to a cross-cultural and broadly anthropological approach to design (Clarke 2016b).

Under the title 'Design and Underdevelopment' ['Design e Sottosvillupo'] *Casabella* condemned the design profession for its 'designing exclusively for elites' and rejected outright 'the pollution of the field by non-usable objects' (Anon 1974). The journal's editor since 1971, Alessandro Mendini had quickly established Casabella as a forum of newly honed critical perspective. Emphasizing international radical and counter-design, and the dissolution of antiquated disciplinary boundaries, it became widely understood as 'the primary instrument of diffusion' for the design avant-gardes (Prina 2010: 217).

Casabella's front cover had famously featured an ensemble of radical Italian architects and designers joined together under the auspices of an alternative design movement titled 'Global Tools'. A manifesto of anti-industrial design, the Global Tools initiative revolved around a concept of networked educational, consciousness-raising events and laboratories (Franceschini and Borgonuovo 2015; Prina 2010). Whilst being unerringly avant-gardist, one of the group's principal aims was to see the devolution of design as a multi-disciplinary phenomenon used to counter, rather than affect, alienation associated with industrial life – to quote Mendini himself the Global Tools project meant 'returning to a primordial type of design that was non-designed, primitive and handmade' (2013: 9).

The Italian avant-gardists of Archizoom, SUPERSTUDIO and the Global Tools initiative are the most comprehensively documented design activists of the 1960s and 1970s and thus perhaps the most often cited. While much of their creative output was confined to an elitist audience of fellow architects and designers, they overtly tied their work to the broader politics and theories of Italian post-Fordist politics (Negri and Grafder 2013); the leading Global Tools figure Adolfo Natalini making one of many denunciating statements:

> If design is merely an inducement to consume, then we must reject design; if archi-tecture is merely the codifying of the bourgeois models of ownership and society, then we must reject architecture; ... until all design activities are aimed towards meeting primary needs. Until then, design must disappear (Natalini 2003: 167).

Significantly, as historian Ross Elfline argues, in a backdrop of mass unemployment, the radical Italian designers simply redefined what counts as design labour (Elfline 2016). In the fourteen years the Global Tools group was active (1966–1980) they were not involved in creating actual buildings – their work was unerringly 'post-thing' – they made a profusion of films, installations, architectural plans and interventions. Superstudio and their ilk influenced by the writings of the Italian workers' movements known as "Operaismo" and "Autonomia" adopted a "refusal to work" stance in an attempt to 'locate an affective space in which the individual worker's affects remain his own' (Elfline Ibid. 64).

The shift from design labour was defined by the stripping away of design process in search of an ur-design practice of essential, social value in which immersion in communities, leading to anthropological understandings, took on a new value.

The radical Italian's work reached an international audience in the form of the MoMA, design show Italy: The New Domestic Landscape (1972). By 1976, with the MANtransFORMS/Aspects of Design exhibit at the Cooper Hewitt National Design Museum in New York, the fusing of design and anthropology, and the appropriation of ethnography and ethnological pretexts was evident beyond the experimental design activists. This exhibit, guest-curated by Austrian architect Hans Hollein, brought together leading international architects and industrial designers exploring design as a cross-cultural force tied to the anthropology of the everyday rather than the formal design studio (Clarke 2011).

Italian designer Ettore Sottsass Jr. had shown his iconic fibreglass multi-functional furniture unit designed for the Italian electronics and office firm Olivetti at the MoMA *Italy: The New Domestic Landscape* show. For MANtransFORMS, however, Italy's premier industrial designer disassociated himself entirely from the machinations of corporate industrial design. He presented instead a series of wistful black and white photographs showing design embedded in desolate natural landscapes, and an accompanying text that read as poetic ethnographic notes. Like a type of conceptual folklorist, Sottsass used the designs to provoke the viewer into considering simultaneously the inanity and the profundity of the design process. Verging on the *Arte Povera* tradition, the jarring installations questioned the social purpose of design and its impact on the environment (Clarke 2013b).

Similarly, the anthropological and ethnological projects of the Italian design group SUPERSTUDIO in the late 1960s and early 1970s used indigenous artefacts plucked from their natural settings for pedagogical purposes. Political economic critiques of commodity form, influenced by newly available Italian translations of Marx's *Grundrisse,* bolstered the search for design influence within the pre-industrial and the found. At the School of Architecture at the University of Florence, SUPERSTUDIO design members, led by Adolfo Natalini, conducted a research course titled Extra-Urban Material Culture exploring Italian indigenous peasant material culture that formed the research basis for *Project Zeno*, Venice Biennale 1978 (Lang and Menking 2003).

The otherness of the vernacular and the rise of material culture studies within archaeology and anthropology of the period made a vital impact on the configuration of design curricula beyond Modernism. The new significance of 'stuff' and its associated modes of methodological inquiry, including historical analysis of non-literary cultures through scrutiny of design's materiality and 'use', evolved into a broader post-processual disciplinary shift in which objects of popular design and consumption took on a new significance; so much so that a decade later even a comparative archaeological study of the design of contemporary Swedish and English beer cans proved legitimate within the upper echelons of the academe (Shanks and Tilley 1982).

In 1974, Kenneth Frampton's widely cited piece 'On Reading Heidegger', heading the cutting-edge architectural journal *Oppositions*, had had an enormous influence across practice. *Oppositions* emanated from the New York-based Institute for Architecture and Urban Studies – IAUS – an institute notably embraced by MoMA design curator Emilio Ambasz who initiated a number of co-partnered projects and shared their visions of urban design (Colombina et al. 2012). Heidegger's theory of dwelling as applied to architecture was taken as a shorthand for the more general concerns of phenomenological approaches during this period and signalled a turn from a Cartesian understanding of object worlds as being intrinsically separate from the subject – as seen in Modernist abstracted rationality – to an emphasis on embodied experience. Phenomenology proposed a model in which, to quote Julian Thomas, design 'worked outward from people's everyday involvement with the world, rather than imposing a utilitarian spatial order from above' (Thomas 2006: 49).

For Frampton and his contemporaries this approach to architecture had an overtly politic departure; 'tabula rasa fantasies of the Enlightenment lose a deal of their authority as with the manifest exhaustion of non-renewable resources the techno-utopic myth of unlimited progress becomes somewhat discredited' (Frampton 1974: 4). Inspired by radical ecology and the move towards the de-privatization of resources, Frampton declared that 'design goals, as the motives of our instrumentality, may only be legitimized through the activation of the public sphere' (Ibid.).

Decrying the 'billboard facades' 'roadside kitsch' and 'somnambulism of television' – Frampton's critique of the 'fabricated mirage of somewhere' that made up contemporary urban life, was strikingly redolent of the populist design critiques made so familiar by US Austrian émigré Victor Papanek's Design For the Real World: Human Ecology and Social Change. Papanek, who self-identified as a designer and anthropologist, popularized European activism in the guise of US anti-corporate rhetoric (drawing on the tradition of best-selling cultural critics such as Vance Packard, author of The Waste Makers, 1960) and used outsider and indigenous design as a counterpoise to the inauthenticity of capitalist industrial design.

Papanek's sloganizing book Design for the Real World, first published in English in 1971, acted as a design activist's handbook, advocating co-design, participant immersion and anthropological models of inquiry. The polemic has purportedly never fallen out of print in 40 years; available in over a dozen languages it is arguably the clearest historiographical link to the formation of a contemporary global design anthropology discipline emanating from activist design practice (as opposed to the corporate sector).

A Small but Significant Uprising in Denmark

By 1972, Papanek's treatise on the social purpose of contemporary design had proved so popular in Europe that he was invited as guest professor at the Danish Academy of Fine Arts in Copenhagen, a position that coincided with the release of the Danish version of Design for the Real World, titled Miljø for millioner – Design for behov eller profit (1972) (see Figure 5.1). One national journalist described him as 'a knight in shining armour' and a 'crusader for a better world', drawing parallels between Papanek and the US consumer rights campaigner Ralph Nader; both provoking the ire of industrialists and harbouring grand ambitions to improve the world.[2]

Papanek's presence tallied with, if not inspired, a small but significant uprising at the design and architecture studios of the Danish Academy. In late September 1972, Jens Olsen, a young would-be architecture student turned design activist,

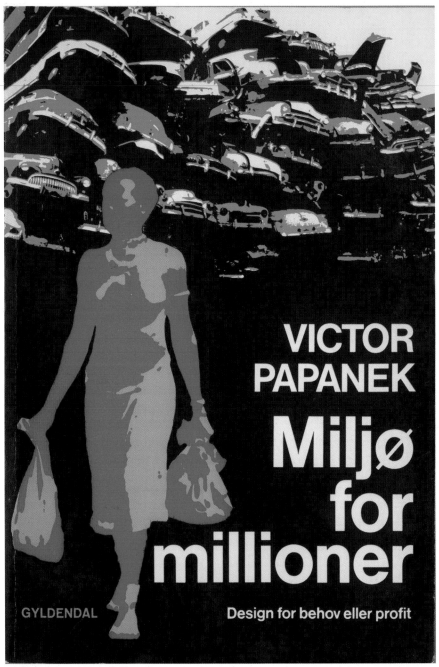

Figure 5.1 Victor Papanek, *Miljø for Millioner*, (Gyldendal: Copenhagen, 1972), cover design © William Saxtorph. Courtesy of Victor J. Papanek Foundation, University of Applied Arts Vienna

rallied together a group of disaffected students who, like himself, had failed to pass the Academy's entrance exam.[3]

Olsen's aim was to expose what he perceived as the unspoken hierarchies at work in Danish design culture – a design culture whose rules ensured that (in Olsen's words) 'only a few people and mostly people from architectural families' made it into the Academy, and consequently the broader national Danish design scene. To Olsen and his dissenting contemporaries, this professional nepotism was inextricably linked to the prolonged observance of an elitist Danish design culture of 'good form'; a culture that focused on design connoisseurship and the notion of distinction (in the crudest Bourdieuian sense). It was this hierarchy of cultural capital, rather than a democratic vision of good form and function for all, that sustained adherence to a design culture based on formal aesthetics and exclusion. Olsen and his disaffected group of would-be students had an agenda for design that envisaged collaboration and 'real' social engagement.

As a counterpoise to the social class bias and dynastic design and architecture structure in which the Danish Royal Academy was entrenched, a group of newly forged design activists demanded that the Academy open itself up as a non-hierarchical interdisciplinary place of learning in which anyone with an interest in design or architecture could participate, regardless of formal qualifications or connections. The politics of inclusion and co-design sketched out in the prominent contemporary discourse around urban space (see Jacobs 1961; Gehl 1971; Rudofsky 1965) was not just extended to design, rather design practice itself turned to anthropology in all its facets – embracing notions and theories that had heavily influenced architectural theory of the period (Otero-Pailos 2010).

On the back of a ground-swell of international student activism, the humanitarian horrors of Vietnam and the Biafra–Nigerian civil war, the notion of 'design for need' emerged as an ever more potent theme. Design took on a new prescience as the focus of protests against consumerism and materialism, with the May 1968 14th Milano Triennale themed 'The Greater Number' ransacked by student and political activists (Nicolin 2008).

Papanek's major thesis, that design could serve a greater social service more integrated to 'real' user needs, drew heavily on his interaction in the 1960s with Scandinavian design students; indeed he lamented in the early 1970s that while Scandinavia provided a fertile ground for his ideas, in the US he had been lambasted as a controversial figure set on undermining the professional design industry.[4] An invitation from the Scandinavian Design Students' Organization (sdo) with whom he conducted a seminar in Copenhagen in the summer of 1969 (Clarke 2013b; 2015) led to one of his most influential designs – a hand-drawn diagrammatic flowchart titled 'Work Chart for Designers' (see Figure 5.2). Drawn up in the course of illustrating a holistic approach to design thinking around the issue of disability, Papanek generated a diagram laying bare 'the social and moral responsibility of the designer and his [sic] position in a profit-oriented society' (Papanek 1971: 277). The pull-out flowchart, featured in the 1971 English-language edition of Design for the

Real World, was intended as an interactive tool to provoke critical design thinking: 'The reader is encouraged to play with the flow chart, to add to it and discover his [sic] own relationships [...], completed, it will form a social and political blueprint for tomorrow – for society as well as design.' (Papanek 1971: 278). A crucial part of the diagram was the drawing of 'The Minimal Design Team' – a team that incorporated anthropology, social and behavioural sciences, structural biology and mathematics, psychology, engineer, media, ecology, the architect, the designer and 'A representation of the REAL '"client" Group'; dubbed the 'Copenhagen Chart', the flowchart was later made into a purchasable poster.

With the abandonment of the Danish Academy's former entrance policies, design education was bordering on chaos as numbers of informal students moved between studios freely, many without formal studio space or structured programmes. In an attempt to appease the chaos of the 'open door' policy – and sympathizing with the social design agenda of the students – one of the Academy design professors invited Papanek to address the newly radicalized student caucus. 'Design', declared Papanek in one of the opening pages 'is a luxury enjoyed by a small clique who form the technological moneyed, and cultural "elite" of each nation' (Papanek 1971). For Danish students like Olsen such polemic must have seemed unerringly apposite in the context of the 'Good Design' tyranny, which he perceived as a form of repression.

By 1973, the Academy still in flux, Papanek tutored students in design projects with overtly social remits: Corn mills for Africa; toys for pre-school children; exercise

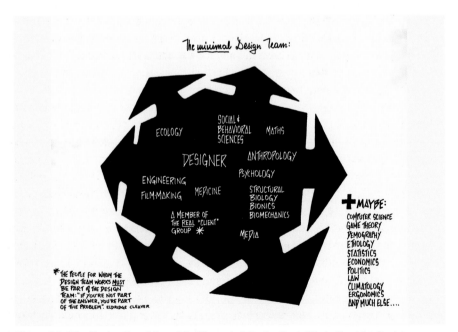

Figure 5.2 'The Design Team' from 'Big Character' Poster No.1: Work Chart for Designers (1973) © Victor J. Papanek Foundation, University of Applied Arts Vienna.

apparatus for pregnant women; jigsaw puzzle for blind children; crutches; an oven for developing countries; desk fan for developing countries; play- and work-cart for kindergartens.

With students re-visiting Rachel Carson's environmental treatise *Silent Spring* (1964), and volumes such as Teresa Hayter's critical *Aid as Imperialism* (1971) and E. F. Schumacher's highly influential *Small is Beautiful: A Study of Economics as If People Mattered* (1973), design had taken on a new prescience in addressing social inequality and challenging top-down solutions. The formerly disaffected student Olsen, for example, worked on a project designing a wagon to transport kindergarten children housed in one of the major squats in Copenhagen to a scout hut in the woods. This project was at once sensitive to the needs of those on the periphery of societal power structures, and overtly political: the presence of the kindergarten group in the squat prevented police from storming the place.

This vignette is illustrative of a pan-European radicalization of design schools that had begun in the late 1960s and persisted into the early 1970s (Colombina et al. 2012). But it is important to mention that the design upsurge was not confined to the art school – it was directly linked to Worker's Unions, ecological groups, pedagogic reform, NGOs, social landscape movement, ergonomics, alternative and appropriate technology, community activism, disability rights, alternative transport activists, health design, occupational therapy and humanitarian relief.

In simple terms this period marked a turning point in design practice in which anthropologically inspired research, collaboration and process took on a new political significance that was the subject of fierce debate and criticism. Danish social anthropologist Mette Bovin, faculty at Aarhus University, was perhaps the most adroit at recognizing the interdisciplinary potential of a new 'design anthropology'. As a young student, Bovin herself had been instrumental, in the late 1960s, in establishing a now well-known relationship with Evans-Pritchard and Aarhus University, and thus with the British school of anthropology (James 2007: 182).

In 1973, in a national left-leaning Danish newspaper, Bovin offered a portrait of the peripatetic design critic under the title 'Victor Papanek's Ideas and Anthropology' in which she highlighted parallels between his and anthropology's methodological approach: the holistic view of the human being, methods of analysis based on participation and in-depth cultural awareness. The fact that Papanek had spent half his life outside of his 'native culture', and that he used this as a productive method of reflective distancing, critiquing power relations and giving voice to the 'client group', made Papanek directly comparable to a contemporary anthropologist by Bovin's account. She concluded that his approach contrasted only in that he did not only locate 'interesting problems' but contributed solutions through design (Bovin 1973).

Under a sub-title 'Anthropology and the failures', Bovin reinforced calls for interdisciplinary team-work, using the example of her own professional experiences as an agricultural advisor in South East Asia to illustrate her point. Her own fieldwork research, she argued, had led to a recommendation for the re-design of ploughs from steel to plastic; the former material being in conflict with the indigenous populations' religious beliefs leading to their abandonment of the tools. Bovin asserted that research conducted by a multidisciplinary team prior to the issue of the ploughs would have foreseen this 'user' problem, taking into account the cultural subtleties surrounding even the most basic functional object. While, for ethical reasons anthropologists, as a matter of course, would normally prohibit such interventions, denying the possibility of 'hands-on' application, Bovin called for a wholesale 'de-mystification' of disciplinary boundaries and the re-thinking of anthropology's intent.

Figures outside the Academy recognized the broader potential of an interdisciplinary design culture. However, Papanek's Danish educative intervention did not escape controversy. Towards the end of his position at the Royal Academy of Fine Arts in Copenhagen, in an open newspaper interview, Papanek criticized the design students for their lack of tenacity and bourgeois romanticism as well as the chaos which reigned within the institution. Finally, sealing his shift away from broader political activism, Papanek argued that good designers should be socially aware, but remain politically unaffiliated. Erik Herløw, head of the design school was forced to defend the cohort in a national newspaper interview explaining the year-long upheaval as an experimental phase. He made assurances that the turmoil and insecurity was merely part of a more general youth upheaval that would soon 'settle down'.[5]

Towards a Critically Reflective Design Anthropology

Ultimately the initiatives of radical designers, design critics and design activists impacted the broader industrial design late post-war community with their explicit turn towards qualitative, participatory design and ethnography and their overt politicization of design practice beyond a modernist, rationalist paradigm. Contemporary design anthropological practice has left the legacy of this proto-design anthropology largely unacknowledged, despite inadvertently and consistently drawing on the major tenets of its legacy in exploring 'the space of the possible'. From the Italian *Global Tools* initiative with its direct relation to Italian worker-politics, to the design critic Victor Papanek's pivotal role in imagining a late post-war pan-Scandinavian counter-design culture, this chapter brings into focus the significance of specific historical encounters and theoretical episodes in the making of design anthropology as a field. It argues that the unpacking of a historiographical trajectory is a vital and necessary part of creating self-reflective and critically informed design anthropological futures.

These earlier encounters between the disciplines emphasized the critical reflexivity inherent in an ethical design practice that engendered global relevance while valuing 'the local' and the specific. As future design cultures marry the demands of a neo-liberal economic agenda with those of a broad sweeping definition of 'the social', maintaining the cultural and political specificity of design and its rootedness in groups outside of the corporate and governmental is of paramount concern.

As anthropologist Keith Murphy asserts in his ethnography of contemporary Swedish design, the ways in which ideology and 'things' intersect, makes design a practice that uniquely 'encompasses both the ways in which the qualities of objects are literally given shape and how those forms come to acquire socially relevant meanings [...] their agency materializes as an achievement, the product of asymmetrical forces that together grant design its politics' (Murphy 2015). The historical contextualization of design is vital in preventing design anthropology from devolving into a project of unfettered relativism. In considering the role of 'design things', the processes of making and collaboration in the context of design anthropology, the tracing of design's relationship to anthropology offers a vital element in reclaiming the area's critical capacity (Clarke 2017). This brief insight into the rise of ethnography, and anthropology as an integral aspect of late 1960s and 70s activism, and its specific historiographical relations to Scandinavian design offers a starting point to this project.

Acknowledgements

The author wishes to acknowledge a Botstiber Institute for Austrian-American Studies (BIAAS) award in support of research related to this chapter.

Notes

1   The emergence of design high schools as an antidote to conventional academic training is an expanding phenomenon – see for example self-organized high school design education on http://designschoolx.tumblr.com/PURPOSE.
2   Anon. (1972), 'Problemløser og missionær', *Ingeniørens Ugeblad*, 10 November.
3   Jens Olsen is the pseudonym for a former student, with whom oral history interviews were conducted with the author in Denmark, November 2013. Olsen, later critical of Papanek's presence in the school, wished to remain anonymous.
4   Jørgen Lind, 'Professorens største succes: NYHED PÅ KONKONSERVESDÅSE' MORGENAVISEN Jyllands-Posten, 8 October 1972.
5   Author acronym, J. S., 'Designskolens leder svarer på gæsteprofessorens kritik', in *Dagbladet Information*, 4/5 August 1973.

References

Anon. (1974), 'Design e Sottosvillupo ('Design and Underdevelopment')', *Casabella,* 385: 42.
Armstrong, L., Bailey, J., Julier, G. and Kimbell, L. (2014), *Social Design Futures: HEI Research and the AHRC. Report for the Arts and Humanities Research Council*, Brighton: University of Brighton.
Banham, R. (1971), *Los Angeles: The Architecture of Four Ecologies*, London: Allen Lane.
Bird, J. (1996), *The BLOCK Reader in Visual Culture*, London: Routledge.
Bishop, C. (2012), *Artificial Hells: Participatory Art and the Politics of Spectatorship*, London: Verso.
Bovin, M. (1973), 'PORTRÆT: Victor Papaneks ideer og antropologien', in *Dagbladet Information*, 11 September.
Carson, R. (1964), *Silent Spring*, New York: Fawcett Crest.
Clarke, A. J. (2011), 'The Anthropological Object in Design: From Victor Papanek to

Superstudio', in A. J. Clarke (ed.), *Design Anthropology: Object Culture in the 21st Century*, 74–87, Vienna and New York: Springer.

Clarke, A. J. (2013a), '"Actions Speak Louder": Victor Papanek and the Legacy of Design Activism', *Design and Culture*, 5 (2): 151–68.

Clarke, A. J. (2013b), 'Ettore Sottsass: The Design Ethnologist', in A. Coles and C. Rossi (eds.), *The Italian Avant-Garde 1968–1976*, 67–78, Berlin: Sternberg Press.

Clarke, A. J. (2015), 'Buckminster Fuller's Portable Reindeer Abattoir and Other Designs for the Real World', in A. Blauvelt (ed.), *Hippie Modernism: The Struggle for Utopia*, 68–75, Minneapolis: Walker Art Center.

Clarke, A. J. (2016a) 'Design for Development, ICSID and UNIDO: The Anthropological Turn in 1970s Design', *Journal of Design History*, 29 (1): 43–57.

Clarke, A. J. (2016b), 'Survival: The Indigenous and the Autochthon', in Franceschini, S. and Borgonuovo, V. (eds.), *Global Tools: 1973–2015: When Education Coincides with Life*, Berlin: Archive Books.

Clarke, A. J. (ed.) (2017) Design Anthropology: Object Cultures in Transition, Oxford: Bloomsbury.

Clifford, D. H. (2015), 'Purpose', http://designschoolx.tumblr.com/PURPOSE (accessed 5 January 2016).

Colombina, B. with Choi, E., Gonzalez Galan, I. and Meister, A. M. (2012), 'Radical Pedagogies in Architectural Education', *Architectural Review*, September 2012, http://www.architectural-review.com/education/radical-pedagogies-in-architectural-education/8636066.article (accessed 5 January 2016).

Drazin, A. (2013), 'The Social Life of Concepts in Design Anthropology', in W. Gunn, T. Otto and R. C. Smith (eds.), *Design Anthropology: Theory and Practice*, 33–50, London and New York: Bloomsbury.

Elfline, R. K. (2016) Superstudio and the "Refusal to Work", *Design and Culture*, 8(1): 55–77.

Escobar, A. (2011), 'Sustainability: Design for the Pluriverse', *Development*, 54: 137–40.

Frampton, K. (1974), 'On Reading Heidegger', *Oppositions*, 4: 1–4.

Fry, T. (1999), *A New Design Philosophy: An Introduction to Defuturing*, Sydney: University of New South Wales Press.

Gehl, J. (1971), *Livet Mellem Husene*, Copenhagen: Arkitektens Forlag.

Hannah, F. and Putnam, T. (1996), 'Taking Stock in Design History [1980 Issue 3 BLOCK]', in J. Bird and B. Curtis (eds.), *The Block Reader in Visual Culture*, 134–47, London: Routledge.

Hayter, T. (1971), *Aid as Imperialism*, Harmondsworth: Penguin.

Hunt, J. (2011), 'Prototyping the Social: Temporality and Speculative Futures at the Intersection of Design and Culture', in A. J. Clarke (ed.), *Design Anthropology: Object Culture in the 21st Century*, 33–44, Vienna and New York: Springer.

Irwin, T., Kossoff, G. and Tonkinwise, C. (2015) 'Transition Design Provocation', *Design Philosophy Papers*, vol 13, no. 1 3–11.

Jacobs, J. (1961), *The Death and Life of Great American Cities*, Harmondsworth: Penguin.

James, W. (2007), 'Appendix: Reflections on Oxford's Global Links', in P. Rivière (ed.), *A History of Oxford Anthropology*, 171–93, Oxford: Berghahn Books.

Julier, G. (2012), 'British Design Consultancy and the Creative Economy', in C. Breward and G. Wood (eds.), *British Design from 1948: Innovation in the Modern Age*, 310–23, London: V&A Publishing.

Mendini, A. (2013), 'The Role of Radical Magazines', in A. Coles and C. Rossi (eds.), *The Italian Avant-Garde 1968–1976*, 7–22, Berlin: Sternberg Press.

Murphy, K. M. (2015), *Swedish Design: An Ethnography*, Ithaca, NY: Cornell University Press.

Natalini, A. (2003), 'Inventory, Catalogue, Systems of Flux … A Statement', in P. Lang and W. Menking (eds.), *Superstudio: Life Without Objects*, Milan: Skira Editore.

Negri, A and Gfader, V. (2013) *The Real Radical in The Italian Avant-Garde: 1968–1976*. EP, 1 . Sternberg Press, Berlin, 200–19.

Nicolin, P. (2008), 'Protest by Design: Giancarlo De Carlo and the 14th Milan Triennale', in D. Crowley and J. Pavitt, *Cold War Modern: Design 1945–1970*, 228–33, London: V&A Publishing.

Otero-Pailos, J. (2010), *Architecture's Historical Turn: Phenomenology and the Rise of the Postmodern*, Minneapolis: University of Minnesota Press.

Papanek, V. (1971), *Design For the Real World: Human Ecology and Social Change*, New York: Pantheon Books.

Poynor, R. (2014), 'Observer: In a Critical Condition', *Print Magazine*, Online, October, 2014, http://www.printmag.com/imprint/observer-in-a-critical-graphic-design-condition/ (accessed 5 January 2016).

Prina, D. (2010), 'The Struggle of Design Criticism: The Case of the Italian Magazine', *MODO*: 216–19.

Rees, A. L. and Borzello, F. (eds.) (1986), *The New Art History*, London: Camden Press.

Rudofsky, B. (1965), *Architecture Without Architects: A Short Introduction to Non-Pedigreed Architecture*, New York: The Museum of Modern Art.

Rydell, R. W. and Burd Schiavo, L. (eds.) (2010), *Designing Tomorrow: America's World's Fairs of the 1930s*, New Haven: Yale University Press.

Schneider, B. and Hussain, O. (2010), 'An Interview with Hal Foster: Is the Funeral for the Wrong Corpse?', *Platypus Review* 22, April 2010, http://platypus1917.org/2010/04/08/an-interview-with-hal-foster/ (accessed 5 January 2016).

Schumacher, E. F. (1973), *Small is Beautiful: A Study of Economics as if People Mattered*, London: Blond and Briggs.

Shanks, M. and Tilley, C. (1992 [1987]), 'Social Values, Social Constraints and Material Culture: The Design of Contemporary Beer Cans', in *Re-Constructing Archaeology: Theory and Practice*, 2nd edn, London/New York: Routledge.

Thackara, J. (ed.) (1988), *Design after Modernism: Beyond the Object*, London: Thames and Hudson.

Thackara, J. (2015), *How to Thrive in the Next Economy: Designing Tomorrow's World Today*, London: Thames and Hudson.

Thomas, J. S. (2006), 'Phenomenology and Material Culture', in C. Tilley, W. Keane, S. Küchler, M. Rowlands and P. Spyer (eds.), *Handbook of Material Culture*, 43–59, London: Sage.

Walker, J. A. (1989), *Design History and the History of Design*, London: Pluto.

Section II
Interventionist Speculations

6 Design Interventions as a Form of Inquiry

JOACHIM HALSE AND LAURA BOFFI

Things Could be Different

This chapter is about research methods that are explicitly oriented towards quali-tative empirical exploration of the open-endedness of the world. In short, we propose that design interventions can be seen as a form of inquiry that is particularly relevant for investigating phenomena that are not very coherent, barely possible, almost unthinkable, and consistently under-specified because they are still in the process of being conceptually and physically articulated. We see design interventions as a supplement to existing research methods, one that favours and explores unsettled and imagined possibility, yet employs empiricist virtues of embodiment, empathy and documentary forms. Interventionist speculation blends the techniques of invention with techniques of description; it carries an activist attitude that oscillates between 'what is' and 'what could be'; it embodies a research curiosity inclined towards experimentation; and as such, it dares to pose as a productive line of connection between design and anthropology.

An underlying assumption of many research methods is that the world is a pretty determinate set of discoverable entities and processes (Law 2004: 9). The dominant image of scientific research methods is that they aim for clarity and precision, seek to eliminate sources of bias, and strive for unambiguous outcomes. The so-called 'randomized clinical trial' poses as the highest standard of rigorous research into human science experimentation, and as a matter of self-evident logic (Dehue 2002: 79). In *Logic: The Theory of Inquiry* (2007 [1938]: 108), John Dewey defined inquiry as 'the controlled or directed transformation of an indeterminate situation into one that is so determinate in its constituent distinctions and relations as to convert the elements of the original situation into a unified whole'. In other words, Dewey's early scientistic work on inquiry is about reducing uncertainty. This is *not* the primary commitment of design interventions as a form of inquiry.

The word intervention literally means 'coming between'. In everyday use it is typically understood as a goal-oriented interfering in a course of events to promote a preferred state, usually defined by an external force, for example diplomatic, military, or medical. In experimental design research, however, the word intervention is less about conflict resolution or correction. Design interventions are used to describe an engaged research method, not to test a prefigured solution to a defined problem as in prototyping, but to enable new forms of experience, dialogue and awareness about the problematic to emerge (see Thompson (2004) for similar usage in art practice). For these reasons, design interventions are often employed as a strategy of complexification (see also Lindström and Ståhl, this volume; Lenskjold and Olander, this volume).

Our task here is to discuss design interventions with the purpose of exploring what they are. We need to take seriously what is implied by intervening as a form of inquiry, both conceptually and practically. Design interventions are currently flourishing as a practice in experimental design, as illustrated in our main case about hospice care in this chapter. However, we see a related but distinct track of more conceptual discourse about intervention in the literatures of Anthropology and Science & Technology Studies (STS), which we will return to below.

Early design mock-ups and prototypes are speculative in the sense that they speculate about a particular direction of understanding and its potential implications, in order to elicit feedback: what if we introduced this feature, or imposed that structure, then what would happen? Design's capacity for evoking alternative opportunities for thought and practice relies on such speculation. Often the process is goal-oriented, but speculation may also be employed in design processes of a much more exploratory nature, as when Carl DiSalvo (this volume) explores how industrial surveillance technology may contribute to the emergence of a public around the issues of informal fruit-picking and urban foraging.

Let us take another illustrative example, and see how the term is being used to de-centre the object in a design research project exploring energy usage in Sweden. Some of the concrete design expressions referred to in this quote are photographic renderings of speculative future scenarios where mundane energy consumption is foregrounded and amplified:

> Replacing notions of objects, products and even services with placeholder concepts such as 'interventions,' Switch! explores a range of alternative design expressions, methods for prototyping concepts and strategies for placing design concepts in discursive contexts. [...] This is part of an ongoing investigation of design interventions (as things or happenings) into systems in order to effect an awareness of the values involved – such interventions might operate to expose habits, norms and standards, or to shift and renegotiate actors/variables (Bergström et al. 2009; see also Mazé, this volume).

The design intervention is here defined as a placeholder concept, which because of its ambiguity allows for a wider range of conceptual alternatives to be explored. And the immediate objective is not so much to arrive at closure, as it is to prompt reflections about the issue in discursive contexts. This attention to further discursive values of immediate material artefacts is shared with Zoy Anastassakis and Barbara Szaniecki (this volume) who suggest the notion of 'conversation dispositifs'; speculative and interventionist research experiments developed to open up dialogue and engagement among researchers, students and inhabitants of an urban setting.

Nilde imagines what would happen if she had put symbols inside her matryoshka for her friend:

> This is like denuding oneself, because maybe later you have to explain why you did this thing ... With Laura, I don't know, it might have been difficult ...
>
> She might have required an explanation for the things I put in my matryoshka. [...] Maybe a person put the symbols in with extreme honesty ... I do not know if you can be so honest when explaining them. We can't ignore that ... you can enter the hospice door, but you will never go out again ...
>
> [...] A relative of a patient can still have some kind of hope, so the symbolic objects you put inside the matryoshka could be symbols of hope. Maybe it could have been ... But I think it could work because it's like another tool to communicate, sometimes it's hard to start a conversation and get more intimate. There's no occasion, maybe. Having objects inside this matryoshka could be a key to opening doors that are difficult to open (transcript from field video, translated from Italian).

The second object, the messaging station, is playing with the possibility of displaced and asynchronous conversations. As the hospice is already working consciously with outdoor space as distinct from the rooms and as an escape from the clinical setting and its constraints on emotional interaction, the station is hung from a large tree in the garden.

Figure 6.1 Laura, a nurse, is using a partly imaginary, partly mocked up, messaging station in the garden of the hospice to write a message to her patient © Laura Boffi

Margot, a nurse, has used it to write to her patient, and reflects on the experience:

I thought of a person who has just passed away ... I spoke to him now, by writing. [...] The tree is the space where we go and say what we feel and think. Maybe we speak about things we never speak about. It gives serenity for the two minutes you are sitting there. We can abandon ourselves to our suffering here (transcript from field video, translated from Italian).

The third object suggests the leaving of an open channel of communication during the last moments of life. It is a blanket, which resembles the large living tree with the communication station in the garden. The body of the blanket is brown and long as a tree trunk; the top of the blanket is green and shaped like the contours of a tree crown.

A nurse, Lorena, is in a patient room and imagines herself with a dying patient under palliative sedation. She holds the blanket tight in front of her with both arms:

The palliative sedation is a particular moment and situation ... For me it is each time special, a particular goodbye. [...] [Lorena stands in front of a bed.] As it often happens, I imagine that if the patient lies here ... before giving him the sedation, I clean him and make the bed neat, and then I use this blanket because it is a symbol of us, I would say ... since we have been using the tree to speak indirectly. And we even shared it with the family [Lorena spreads the blanket over the hospital bed]. But I think this moment is just our moment. It is

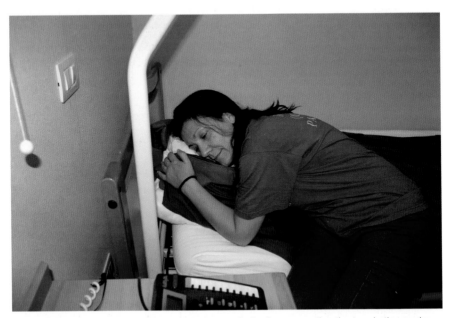

Figure 6.2 Lorena, a nurse, is using a blanket symbolically representing the tree in the garden. She has draped it over the imagined body of a patient, and enacts a moment of caring for the dying © Laura Boffi

the patient's and my moment [...] I actually imagine the body being all wrapped. On the cheeks as well, like if there was a baby [arranging the blanket so as to tuck a person in]. If this was the face ... hmmm ... It's too big, this face [Lorena tries to form the pillow as if it were a person's head and smilingly speaks directly to the researcher]: if you prefer I can lie down myself. [A light giggle from the researcher.] And so ... I would put the blanket close to his body and ... As I usually do, I hug my patients. We stay like this as long as we feel like it. And I sit like this ... At the bedside [Lorena gives a long hug to the pillow wrapped in the blanket]. We stay close for a while. And then it depends on what the patient asks for, if he can speak. And I let the sedation go to him [Lorena points to an imaginary tube from the medication holder towards the bed], I stay there and sit on the bed. I do not like to stand while the patient is over there, you know. Well ... As I usually do, I will say to let himself go and not to be afraid ... Because there will be me here to watch over him, and ... Have a nice journey [smiles gently] (transcript from field video, translated from Italian).

The sensitivity of the researcher has been crucial for establishing this kind of intimacy grounded in the field encounter around an issue as serious and delicate as end-of-life-relationships. But just as important for the effect of the design intervention has been the interventionist stance of the designer, who dares to propose and put forward in material specificity three artefacts to sketch out new modes of interaction, despite the uncertainty about what constitutes 'good' end-of-life-communication. This short account of the project Weaving Relationships has shown both ethnographic methods for exploring hospice practice and designerly methods of prototyping early ideas. However, what we are really after in this chapter is where they blend. There are strong components of material sensitivity and expression within the ethnographic exploration, just as open-ended curiosity and empathy is guiding the designerly staging of a prototypical practice. The design intervention is a material way of trying out a hypothesis regarding what the important features of end-of-life relationships and hospice care are, but also, and just as importantly, it is a way of bringing their alternative forms into corporeal reach and practice.

How is a Design Intervention a Form of Inquiry?

The account of a passionate encounter around end-of-life relationships serves here as an excellent example of the concept and practice of design interventions as a form of inquiry. In getting closer to a delineation of design interventions as a form of inquiry, let us briefly distinguish them from a number of related forms of intervention.

Design interventions are related to what Harold Garfinkel named breaching experiments (1984 [1967]), where commonly accepted, but unwritten, social norms are deliberately broken, in order to generate reflections about what 'counts' in any given social situation. A breaching experiment is both an intervention and a form of inquiry. But compared to the methods discussed here, where the design researcher cares deeply for the people in the situation, an important distinction is that Garfinkel was essentially not interested in the particular people whose norms he or his students were breaching; the concern was with the general patterning of social norms.

If we compare design interventions as a form of inquiry to other forms of intervention with a more violent engagement, like injecting a medical drug under a compulsory treatment order, or a lethal military strike on the enemy, we are here concerned with intervening by proposal rather than dominant force. In the cases we discuss, design interventions are seeking to create local actionability in a reflective way, despite ambiguity, inaccessibility and uncertainty. Agency is thus a dear achievement, a hopeful outcome of the intervention, rather than a necessary precondition for it as in the case of medical and military interventions.

There are no clear demarcations of when design interventions as a form of inquiry deal with describing the existing world as is, and when they prompt the human and non-human actors of the field to enact new imaginaries. These methods assume that we can *at the same time* learn about the socio-material practices around dying and appreciate that these same practices are being unsettled, re-imagined and reinvented. Design interventions deal with something that resists full articulation; what they circle around is messy, ephemeral and only almost possible. They aim to expand the scope of possibilities, and to situate these empirically by bringing them into corporeal reach for a larger audience.

We do not wish to distort this ongoing mess into clarity. Rather, we propose design interventions as a particular form of messy inventive inquiry that has little in common with the experimentation of the randomized clinical trials that set the current standards for scientific approaches to hospice practice. The methods demarcated by the notion of design interventions as a form of inquiry are not standardized, nor are they rigorous, and notably, they do not produce clarity, which are all distinguishing them from the scientist ideals of Dewey's inquiry (2007). Design interventions as a form of inquiry are highly contingent and locally invented or adapted, they are employed opportunistically and unsystematically, and most importantly, they produce complexifications, bifurcations and multiplicities.

Design interventions as a form of inquiry generally share this orientation towards difference and multiplicity with many researchers of anthropology and STS who are identified (by themselves or by others) with the 'ontological turn', as exemplified by Annemarie Mol's famous ethnography of atherosclerosis (2003). The 'ontological turn' has brought an important insistence on the integrative relationship between representations and what they represent. But this does not mean that all representations are equally effective instantiations of ontological change. The authors' re-labelling ethnographic analysis and description as intervention, recounted above (Vikkelsø 2007; Winthereik and Verran 2012; Jespersen et al. 2012) is concerned with re-establishing links between their ethnographic representations and the worlds they represent. With design interventions as a form of inquiry we are more concerned with the opposite, to re-establish links between corporeal interventionist practice and the knowledge production entailed in this. We are not suggesting a radical counter steering, as in a designerly 'turn to the epistemological', but we *are* seeking to qualify design interventions as an epistemological practice. Design interventions is a practical means of generating knowledge around emerging social and cultural issues, akin to Hans-Jörg Rheinberger's concept of 'epistemic things' hovering between material and conceptual entities (1997). By this onto-epistemological manoeuvring, we may not obtain solid scientific knowledge of our field, but we will be able concretely to explore a wide range of realities, and engage consciously in their contested making and remaking.

The brief account of Weaving Relationships begins with concrete usage of photography, embroidery, pebble stones, textile bags and diaries, alongside interview and observation techniques that together constitute a kind of multisensory ethnography. But let us reconsider the design intervention: staging of three empirical encounters at the hospice around 3D printed matryoshka dolls, a messaging station mocked up in cardboard and string, and a sewn textile blanket. What should we make of them? Are they ethnographic encounters about everyday hospice practice? Not exactly. Are they staged prototype tests of fictitious future products? Not quite that either. Our proposal is that they are both. As an open experimental moment between modes of existence, this is a design intervention playing with situated possibility and constraint in the present.

This design intervention and the issue it explores are deeply implicated in one another. Understood as a research method, the design intervention does not afford a transparent representation of the issue, free from personal interpretative bias. On the contrary; the researcher's personal experiences with loss are arguably an important precondition for establishing this kind of empathic exploration in such a sensitive field, normally so difficult to access. The specific artefacts are suggestive of a particular direction, but at the same time exposed to critical assessment by the people they concern.

In sum, design interventions can fruitfully be employed as an exploratory design anthropological research device that stages qualitative empirical dialogues about possibility, and deploys evocative probes, props and prompts to inquire into people's concerns, aspirations and imaginative horizons.

Note

1   All the patients participating in the initial field study had in the intervening period passed away. However, the niece of one of the patients who had taken photographs contacted Laura to see the last pictures her aunt had taken, thus extending the reciprocal conversation between researcher, patient and relative on memories.

References

Bason, C. (2010), *Leading Public Sector Innovation: Co-creating for a Better Society*, Bristol: The Policy Press.

Bergström, J., Mazé, R., Redströmand, J. and Vallgårda, A. (2009), 'Symbiots: Conceptual

Interventions Into Urban Energy Systems. Engaging Artifacts', in *Proceedings of Nordic Design Conference Nordes 2009 – Engaging Artifacts*.

Binder, T. (1999), 'Setting the Stage for Improvised Video Scenarios', in *Proceedings of the CHI '99: Extended Abstracts on Human Factors in Computing Systems*, 230–1, New York: ACM Press.

Bleecker, J. (2009), *Design Fiction*, San Francisco: Near Future Laboratory.

Brandt, E., Messeter, J. and Binder, T. (2008), 'Formatting Design Dialogues – Games and Participation', *CoDesign – International Journal of CoCreation in Design and the Arts*, 4 (1): 51–64.

Brown, T. (2009), *Change by Design*, New York: Harper Collins.

Buchenau, M. and Suri, J. F. (2000), 'Experience Prototyping', in *Proceedings of the Conference on Designing Interactive Systems*, 424–33.

Clifford, J. and Marcus, G. E. (1986), *Writing Culture: The Poetics and Politics of Ethnography*, Berkeley: University of California Press.

Dehue, T. (2002), 'A Dutch Treat: Randomized Controlled Experimentation and the Case of Heroin-maintenance in the Netherlands', *History of the Human Sciences*, 15: 75–98.

Dewey, J. (2007 [1938]), *Logic: The Theory of Inquiry*, New York: Saerchinger Press.

Dourish, P. (2006), 'Implications for Design', in *Proceedings of the SIGCHI Conference on Human Factors in Computing Systems*, 541–50, New York: ACM Press.

Dunne, A. and Raby, F. (2013), *Speculative Everything: Design, Fiction, and Social Dreaming*, Cambridge, MA: MIT Press.

Elsass, P. (2012), 'Livet og Dets Afslutning på Tværs af Virtuelle og Realistiske Rum', workshop, School of Communication and Culture, Copenhagen University.

Garfinkel, H. (1984 [1967]), *Studies in Ethnomethodology*, Englewood Cliffs, NJ: Pearson Education, Prentice-Hall.

Hacking, I. (1983), *Representing and Intervening: Introductory Topics in the Philosophy of Natural Science*, Cambridge: Cambridge University Press.

Henare, A., Holbraad, M., and Wastell, S. (eds.) (2007), *Thinking Through Things: Theorising Artefacts Ethnographically*. London and New York: Routledge.

Jespersen, A. P., Krogh Petersen, M., Ren, C. B. and Sandberg, M. (2012), 'Cultural Analysis as Intervention', *Science Studies*, 25 (1): 3–12.

Kelley, T. (2005), *The Ten Faces of Innovation*, New York: Doubleday.

Koskinen, I., Zimmerman, J., Binder, T., Redström, J. and Wensveen, S. (2011), *Design Research through Practice: From the Lab, Field and Showroom*, Waltham, MA: Morgan Kaufmann/Elsevier.

Law, J. (2004), *After Method: Mess in Social Science Research*, London: Routledge.

Löwgren, J. and Stolterman, E. (2004), *Thoughtful Interaction Design: A Design Perspective on Information Technology*, Cambridge, MA: MIT Press.

Lury, C. and Wakeford, N. (eds.) (2012), *Inventive Methods: The Happening of the Social*, London: Routledge.

Marcus, G. E. and Fischer, M. M. J. (1986), *Anthropology as Cultural Critique: An Experimental Moment in the Human Sciences*, Chicago: University of Chicago Press.

Mol, A. (2003), *The Body Multiple: Ontology in Medical Practice*, Durham, NC: Duke University Press.

Olander, S. (2016), 'Texts As Events – Or How to Account for Descriptions as Intervention', *STS Encounters,* 8 (1): 1–26.

Polaine, A., Løvlie, L. and Reason, B. (2013), *Service Design: From Insight to Implementation*, New York: Rosenfeld Media.

Rheinberger, H.-J. (2010 [1997]), *An Epistemology of the Concrete: Twentieth-century Histories of Life*, Durham, NC: Duke University Press.

Testoni, I. and Sposito, D. (2010) *Ecce Homo – Ma se Questo è un Uomo: Umanizzazione e de Umanizzazione del Dolore nel Morire*. Padua: Padova University Press.

Thompson, N. (2004), *The Interventionists: Users' Manual for the Creative Disruption of Everyday Life*, Cambridge, MA: MIT Press and Massachusetts Museum of Contemporary Art.

Vikkelsø, S. (2007), 'Description as Intervention: Engagement and Resistance in Actor-Network Analyses', *Science as Culture*, 16 (3): 297–309.

Winthereik, B. R. and Verran, H. (2012), 'Ethnographic Stories as Generalizations that Intervene', *Science Studies*, 25 (1): 37–51.

Zuiderent-Jerak, T. and Jensen, C. B. (2007), 'Editorial Introduction: Unpacking "Intervention" in Science and Technology Studies', *Science as Culture*, 16 (3): 227–35.

7   Jostling Ethnography Between Design and Participatory Art Practices, and the Collaborative Relations It Engenders

GEORGE E. MARCUS

Beginning with a particular critical history of ethnography in which I have been engaged, I want to examine further the nature of the ethnographic method in anthropology that is more convergent with design practices and the social interventions of art movements than ever before. The identity of anthropology remains, but the nature of its own game has changed. This is most apparent in the forms that ethnography increasingly takes between its key modes of traditional writing: the private archives of field notes and the finished genre of the ethnographic text. So my concern here is not an anthropology *of* design or anthropology *as* design, but how design (especially collaborative studio methods) works its way today into the long-standing production of anthropological research by ethnography (for related arguments, precedents, and parallels, see, for example, Gunn, Otto, and Smith 2013; Murphy 2015; Dunne and Raby 2013; Lury and Wakeford 2012). The most notable 'making strange' effect on the past habits of ethnographers is the encouragement toward an active 'making' with others of things, events, or occasions in the fieldwork process that begins as profoundly individual and still concludes that way.

In late 2011, a conference was held at Duke University organized by the current editors of the journal *Cultural Anthropology*, to recognize the 25th anniversary of the publication of the volume *Writing Culture* in 1986. It was both an occasion and an assessment of what that volume marked in the history of ethnographic method. Presented were readings by six contemporary and noted writers of ethnography in the U.S., reflecting a range in the diversity that that moment of broad discussion licensed in the production of ethnographic writing, just as the research agendas of anthropology and other disciplines were reforming and becoming diverse, even eclectic.

James Clifford and I had the honour of leading off with prefatory comment and reflection. Clifford, in his talk, 'Feeling Historical', was characteristically elegant and elegiac, casting a look backward to the near past from the perspective of vast present changes. And I, writing in my characteristic style of the 'bricklayer', was interested in the next brick, the next wall and its architecture in the near future of ethnography

(Marcus 2012). Writing beautiful texts, keyed to inventive narrative, analytic creativity, and reflexive awareness, as especially licensed by the Writing Culture exposure of the representational history of ethnography in anthropology, remains the standard in guaranteeing academic careers. However, for me, the present and near future challenges for ethnography as textuality, performance, and representation are all about developing the latters' forms and making them accessible within the design, politics, and conditions for establishing the 'field' of fieldwork, project by project, in a world full of diverse projects, of global scale and portent, of self-awareness, and where textuality is synonymous with sociality. Responses to one's work, in the making, among one's subjects and other publics, matter more than ever to the standing and influence of anthropological writing and thinking as knowledge. Theory work thus does not just precede the production of anthropological texts as a mode of communication to colleagues, but surrounds this professional context on all sides. Indeed, the creation of concepts and theories occurs significantly in the field ('in the wild' in Michel Callon's 1998 terms) and circulate as prototypes among diverse publics before they ever reach colleagues through publication. Professional discussions of research in anthropology seem increasingly to define themselves in the middle of projects without making the dimensions of research significantly clear.

Anthropological knowledge is at the same time expert knowledge and publicly recognized as such. The question is, what forms of representation in the contemporary make this so? And how are these forms of representation synonymous with method? How, then, do we sustain, or morph, the regulative ideals of ethnographic writing in relationship to, and more importantly within, the fieldwork experience itself – operating as research in the world? So, 'Writing Culture', beyond the private archives of field notes, is somehow synonymous with and publicly implicated in the messy track of contemporary fieldwork that is both dwelling and moving. But just how?

What is unique to ethnography is the building of its ideas – and its concepts and theories – from those of its subjects and found partners in fieldwork. In this sense, theory is a primary form of data – not its result – but as such, it must be engageable thought located in the sites and situations of fieldwork (see Boyer, Faubion and Marcus 2015). This requires dialogic forms of reception that the anthropologist has to make, stage, design, and incorporate into classic notions of fieldwork and the production of ethnographic texts from them. How all of this can be staged, mediated, and circulated in a 'standard' project of contemporary anthropological research is a matter of keen interest to me as I have emphasized in recent writing (Marcus 2015; forthcoming).

My impulse is to push the production of ethnography – its published texts – back into the contemporary experience of constructing the field of fieldwork. And this needs its forms and norms for remediating the textual forms that we have, making them performative and more actively interventionist in part, and rescaling the classic regulative ideals of ethnographic method themselves. So, forms of enactment, emplacement, and textuality within and alongside fieldwork are what I am after.

Appearing to become theatre, performance, or experimental in the aesthetic sense, on one hand, or the studio work of designers, on the other, these alliances create the forms for achieving the distinctively historic analytic and theoretical ends of anthropological inquiry as these have evolved since the 1980s.

Issues in the Contemporary Pursuit of Ethnographic Method

Organizing a Center for Ethnography at the University of California has provided me and others with an opportunity to think through and experiment with these forms of producing ethnography within and alongside the politics and dilemmas of establishing sites and conditions in the spirit of classic fieldwork (where sustained participant observation, dialogic engagements, and deep relationships significant for research could be cultivated).

These are means for experimenting with textualizing of ethnography in the real time of fieldwork. The Center has offered an opportunity to think about forms that would push the process of ethnographic writing back to the practical, on–the-ground problems of constituting fieldwork in differently constructed worlds from the ground up. I think of this as anticipated in my interest in the emergence of 'multi-sited ethnography' in the 1990s (Marcus 1995) with its 'following' metaphor, as a condition of producing this kind of research, similar to other research and theory imaginaries about mobile or circulating processes of knowledge making that were in high fashion during that period, the most influential remaining actor-network theory. However, today, that view of the social life of the ethnographic method is far too lonely. It should be re-imagined and challenged in addressing the problem anew of situating the virtues and effects of micro-scale, ethnographic work in a networked, globalizing world of which collaboration has come to be the key, almost universal normative expression of desirable social relations. Ethnography remains multi-sited but its composition cannot be comprehended by following and explaining processes that are authoritatively and aesthetically realized in resulting accounts.

A key problem is that the evocation of multi-sited ethnography came to be understood in a literal way as the reproduction and multiplication of sites of individual research where the modes and standards of inquiry applicable to one would be produced in each. Of course this was open to obvious critiques of feasibility, which I anticipated in the original essay. What I was personally more interested in was how work in one place evoked often hidden routes to others, precisely through the theory or concept work that the ethnographer could do with specific subjects and not others (the key informant becoming epistemic partner in complicit relations [Marcus 1997]). In this trajectory, I saw the multi-sited construct becoming something like the emergent connectivities and paths of recursion that were generated by collaboratively produced and distinctive ideas of ethnography emerging in the scenes of fieldwork – as a technology of question asking that sent one on a trajectory that was in fact multi-sited. What was missing was thinking about the literal forms that might materialize this sense of fieldwork process. Changes in the way the world presents itself to ethnographers for fieldwork projects and dramatic changes in media and communication technologies have finally made explicit and pressing the question of doing things differently with the classic method. In the original multi-sited formulation, this question was not far under the surface, but it only became gradually, and never clearly, sayable until the present and the recent past. These issues, then, have been the major preoccupations and experiments with form that have emerged in the Center at UCI and that are also important elements in the formation of the field of design anthropology:

Collaboration

Collaboration was the first obvious topical interest of consideration, and it has been sustained. Quite aside from *de facto* collaboration being a more or less explicit component of individually authored ethnographic projects from the method's inception, collaboration is everywhere now a standard, and a normative expression of association. It is a universal 'good' to be promoted with very few shadows. It is thus the practical, formal, and found entre as well as the on-the-ground medium of access in constituting fieldwork amid assemblages, projects large and small, locations, sites, and places. It is both the ether and the cocoon of still individually conceived research projects that become collaborative everywhere, by push or pull. In short, collaborations are not a choice in fieldwork, they are a condition for constituting it. Experiments within collaborations, and their politics of research relations, defines the degree of freedom that ethnographers can reserve to pose their own questions.

Pedagogical Experiments

The students who become anthropologists now, and who pass through its initiation by ethnography, are distinctive by often having already been where they want to go (e.g. as journalists or as workers in NGOs of a variety of sizes and causes), having both experience and knowing languages relevant to the once-defining alterity of place of the ethnographic subject. They arrive, and we recruit them, on the basis of their already formed commitment to and curiosity about problems that becoming anthropologists will help them know afresh or more deeply. Thus, regulative norms of classic method bend pragmatically to suit what is brought by contemporary students.

The impulse is to push the production of ethnography back into the experience of the field, but it needs its forms of pedagogy for so doing. The prevailing Malinowskian regulative ideals are still very much training in theory and method before venturing into the literally unknown. Instead, experiment with ethnographic form – in the studio or charrette – expands the imagination for projects to which students come already committed.

The experimental possibilities increase considerably in post-doctoral revision of dissertations, and in the imaginaries for second projects, when newly minted anthropologists are on their own. Post-dissertation work and later projects are never so Malinowskian again. But, first fieldwork is messy, especially amid networked entanglements of collaborative projects large and small, highly reflexive, and sometimes even para-ethnographic in outlook. It might just as well be served by alternative forms and contraptions, if only they were encouraged by pedagogical experiment.

Third Spaces, Studios, Para-sites and Intermediate Forms of Concept Work Within and Alongside Fieldwork

Third spaces have been evoked in the work of Michael Fischer in his efforts to envision a distinctive anthropology of science and technology (Fischer 2003). They emerge at 'plateau' moments in fieldwork settings, which are dialogic opportunities for anthropologists, when ethical issues get debated and articulated by social actors in process. Their emergence suggests alternative, performative strategies of ethnographic elicitation.

Para-sites (Marcus 2007) evoke experiments with the actual staging of such third space events, in the spirit of studios, rather than seminars, in the midst of fieldwork or alongside it, as a means of developing lines of thinking or concept work among relevant and willing parties. 'Third-spaces' and 'para-sites' are specific expressions of, and prototypes for, the intermediate forms that I have in mind.

Platforms, and Digital Experiments With Composition, Commentary, Relationship, Reception, Micro-Publics and Textualities

Digital platforms, in their design and care, are indeed third spaces, becoming primary genre forms for ethnography – they subsume texts and fieldwork. They also promise to condense many of the functions that I imagine intermediate forms to enhance, if not displace, in the traditional production of ethnographic texts from fieldwork. But they are major collective undertakings, involving considerable coordination, devotional managerial and curatorial labour, and struggle for resources if these do not come externally. Interesting projects include, for example, the Digital Natives research, undertaken by Rachel Smith and Ton Otto (see this volume), and the Asthma Files conceived and nurtured over several years, by Kim and Mike Fortun, who have written in detail about the derivation of the design of their platform from the lineage of Writing Culture, and more generally, of cultural theory ferment during the 1980s and 1990s (see, for example, Fortun 2011). Some remain small, and productively struggle. Others start within or become assimilated by huge, well-funded philanthrocapitalist projects.

... And Contemporary Contraptions In General: Nestings, Scaffoldings, Recursions, Receptions and Micro-Publics

Digital experiments and designs for ethnographic research and writing are particular sorts of contraptions, improvisations with the classic ethnographic form within the constraints and possibilities of media technologies. I am personally more involved in a kind of contraption that works with the classic, technologically primitive forms of the ethnography (participant observation, immersion, field notes, and writing therefrom, etc.). These constitute experiments in contextualized inquiry and thinking in natural contexts with found partners and collaborators, marked by inclusive developments, addressing the issues of scale and circulation raised by my original interest in the emergence of multi-sited ethnography in the 90s. Such ethnographic projects as contraptions require frequent use of design methods and thinking, alongside, or in mid course, to see where they are going (see Rabinow et al. 2008, and Marcus 2015).

The multi-sited frame entailed the idea of moving among intensively investigated sites of fieldwork, imagined as following processes. Contraptions signify a refunctioning of this style of multi-sited research from following processes, intensively investigated at appropriate and found sites, toward the idea of building and staging micro-publics and receptions for insights discovered in initial arenas of investigation and transformed as argument, as ethnographic data, as theory, as they move. This is movement of the modest ethnographic research project toward an eventual 'docking' or limit in authority. Yet, this project does not arrive definitively as a report to the academy, with a presentation of a model, an explanation, or analytic description, in the mode of endpoint or product, but with yet another call for reception, among a history of others, on a recursive pathway of circulation. Though paused for discussion, that may indeed be articulated in the language of models, outcomes, and knowledge by a project's assessors in the academy or elsewhere, the contraption is most loyal to an opportunistic, more inclusive, and open-ended methodological strategy.

My argument here joins a call for the preservation and progressive refinement of prototypes as the core of ethnographic research (Corsin-Jiménez 2014), and what in a current collaborative project we are evoking as 'productive encounters' (Cantarella, Hegel and Marcus 2015). Prototypes are in phase both tentative and committed forms of innovation, of speculative, imaginative, ideas, yet they are tied to the reality of a product that will work, in technologically driven societies today. In technology, prototypes are eventually disposable, perhaps remembered by 'techie aficionados', but otherwise they are created to be inevitably forgotten. Anthropologists, in their conceptual thinking, also deal in prototypes, but they invest more in them. The richness of what they have to offer perdures as such in the field. The firm and authoritative ideas that anthropologists produce as concept or theory are often no stronger or longer-lasting than prototypes. Current anthropological debate depends on preserving prototypical ideas, as a form of data, re-enlivening them for other possibilities, and sometimes excavating them back from the 'finished' concepts as they appear in texts and publication, for continuing inquiry. In anthropology, proto-typical ideas span the space of the experimental and the authoritative. The 'gift' (with its intellectual origins in Marcel Mauss's legendary essay), for example, is one of anthropology's most enduring prototypical ideas.

Multi-sitedness here is moving such prototypes of thinking in the field proactively to sites of receptions and micro-publics, variously staged, for whom these ideas may not be otherwise presented, or not presented in composed forums. The envisioned role of experiment is to enfold receptions in evolving fieldwork before it reaches or 'docks' in points of authority, offering reports to, and debates with, the academy, or assimilation by powerful forms and projects of philanthrocapitalist sponsors. Formerly, something like this would be the endpoint of ethnographic research in the role and exercise of anthropological expertise in 1950s and 1960s development paradigms. Its successors are collaboration-based philanthrocapitalist projects (e.g. the Gates Foundation, but many others worldwide based on its model). Ethnographic research in its traditional modest scale can work outside such realms of authority for considerable periods, although these define an inevitable limit for it, what I have called its 'docking' points. In the meantime, such a multi-sited paradigm for ethnography is capable of a trajectory that does not follow processes but moves ethnographic results as thinking, concepts, grounded speculations – prototypes – among different micro-publics that it modestly constitutes for its purposes through collaborations with, for example, designers and artists, to which I now turn. The university research project is enough, or will do, to provide the means to create a scale of diverse reception in research as a varied communicative field of experiment.

Close working collaborations, specific to the project, are essential for the production of this kind of multi-sited ethnography even when the latter is still imagined as the work of the lone fieldworker. For example, Kim Fortun (2001) in her ethnography, *Advocacy After Bhopal*, gives a very good account of working within circuits of activism that define the sorts of micro-publics and granular receptions (she calls them enunciatory communities) that an embedded ethnographic project can conjure for its own purposes – for example how media representations, advocacy campaigns, and legal responses all recursively contribute to making an incident into an event, and how ethnography creates its own receptions, proofs of concept and the like, alongside. We intend, in Center projects, the same kind of partial and measured embedding of ethnographic inquiry in the practices of relevant others, but in our case, the inspirational partners, or referents, have been design thinking and methods on one hand, and certain contemporary art movements (site-specific and participatory art and its predecessors) on the other.

Jostling Ethnography Between Design and Art

I like this term 'jostling' to evoke the relationship of an experimentally oriented ethno-graphic method to design on one side, and to contemporary art movements on the other, as the two key creative sources for shaping a more active, interventionist role of ethnographic research in its sites of fieldwork. I give a priority concern to ethnography within its distinctive histories rather than to examining its already existing considerable record of collaborative relations with each broad arena. Ethnography is not new to design and art movements (see Gunn, Otto, and Smith 2013), but in the former's own disciplinary history and agenda in anthropology, the latter are relatively new to it. So, what can ethnography absorb and experiment with from various design and art movements?

The inspiration of design methods and thinking have tended to incorporate ethnography through the use of cultural probes as well as the space they make for knowledge of end users. But reciprocally for ethnography itself, design disciplines offer, first, a rationale and ideology for operating creatively and, sometimes, experimentally within structures of business, markets, governance, and policy (this is captured in Bruno Latour's, 2008, delicious characterization of design as 'cautious Prometheus', capable of morphing matters of (even critical) fact into 'matters of concern'). Second, and in terms of tradecraft, design venues offer most crucially actual technologies and experience for developing new spaces for ethnographic research alongside and within fieldwork. These are the third spaces, studios, and sites for collective or collaborative work within fieldwork. Design methods provide, in sum, cunning, ingenuity, and process – cocoons, and a certain kind of mimicry in effect – by which ethnography can produce intermediate forms that are necessary for it to be multi-sited in the way that I have described.

Parallel attention to the creativity and imagination of certain contemporary art movements (such as the idea of 'relational aesthetics' developed by Nicolas Bourriaud, 2002) can enhance the contexts of design thinking and methods in which ethnographers have begun to produce the intermediate forms that I have described as spaces of experiment with intervention in the course of long-term fieldwork projects. For the experiments that I am evoking here, I have been especially engaged by Claire Bishop's *Artificial Hells* (2012) as providing a thrust for anthropological ethnography that, frankly, it would not be as likely to do for itself. Drawing on her observations will lead me into a concluding discussion of the '214 Square Feet' project, which has 'contraption' qualities, the logic of which is captured by Bishop's discussions of the key binds and qualities of participatory art projects. These features are also the source of designs for interventions that come to define the core dynamics within ethnographic projects that seek to constitute micro-publics for successive, prototypical iterations of ethnographic argument in the field.

'Artificial Hells': How Participatory Art Informs the Design of Ethnographic Interventions

Claire Bishop takes her title from Andre Breton's post-mortem on Dada's 1921 movement into the streets. But it could stand half humorously for what the twentieth-century avant gardes have sought to produce directly in social settings. While she narrates an original and rich history of such largely European avant gardes through the twentieth century, her intent is to focus on post-studio artists, who operate in natural and found social settings, who give up works 'for projects', and who, while they produce site-specific events, are interested above all in participation that effaces the distinction between artist and spectator. Bishop herself is not interested in ethnography; in fact she does not mention it. But many of the projects she discusses resonate with a more interventionist experience of fieldwork, as well as with the long-standing modes of incorporating subjects of ethnography as participants and interlocutors in its agendas.

I summarize some of Bishop's points useful for viewing ethnographic projects as contraptions that construct chains of micro-publics from the experience of fieldwork. These might shift the classic ethnographic project and its more recent multi-sited characterization to summon granular receptions as the rationale for its movement and its terms of completion before it 'docks' or plateaus in an authoritative form for response as a text or document of the expert. In this way, the intermediate or prototypical texts and experiments of fieldwork become its results, rather than sketches and drafts, intolerably messy and hidden from view, as much as the formal textual artefacts that we now have. This requires modes of textuality, commentary and composition, not anticipated by the Writing Culture or other critical discussions of the ethnographic form since (see Fabian 2008; Kelty 2009). Ethnographic writing remains largely composition after fieldwork. It presumes and privileges at least a professional readership for its performance just as art presumes spectators. In my view, ethnographic texts are part of a broader process of production whose earlier forms are of equal and sometimes more enduring importance than monographs or articles.

While Bishop does not mention ethnography, her work in fact revises Hal Foster's famous mid 1990s article, 'The Artist As Ethnographer?' (1995), that clearly distinguishes site-specific and associated forms of art from ethnography – a fashionable association at the time – but only by formally delimiting the latter as method, something rigorous, less imaginative, stiffer than the site-specific art that beckons toward it. For ethnography in the 2000s, this characterization of the relation between art and ethnography will no longer do. The relation between participatory art, at least, and multi-sited ethnography redux deserves a new trading language. Bishop's study reopens the question in ways that ethnography has not done, and in so doing strengthens ethnography's re-identifications, not necessarily with its collaborations with specific art movements, but rather with its current, stronger relationships to a range of design disciplines.

Bishop's key observations resonate with an ethnographic method that focuses attention upon its middle terms and prototyping processes. In my view, she injects *de facto* an ethos of classic ethnographic immersive engagement into participatory art practices, without saying so, and thus provides terms that anthropologists might use to reposition their method for design interventions and collaborations. Her recurrent key issue is the lack of a secondary reception or spectatorship for participatory art – and with no obvious sense of how this will be achieved. This gap is one that suggests methodological innovation and experiment – an impulse that both participatory art projects and ethnographic ones share. A contraption in either anthropology or participatory art seems to develop from a period and experience of intensive site-specificity toward its dialogic sources. In terms of multi-sited ethnography, it is not so much a matter of following a path, as being pulled by the polyphony in a site toward the speculative designing of related receptions elsewhere.

Nested and scaffolded commentaries and re-presented thinking in carefully staged and composed venues, at least for the purposes of ethnography, do have extraordinary cumulative value. Recent interest of anthropologists, who came up through the same basic technology of question-asking and note-taking, are now producing exemplary texts, in open access, platform experiments (Fortun 2011), recursive publics (Kelty 2008), and ethnography as commentary (Fabian 2008). These are all exploring the kind of contraptions that projects of participatory art seeking spectators, or commentary from publics beyond the act or event of art, produce with ingenuity and creativity.

Both ethnography and participatory art share this problem of doing something about the issue of secondary publics and incorporating them in their projects. This defines a shared logic to other sites and creating forms of reception and their documentation as micro-publics – folded into 'results' for eventual authoritative limit or docking. Ethnography may have more obvious play or direction in this regard than participatory art projects, but the logic of impulse to experiment is no different.

'214 Square Feet' – An Exemplary Project, in Conclusion (co-authored with Luke Cantarella and Christine Hegel)

As a sustained collaboration with two artists that has spun off from our Center for Ethnography, Luke Cantarella, Head of Theater Design at Pace University, Christine Hegel, anthropologist and artist, and myself, are writing a text in the form of a workbook or manual that concerns how projects that merge ethnographic, design, and participatory art methods produce interventions, or what we call 'productive encounters' in relation to ongoing ethnographic research projects at different stages of development (see Cantarella, Hegel and Marcus 2015). Our orientation is explicitly toward the ethnographic method and our purpose is to rethink or performatively and theoretically expand, with organized, relevant publics, aspects of fieldwork projects. A 'productive encounter' is doing something different with fieldwork materials. This involves an interesting rethinking of fundamental methodological concepts, and the differences between performance concepts in art and design and the same ideas deployed in anthropological ethnography.

For example, Hegel rethinks and expands the concept of 'immersion' central to the professional culture of method in anthropology, as 'amplification'. 'Productive encounters' have the potential to amplify existing dynamics/conversations/debates/ phenomena. This runs counter to how classical ethnography works in the sense that,

Figure 7.1 '214 Square Feet' Exterior © George E. Marcus

Figure 7.2 '214 Square Feet' Interior © George E. Marcus

through immersion, one seeks to overhear and observe 'natural' phenomena that occur in the course of everyday life. This tacit knowledge is unamplified, and thus is only accessible by the 'fly on the wall' approach.

Being an ethnographer has long been associated with a kind of sublime and gifted insight. But this can be opposed to the model for experiment that we are creating, which relies upon techniques to open up, share, and morph anthropological hunches or insights by creating expressions for them, not as true or false, but as situations where such ideas are explored or amplified directly or indirectly by social actors. The imaginaries of pioneer situational ethnographers like Erving Goffman and Harold Garfinkel posed ethnographic insight in these dramatistic terms, but we are breaking the frame of the bounded fieldwork concept, for instance, while keeping clear of the specific assumptions and aesthetics of theatre craft.

One project that we have collaborated on is '214 Square Feet', created principally by Cantarella and Hegel, and advised by me (see Figures 7.1 and 7.2). The title refers to the living space of entire working poor families in rundown but high-priced motels situated in the very wealthy, religious and politically conservative enclave of Orange County south of Los Angeles, notable for the original Disneyland, huge and wealthy churches, extravagant malls and sterile corporate business parks – it is also where the University of California, Irvine is located. The concept of the project was not so much to examine the conditions of the virtually homeless, but to probe the relation, or non-relation, of the wealthy and the privileged to them, and especially to stimulate and clarify ideas of charity, responsibility, and injustice.

'214 Square Feet' is an immersive scenic environment created in collaboration with the Project Hope Alliance, a non-profit organization that serves the homeless population of Orange County. For such families, a motel room is an impermanent home, made homelike through the personal objects that fill it and the daily activities of home-life within its walls. The environment has travelled throughout Orange County creating encounters at various non-traditional sites of performance such as the Balboa Bay Yacht Club, the central plaza of the School of Social Sciences at the University of California, Irvine, the Second Harvest Food Bank and Saddleback Church.

Existing on the border between theatre practice and anthropology, 214 Square Feet is conceived as a research environment that collects ethnographic data through the activation of an experience. Fictional and personal narratives of homelessness in Orange County have been materialized in a staged environment, which in turns serves an ethnographic purpose by inviting audiences to experience this environment sensorially and to offer responses. The scenic environment is a full-sized replication of a motel room inhabited and lived in by a fictional family of six who function as unseen characters. The audience entering the front door and exiting through the bathroom traverses the roughly 214 square feet. Furniture typically found in motel rooms has been rearranged and augmented, showing the creative solutions to the practical problems of poverty and limited living space. Found objects, purchased from auction at the Goodwill of Orange County, represent the personal effects of a composite family.

Audio and video recordings emanate discretely from objects such as a heat vent, a bedside alarm clock, and other objects, and intimate proximity is required to experience some of these media elements. For instance, only by sitting on the bed closest to the clock can one overhear a child's story. The experience overall is an open-ended participatory performance in which audience members open drawers, peek into storage bins, and otherwise touch and move objects as they walk through the space.

In one respect '214 Square Feet' is in the tradition of participatory performance in contemporary art that Claire Bishop chronicles, especially strong since the 1990s.

The project employed classic strategies from theatrical production to create a designed space infused with embedded narrative. Hegel, an anthropologist, functioned as author by other means, substituting the text of the playwright with a body of ethnographic data. Cantarella, whose practice is set design, enacted a traditional design process that 'read' the ethnographic data as a play text and from this reading generated a theatrical setting.

'214 Square Feet' adopted familiar strategies of the site-specific art tradition, but it added to them a strategic dimension of temporality, as well as multi-sited circulation, similar to the emergence of multi-sited fieldwork that so transformed the look and structure of ethnography from the 1990s forward. The '214 Square Feet' project is most ethnographic in these strategies of movement and elicitation among related but diversely positioned subjects – not the working poor themselves, but the privileged in different degrees and situations, of whom the former are of varying interest, reflection, and consciousness. The anthropological root of the project is, at base, about the spatial and conceptual subtleties of variant degrees of awareness of inequality among the privileged.

The initial site, the Balboa Bay Yacht Club, not only transposed one of the poorest motel rooms in Orange County into one of the most exclusive hotels, but it also occurred during the specific time of a gala benefit. Attendees of the gala encountered the materialized performance within the specific context of a benefit and thus had to synthesize visual, spatial, and temporal disjunctures. In this context, the subject of the work became the nature of the charitable act and how it functions to assuage guilt and assert social status while simultaneously creating intimacies across class and between patron and benefactor.

A similar process occurred as the piece travelled to different sites throughout Orange County. At the same time, the terms and the subject of the staged encounter shifted. For instance, during the installation at Saddleback Church, a mega-church with a congregation of over 20,000, the subject became how fundamentalist Christianity resolves its principles of ministering to the poor with its dominant political discourse of libertarianism. Later, when installed in the plaza of the School of Social Sciences at the University of California, Irvine, the installation revealed how works of advocacy, reliant on emotion, are problematic for social theorists and researchers, trained to operate within rational, intellectual structures, and a presumed left-liberal political mentality.

The multi-sited circulation of the project thus engaged fundamentalists, philanthropists, social climbers, social scientists, and self-regarding decent citizens.

In fact, the performance experience is construed as extending beyond the time of encounter into process and installation. For each installation, instead of hiring a strictly professional crew, volunteers were solicited from the different partner organizations to help assemble the structure. The process of installation was seen as a crucial time in which dialogues around the work's themes were rehearsed. Volunteers, having participated in the labour of building and restaging the environment, acquired a kind of ownership in it and often became guides for the viewing audiences. This was particularly notable during the performance at the Balboa Bay Club where a member of the Project Hope Board, costumed in black tie, adopted the role of a narrator, guiding patrons through the motel room and instructing them to specific ways of seeing and interpreting. As in a traditional narrative performance, a definitive statement about meaning voiced through a figure of authority both assert their truth while inadvertently suggesting their inverse. A kind of ethnographically valuable language game emerged. This duality reflected a central question of the gala site, namely, does the charitable act spring from a desire to do 'good work' or from a need to suffer symbolically to cleanse one's guilt as a member of the upper class? This is, of course, a question or an observation that arises in ethnographic participant observation and perhaps explicitly in conversations of classic fieldwork. Here it is performed through the production of the installation in richly generative expressions and reflections by a kind of elicited and interested collaborative doing or making, as ethnography by design and speculative intervention.

This project remains in prototype; we do not yet consider it to have 'docked' in authority. It has no need to, to constitute the richest kind of analytic-descriptive knowledge form that the ethnographic method was invented to produce.

References

Bishop, C. (2012), *Artificial Hells: Participatory Art and the Politics of Spectatorship*, London: Verso.

Bourriaud, N. (2002), *Relational Aesthetics*, Dijon: Presses du Réel.

Boyer, D., Faubion, J. D. and Marcus, G. E. (eds.) (2015), *Theory Is Much More Than It Used To Be: Learning Anthropology's Method In a Time of Transition*, 2nd edn, Ithaca, NY: Cornell University Press.

Callon, M. (ed.) (1998), *Laws of Markets*. London: Wiley-Blackwell.

Cantarella, L., Hegel, C. and Marcus, G. E. (2015), 'A Week In Pasadena: Collaborations Toward a Design Modality for Ethnographic Research', *FIELD: a Journal of Socially Engaged Art Criticism*, 1: 53–94.

Corsin-Jiménez, A. (2014), 'Introduction. The Prototype: More Than Many and Less Than One', *Journal of Cultural Economy, Special Issue: Prototyping Cultures*, 7 (4): 381–98.

Dunne, A. and Raby, F. (2013), *Speculative Everything: Design, Fiction and Social Dreaming*, Cambridge, MA: MIT Press.

Fabian, J. (2008), *Ethnography As Commentary: Writing From the Virtual Archive*, Durham, NC: Duke University Press.

Fischer, M. M. J. (2003), *Emergent Forms of Life and the Anthropological Voice*, Durham, NC: Duke University Press.

Fortun, K. (2001), *Advocacy After Bhopal: Environmentalism, Disaster, New Global Order*, Chicago: University of Chicago Press.

Fortun, K. (2011), 'Experimenting with the Asthma Files?' Paper presented at the *Digital Anthropology: Projects and Projections Panel*. Meetings of the American Anthropological Association, Montreal, Canada.

Foster, H. (1995), 'The Artist as Ethnographer?' in G. E. Marcus and F. R. Myers (eds.), *The Traffic in Culture: Refiguring Art and Anthropology*, 302–9, Berkeley, CA: University of California Press.

Gunn, W., Otto T. and Smith R. C. (eds.) (2013), *Design Anthropology: Theory and Practice*, London and New York: Bloomsbury.

Kelty, C. (2008), *Two Bits: the Cultural Significance of Free Software*, Durham, NC: Duke University Press.

Kelty, C. (2009), 'Collaborations, Coordination, and Composition: Fieldwork After the Internet', in J. D. Faubion and G. E. Marcus (eds.), *Fieldwork Is Not What It Used To Be*, 184–206, Ithaca, NY: Cornell University Press.

Latour, B. (2008), *A Cautious Prometheus? A Few Steps Toward a Philosophy of Design*, Paris: Mendeley Universal.

Lury, C. and Wakeford, N. (eds.) (2012), *Inventive Methods: The Happening of the Social*, London: Routledge.

Marcus, G. E. (1995), 'Ethnography In/Of the World System: the Emergence of Multi-Sited Ethnography', *Annual Review of Anthropology*: 95–117.

Marcus, G. E. (1997), 'The Uses of Complicity in the Changing Mise-en-Scene of Anthropological Fieldwork', reprinted in G. E. Marcus, *Ethnography Through Thick & Thin*, Princeton, NJ: Princeton University Press.

Marcus, G. E. (ed.) (2007), *Para-sites: A Casebook Against Cynical Reason*, Late Editions 7, Chicago: University of Chicago Press.

Marcus, G. E. (2012), 'The Legacies of Writing Culture and the Near Future of the Ethnographic Form: A Sketch', *Cultural Anthropology*, 27 (3): 427–45.

Marcus, G. E. (2015), 'The Ambitions of Theory Work In Contemporary Anthropological Research', in D. Boyer, J. D. Faubion and G. E. Marcus (eds.), *Theory Is Much More Than It Used To Be*, Cornell, NY: Cornell University Press.

Marcus, G. E. (forthcoming), 'Art (and Anthropology) At the World Trade Organization: Chronicle of an Intervention', *Ethnos: Journal of Anthropology*.

Murphy, K. (2015), *Swedish Design*, Ithaca, NY: Cornell University Press.

Rabinow, P. and Marcus, G. E. with Faubion, J. and Rees, T. (2008), *Designs for an Anthropology of the Contemporary*, Durham, NC: Duke University Press.

8 Conversation *Dispositifs*: Towards a Transdisciplinary Design Anthropological Approach

ZOY ANASTASSAKIS AND BARBARA SZANIECKI

Setting up a Research Environment

This chapter discusses the possibilities of combining design and anthropology through the notion of conversation *dispositifs*: speculative and interventionist research experiments developed to open up dialogue and engagement among researchers, students and inhabitants in the urban setting. Through this concept, we discuss the possibilities of developing an experimental research practice that results, simultaneously, in an anthropology by means of design, and in an anthropologically oriented design practice.

More specifically, as researchers and citizens, we pursue an agenda of correspondence (Gatt and Ingold 2013) with the inhabitants of the city of Rio on emerging issues and alternative ways to consider and visualize (Ingold 2000; Ingold and Hallam 2007) the urban environment where we all work and live, creating new forms of participatory engagement (Halse et al. 2010). We believe that the dialogue-inducing qualities of the conversation *dispositifs*, understood as a kind of transdisciplinary design anthropological concept and tool, can help us in accomplishing this goal.

In the experiments described here, the downtown area of Rio de Janeiro was treated simultaneously as research theme and context. Recently, this area has been strongly affected by an urban development agenda designed by governments in partnership with the private sector without greater citizen participation. Therefore, it seemed the ideal ground on which to establish an experimental research agenda bringing together design and anthropology in order to correspond with the citizens in the challenges they face when trying to establish dialogue and participation with the government.

Through the conversation *dispositifs*, we envision the possibility of making room for the collective imagination of alternative possibilities (Hunt 2011) for the city by challenging dominant forces and establishing new forms of public dialogue or conversations which contribute, from a design anthropological perspective, to building a transdisciplinary bridge that reconnects social sciences and society.

Conversation *Dispositifs*: An Emerging Concept

The concept of conversation *dispositifs* emerges from an experimental research agenda initially formulated to explore the possible combinations between modes of knowledge production in design and anthropology (Anastassakis 2012; 2013; Szaniecki and Anastassakis 2014). Through the first research encounters we realized that combining design and anthropology from a fieldwork experience led us to develop a series of experiments in which design means and methods were triggers to open up issues, from an anthropological perspective.

Initially, we were interested in investigating what it means to be a public design school located in the city centre of Rio de Janeiro. We were also interested in developing a design research practice addressing the huge urban renewal of Rio, considering that all of us, teachers and students, are also citizens, affected as everybody else. Henceforth, we engaged in inquiries in which we were not only assuming our professional commitment but also positioning ourselves as citizens-designers. To pursue what this implies, we ask what these inquiries can bring to the design practice itself and also to design anthropology by establishing 'conversations' between these fields.

We started a fieldwork investigation into the school surroundings and looked for the impact urban renewal has therein. With our students we worked in groups walking together back and forth, observing, drawing and discussing. This opened up space for the first experiments on collective imagination about possible alternatives, different from the main urban infrastructure redesign we encounter in the surroundings.

These experiments were done as visualizations of what we had met in the field. The images were created in order to establish conversations with people we met, drawing together (Latour 2008) possible alternative visions for life in the city, considering citizen participation. In this open-ended process, the iterative movements and the speculations across domains served, primarily, to create engagement and bring out issues by connecting researchers, students, citizens and the urban setting itself as the experiments that will be described here will show.

As we continued to create images that led to new alternative visions, formed from these conversations in the streets, we decided to focus our research attention precisely on the graphical materials that were serving us as means by which we engage ourselves in fieldwork. We looked for their potential to act as *dispositifs* of public dialogue in the urban setting, understood itself also as a *dispositif*.

About *Dispositifs* and Conversations

The concept of conversation *dispositif* arose from our own perception of finding ourselves, as designers but also as citizens, acting inside very complex power relations. Our conviction was that even in this tense situation, we could collaborate with our specific professional tools.

For Michel Foucault (1994), the *dispositif* is, firstly, a heterogeneous set of discourses, organizations and decisions, sometimes stated, sometimes not. It is the network that can be established among all these elements. Secondly, between all these elements, discursive or not, he considers that there might be position changes or function modifications of different kinds. Finally, Foucault states that the *dispositif* has a dominant strategic function that implies some manipulation of power relationships by organized intervention in order to develop, to stabilize, or even to block them. In short, 'The *dispositif* is precisely this: a set of strategies of the relations of forces supporting, and supported by, certain types of knowledge' (Foucault 1994: 300), but still open to changes of position.

Later in 'Security, Territory, Population' (1997), Foucault defines the concepts that constitute the new governmentality. The disciplinary mechanism could not handle the management of cities anymore. The concept of 'security' was born to complement it. Cities demanded modulations of livelihoods through safety *dispositifs* that acted on the 'population', conceived as a modular environment neither totally natural nor fully cultural, and in its 'territories', conceived as circulation spaces.

The safety *dispositif* is in full operation in Rio. The area extending from Esdi, the design school where we work, to the port zone is particularly targeted. But, security is not the only function of the *dispositif*. For Foucault, 'population' can be modified by the use of laws, as well as through social awareness, commercial advertising and political propaganda. But, despite the large scale on which it is designed and implemented, the concept of *dispositif* does not support power macro analysis. On the contrary, it is located in a microphysics of powers. The processes of urban renewal are formulated inside the city hall and legitimized by communication in unilateral procedures. We felt that we are part of a *foucaultian dispositif*, not a kind of empty structure, but something that we constitute and, thus, can change.

Unlike communication, conversation is based on other conceptions of society and, possibly, of the city. Communication was, and still is, designed by the social and human sciences, particularly by sociology and history with their great subjects (society, state, working class and capital). Conversation is understood by Gabriel Tarde as an infinitesimal constructivism, without distinction between nature and society, human and non-human. Conversation is the infinitesimal cause for all formations and social transformations, not only linguistic, but also religious, political, economic, aesthetic and moral (Tarde *apud* Lazzarato 2006).

Mikhail Bakhtin (2003) calls conversation subjective processes understood as a constitution 'of each other' through words. These considerations of Tarde and Bakhtin are updated by authors such as Bruno Latour (2006), who conceives the social as a singular way of association through the 'actor-network' (ANT), and such as Maurizio Lazzarato (2006) who observe that, in the cooperation between 'brains' characteristic of the current mode of production, 'others' are not passive recipients but co-creators of our speech and co-updaters from other worlds.

By its persistent continuity, conversation may form new worlds, real or virtual 'possible worlds' and, in our case, 'possible cities'. For its varying scale and molecular dynamics, the 'spaces of conversation' opened by the *dispositifs* that we are seeking to develop differ from 'spaces of public opinion' formed through communication. *Dispositifs* are an open-ended set of heterogeneous elements and relations, and thus we should not consider that 'conversation *dispositifs*' are inside a bigger and urban one. Conversation *dispositifs* and urban settings (also understood as *dispositifs*) are just different and establish network connections between each other rather than hierarchical structures.

If governments use communication *dispositifs* to legitimize and even impose urban projects as being top-down oriented, we rely on conversation *dispositifs* to build multilateral and horizontal processes (between private and public powers and publics and between citizens with designers among them), and especially transversal processes without distinction between nature and society, human and non-human. So, with the concept of conversation *dispositifs*, we enter the dimension of transversality among the heterogeneous agents with their different knowledge and practices that lead, in turn, to transversal and transdisciplinary approaches.

Resources for a Transdisciplinary Design Anthropological Approach

In *Design Anthropology: Theory and Practice*, Gunn, Otto and Smith (2013) define design anthropology as an academic field that combines elements from design and anthropology, carrying forward a debate launched by prominent anthropologists such as Tim Ingold (2011; 2013), and George Marcus and Paul Rabinow (2008). However, according to Otto and Smith (2013), design anthropology has the potential to create a new paradigm for knowledge production not only in anthropology, but also in design, opening up a third space, with its own research and training practices. Promoting correspondence and collaboration among designers, anthropologists and other citizens implies that all of us are co-creators of significant practices that can transform the present while creating alternatives for the future.

Gatt and Ingold (2013) consider ways of thinking anthropology beyond the mere description and analysis of contexts proposing a restoration of the 'designerly' dimension in anthropological research practice. An open concept of design creates space for dynamics of improvisation in everyday life and therefore an anthropology constituted by means of design becomes inherently experimental. From this position, the key to the creation of a combination between design and anthropology lies in the concept of correspondence.

According to these authors, corresponding with the world is not to describe or represent it, but to respond to it, in collaboration. Thus, while anthropology by means of ethnography is a descriptive practice, anthropology by means of design is a practice of correspondence, which, however, should not be limited to predicting, as traditional designers do. To shift from prediction to correspondence, emphasis must go from the form itself to the process of conformation.

In this perspective, design creativity does not lie in the novelty of prefigured solutions, but in the ability of the inhabitants of the world to respond to the changing circumstances of life. Correspondence is related to the notion of foresight, which significantly differs from prediction. More than projecting from an extrapolation of the present, foresight is related to imagining alternatives in the midst of collective processes of social imagination.

In the article, 'Anthropological Fieldwork and Designing Potentials', Kjærsgaard and Otto (2012) also discuss the role of anthropology and ethnographic fieldwork in design processes. Focusing on material interventions developed in fieldwork research and project-development processes, the authors observe the use of design artefacts such as 'props', 'mock-ups' and prototypes within real contexts.

Here lies design anthropology's main contribution to design: anthropologists not only co-design and participate in the creation of these material interventions, but also study the design process as a whole in order to identify its underlying assumptions. By doing this, it is possible to displace design activity and sensitize it to the skilful ability of 'users'. This proposal challenges the ways in which ethnographic practice has been historically appropriated by design (Wasson 2000). It defends a design anthropological approach that operates at the intersection between the practices and contexts of use and design through a holistic engagement that is both critical and material and takes place between the field and the design studio.

Kjærsgaard and Otto reframe design as a form of fieldwork, which is not only a critique of participatory design's methods and prescriptions for developing meaningful design solutions but, above all, a challenge to the classic ethnographic fieldwork that became the defining character of anthropological research practice. In this sense, the practical combination of design and anthropology challenges both areas and reconfigures their organized modes of knowledge production.

While Rabinow and Marcus (2008) approach design as a metaphor or model for having a glimpse of a different way of doing anthropological research, Kjærsgaard and Otto (2012) are interested in design as a way of making anthropology, and anthropology as a way of making design. According to them, design and anthropology not only reflect themselves, but, in a complementary way, they engage actively with each other, through their practices and perspectives.

The design anthropological fieldwork is a collaborative effort between designers and anthropologists in order to study, conceptualize and experience with potential relationships among people, practices and things. It is not about providing detailed descriptions but about exploring concepts and reframing relationships in order to highlight the common creative potential among anthropologists, 'natives', designers and 'users', all of them defined as inhabitants of the world.

Prototypes, Provotypes and Other Design Things

To do this exploration of concepts and relationships, some design artefacts come to play a special role. Authors such as Halse et al. (2010) and Gunn and Donovan

(2012) challenge the role of prototypes in design processes by transforming them from mere drafts of future products to supporters of 'user' participation in the imagination of future scenarios.

This broadening in the understanding of prototypes relocates them from the end to the midst of design processes. Unlike prototypes understood as design solutions, these design artefacts establish relations between past and present practices with future possibilities by provoking reflections on latent issues or emerging alternatives (Gunn and Donovan 2012). This conceptual requalification leads to rethink prototypes as provotypes (Mogensen 1991) or design things (Binder et al. 2011), i.e. as materials involved amid collaborative design practices.

Along the same lines Lenskjold (2011) proposes emphasizing design as a practice of asking questions rather than posing solutions. Following Heidegger (2010), Binder et al. (2011) propose to speak about design work in a reflective way, suggesting a deconstruction of the individual designer and the object of design by the notion of design things. This also implies a shift in the role attributed to designers, because design things may open up space for people's conversations during its very production and circulation. This would contribute to reframing social relations among those involved in participatory design processes such as 'users' or clients. Meanwhile, designers become dream catchers and improvisation facilitators (Ingold and Hallam 2007) instead of providers of solutions.

To fully realize their speculative features, these provotypes or things should be open to interpretations beyond the control of the designers (or anthropologists) in order to support by conversation a more collective production of meanings and knowledge. In this way, these design artefacts create the possibility of approximating the user domain to the design process, investing in it all the controversies, challenges and implications that take place when artefacts are engaged by people in real situations. Less prescriptive, design becomes a critical activity.

Design and Public Issues

In this way, it is important to consider the implications of public issues to design. In 'Design and the Construction of Publics' (2009), Carl DiSalvo refers to John Dewey's text *The Public and its Problems* (1927) where Dewey states that his philosophical investigation cannot be settled apart from everyday life. Thus, Dewey's approach to the public issue as a philosophical theme supports itself with concrete situations, experiences and materialities. For Dewey as for DiSalvo, the public is a broad, inclusive and multiple domain that is, above all, constructed, and this leads DiSalvo to discuss the means for such a construction and, especially, the possible contributions of design in these processes.

Referring to De Certeau (1994), DiSalvo formulates the idea of design tactics. While strategies are acts of power exercised by institutions seeking to prescribe behaviours and ways of life, tactics are developed by people in order to negotiate strategies that fit with their own goals and desires. DiSalvo argues that design means are both strategic and tactical. However, he suggests emphasizing design tactics to build up the public by extending its participation. Tactics can be used in design projects that are constituted beyond what is commonly considered design and with the participation of people who are not designers.

The author highlights two kinds of design tactics – projection and tracing – and how they behave in relation to temporality. While projection begins in the present and is directed to the future, tracing launches into the past forcing it to be known in the present. Neither of the design tactics consider past, present and future as crystallized instances of a linear time, but as a continuum referenced dialectically. Design tactics identify and articulate issues and thus may allow the formation of a common public field around them.

In addition to projecting and tracing, Lenskjold (2011) highlights the tactic of mapping as another mode of critical engagement. Mapping articulates relevant issues, by composing an indiscriminate representation of objects, people and events that influence an issue over time. Following Latour, he comments on the potential of an investment in the mapping of controversies amidst the design field. They may show relevant issues that have been cleared in a given situation and open new perspectives on key issues.

Provotypes, design things, critical artefacts and design tactics can support a critically engaged design activity, making space for a redirection of the role of design research and practice. They may also facilitate a new way to integrate ethnographic issues and anthropological knowledge in the midst of design processes. This type of critical design can enable the transgression of linearity with which traditional ethnographic materials have been used merely as initial inspirations for the design process.

Importantly, discussing the ways in which design can participate in the contemporary complexity reinforces the validity of a combined approach of design and anthropology. Understanding design as a mediation field, we propose that its combination with anthropology contributes to a renewal of design means, methods and goals, at the same time as it can refresh anthropological knowledge production. We are talking about an anthropology with design. It is a transdisciplinary gathering or approach that accumulates mutual exchange among theories, methodologies and tools aiming at dealing with the challenges for the establishment of public dialogue.

First Set of Experiments: Establishing Public Dialogues by Means of Design and Anthropology

Moving from the conceptual origins of the notion of conversation *dispositifs*, we will return to our first set of experiments: in the early moments, we proposed to the students a series of walks around the school to find out what went on there. During fieldwork, design students noticed that their drawings had facilitated interactions with people who approached them.

Together, we perceived that the artefacts (notebooks and pencils) used to draw, as well as the images produced, lessened the distance between them and the

Figure 8.1 First set of experiments: Experiment 'What if this street were mine?' realized at Lada/Esdi/UERJ: speculating about possibilities for the street where the school is located © Zoy Anastassakis

others, opening spaces for conversations. So, we decided to invest more deeply into experiments around the concept of conversation *dispositifs*, experimental artefacts and graphic pieces that could facilitate conversation and engagement with passers-by.

The students gathered, exchanged impressions, quotes, drawings and photographs. Through compiling these materials and trying to organize and make the data visible, they created different kinds of visual mappings. With these graphic pieces, they defined a new fieldwork cycle, focused on a speculative inquiry about alternatives for the city centre. Coming back from this second fieldwork, they created a new set of graphic pieces, this time in the form of scenarios and visions (Hunt 2011; Lenskjold 2011; Reyes 2010). Finally, posters presenting these visual projections were shown on the outside wall of the school.

The posters were shown with the results of a workshop around the issue: 'What if this street were mine?' With this question, we speculated more specifically about possibilities for the street where our school is located. One day, we invested time in fieldwork, registering what we had noticed and talking with passers-by. Then we printed images from Google Street View and created panels so those who passed could interact with us not only by talking, but also by drawing and writing, contributing to the collective imagination about the alternative possibilities for this street.

Showing the results of that work was important to understanding how the interactions with people could be mediated by the graphic materials, and to refine our understandings of what was at stake in that urban setting, not only according to our own perspectives, but as a result of a public dialogue established among all the participants of this open activity.

The interactive exhibition in the street turned out to function as a kind of design tactic. More than simply presenting our research work, the exhibition gave us the opportunity to interact with people who normally pass by the school gate and with whom we never engage in conversations. They also had proposals about this street, so sharply thwarted by the managers of the urban renewal process that continues to affect the entire city, and this street as well. So, the interactive exhibition was one more step in imagining possibilities for the future of the area.

However, these dialogues were quick. The exhibition did not open enough space for the expansion and deepening of interactions. It seemed to us that it was necessary to experiment with ways of being in the field and becoming part of conversation *dispositifs* that go beyond instant interactions, and enable longer exchanges that might turn into more stable collaborative engagement and co-design processes.

Second Set of Experiments: Staging Mutual Local Partnerships

Shortly after the first experiments, LaDA was invited by an NGO (Agency of Networks for Youth) to collaborate in a programme in '*favelas*' (Portuguese word for slum) that were until recently in the power of drug traffickers and now are under the control of a 'Pacifying Police'. Young people living there were encouraged to develop social,

Figure 8.2 Second set of experiments: Results of the partnership between Lada/Esdi/UERJ and the NGO Agência Redes para Juventude: cartographies of the impact of the project in the neighbourhood and of the methodology of the projects themselves. © Carolina Menezes and Joyce Pires for the project Boca de Lixeira

cultural, or commercial initiatives. At the end of their project development, they realized the need for graphic materials to establish conversations with possible partners and supporters in order to gather resources for its implementation. So, the NGO invited us to codesign the visual communication with them.

For over four weeks, eighteen design students worked in pairs with young people from the NGO in the development of visual identities and their application in two graphic pieces. One had the objective of illustrating the impact of the project in the neighbourhood, and the other of explaining the methodology of the project itself. It was not a mere diagramming of information already organized. As their first task, the pair had to systematize information about the project and select what should be communicated graphically.

The two posters would stimulate the potential partners and sponsors to engage in the processes. Over the meetings, the pairs co-designed visualizations of information, negotiating what would be essential to show. Simultaneously, they created visual identities. Thus, the process of graphic design was in itself a catalyst for the establishment of partnerships between students from Esdi and youth leaders in the communities' projects.

We realized that the design process was a means for creating dialogue and engagement not only with future partners or sponsors, which was the greater goal of the NGO, but, more so, between young community leaders and design students, at a micro level. Co-designing was a means to foster social relations necessarily mediated by the anthropological sensitivity of the design students who, through design tools, sought to correspond with other youth.

The great challenge of this collaboration was to enable relationships beyond traditional provisions of design services and in the direction of alternative creative processes to the development of these areas, as the very notion of development (and the practices of security that comes with it) was at issue. These experiments acted in different levels and sets: between the students of Esdi and the youth from the NGO, but also between them and the set of relations of forces supporting and supported by knowledge where they take place, i.e. the city of Rio de Janeiro in a time of infrastructural preparations for events such as the Football World Cup (2014) and the Olympic Games (2016).

In the end, some students even joined in the youth's projects, taking forward their partnerships through infinite and infinitesimal conversations by their own means and according to their own goals. While on our part, we temporarily interrupted the partnership between LaDA and the NGO in order to avoid a purely functional practice of design in the urban *dispositif* and to affirm a disposition to establish partnerships in a more collaborative and symmetric way.

Third Set of Experiments: Negotiating Design Issues

After that, LaDA was invited by SEBRAE, an entrepreneurship development agency that started a programme to support culture and tourism using design tools, in Morro dos Prazeres, a *favela* located near Esdi. For fifteen weeks, we developed mappings and design experiments in collaboration with residents and local entrepreneurs.

SEBRAE had requested the development of design experiments related to existing or emerging community projects involving tourism, trade and services, waste management and/or environmental preservation, issues considered central to the initiatives in micro-entrepreneurship in these areas. For us, the main objective was making contact with the community residents through design processes to understand their own practices, needs and wishes so that, in partnership, we could imagine opportunities for their businesses as well as other activities.

Mapping the ways of life and creative practices in which the community inhabitants were engaged, was more than using graphic material to correspond (Gatt and Ingold 2013) to the broader challenges they confronted as in the first experiment. Rather, we sought to awaken in the students an engaged (Ingold 2000; 2011) sensibility by taking them to the field – in this case, segregated spaces of the city – and by encouraging them to relate to other people in their everyday life through design processes.

Design experiments were the means by which we placed ourselves in this context and the way through which we understood the possible relationships that we could develop with our partners. For us, bringing out new ways of understanding design in contemporary times was more important than fulfilling SEBRAE's expectations. So we directed the emphasis of the design activity towards the process itself, addressing alternatives informed by the practices and issues that corresponded to the context.

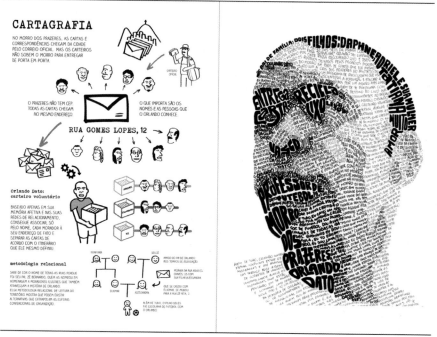

Figure 8.3 Third set of experiments: Results of the partnership between Lada/Esdi/UERJ and the SEBRAE: developing maps and design experiments in collaboration with residents and local entrepreneurs. Photographs © Barbara Szaniecki. Illustrations © Daniel Rocha and Thiago Dias

In some cases, as many of the activities conducted by these micro-entrepreneurs went unnoticed by the community itself and by institutions related to them, making them visible was very important. Bordering the formal and informal economies, these businesses garnered SEBRAE's interest in exposing their activities to alter their socioeconomic value. But, through conversations, we noticed that SEBRAE's intentions and communities' wishes didn't seem to coincide.

The very idea that was presented to us – the development of the 'productive chain of tourism' – didn't seem to have been sufficiently discussed. For the community, the promotion of tourism was less important than solutions to pressing issues such as excessive trash or absence of mail. A pair of students developed a friendship with the volunteer postman, Orlando, which led to the understanding of a relational methodology of distribution of letters in the community.

In these particular sets of experiments, our conversation *dispositifs* relied heavily on visuality by the development of different mappings: cartographies (processes in the territory, with its spaces and participants), chronographies (processes in chronological time or methodologies) and infographics of different goals (information and narratives). But, beyond these visualities, the conversation *dispositifs* have turned out to be necessary before the development of design projects in territories disputed by different powers and whose reintegration into the formal city and citizenship generated many controversies and conflicts.

The touristic and micro entrepreneurship aspects or elements – stated or not – of the urban setting were partially reshaped by these experiments in their immaterial and material dimensions (discursive and non discursive, to use Foucault's terms). For example, the relational system developed by students for letter distribution points to a strong local agency and thus the possibility that the community has to enforce its point of view on the process of integration, through tourism, into the formal and globalized city.

Fourth Set of Experiments: Rehearsing New Forms of Public Dialogue

Eventually we asked ourselves: How can we return to fieldwork in an interactive and thought-provoking way, while also speculating about the protests that took the networks and the streets of Brazil, considering limits and potentialities of the often-unexplored use of public space and of the political sphere? How could we extract new possibilities from these interventions to correspond with, drawing together with (Latour 2008) those who live the challenges of the urban renewal and a city governance?

Having already explored some input from the use of design experiments as a means of engagement and mobilization around emerging themes, we wanted to deepen their potential for using the territory itself where these issues and controversies (Latour 2006) emerged. Consequently, we sought to go further in the direction of design speculations concerning alternative ways of life and interplay

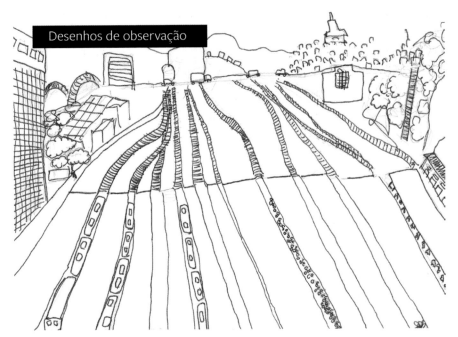

Figure 8.4 Fourth set of experiments: Rehearsing new forms of public dialogue. (Top) Drawings from the project Central do Brasil. (Bottom) Cartographies from the project Central do Brasil. © Ana Almeida, Ignez Carioca and Luana Moreira

with the city, formulating design concepts by means of participant observation and speculative interventions in the field.

In this process, the mediation of design artefacts produced by students gained central focus as they could facilitate interaction with residents and passers-by, as well as encourage collective imaginative experiments about alternative ways of life in the downtown area. Far from being prototypes, such materials should primarily mediate conversations and stimulate imaginations.

We realized the need to expand critical conversations beyond our research lab, within the university environment. So we answer to an open call of the City of Rio de Janeiro and obtained the funds for a seminar in the Carioca Design Centre (CCD), which is also located in the city centre. More than just a seminar, it was both a research event and an activist intervention. It was part of the conversation *dispositif* we intend to assemble.

We sought to approach public management, aiming to build, in a collaborative way, desirable future design plans for this city and its inhabitants. We hoped to cooperate in order to create a greater articulation between engaged knowledge, ways of life and creative practices of the citizens; and practices of planning and management of urban life undertaken by political representatives and public administrations.

Alongside workshops, speeches, round tables and panel presentations, we set up a temporary design anthropology lab where participants were stimulated to develop speculative interventions around the neighbourhood. Unlike the other activities of the seminar, we had no idea of what would be produced and the participants took advantage of the situation by freely creating in the public square in front of the CCD a series of creative and critical provocations to the urban renewal.

Having the seminar in a space of the municipality meant adopting a conversational tactic in order to act in the *dispositif* assuming ourselves – researchers and citizens – as part of this set of heterogeneous power relations and thus investing in the possibility of subverting the current game of urban renewal.

Opening Spaces for Citizenship

Exploring the alternative possibilities for life in the city from an agenda based in experimental research organized in the interface between design and anthropology, we sought to elaborate a series of design interventions conceptualized as forms of inquiry (Halse and Boffi, this volume). With this goal, we hoped to reinforce the construction of each set of experiments from our consolidated findings in the previous interventions.

Undoubtedly, the transition between each of the experiments guided our experimental research practice, and reframed the initial programme (Brandt et al. 2011) while also qualifying our subsequent questioning. The second set of experiments (with the NGO), for example, strengthened our commitment in exercising a design anthropological attitude as more than just an interventionist design practice. From the third set of experiments (with SEBRAE) resulted the perception that even from within the framework of an instrumental demand, it is possible to explore and strengthen local associations. And with the fourth set of experiments we realized that also in the broader urban setting there are opportunities for critical changes of position.

The concept of conversation *dispositifs* set in motion the proposal to combine modes of knowledge production in design and anthropology, in order to correspond with people and the emerging issues in the urban space that surrounds us, not only as teachers, researchers and design students, but as designer-citizens. In this regard, we formulated the notion of conversation *dispositifs* based on its conceptual and practical openness. Openness in political thinking and making: no longer a conception of power located and determined but power understood as power relations in an ongoing game (even if often violent).

This openness doesn't mean to ignore the relations between knowledge and power of the conversation *dispositifs* but to assume them whenever democracy seems to require it. As, for example, when governments ignore the murmurs of citizens but may hear the voice of the university. And openness brings the kind of involvement that the designer, among other 'creatives' may have in this *dispositif*: an acting or performance that stimulates the continual conversations through design experiments more than a one-way communication that directs the city project.

Thus, the city is no longer a mere urban area with features fully focused on the efficiency of production. It may regain its policy sphere dimension with collective decision-making processes in which the designer fully participates along with all citizens. Conversation *dispositifs* are not only a good alternative to top-down planning, but a possible way to contribute to the democratization of democracy by means of design.

References

Anastassakis, Z. (2012), 'Design and Anthropology: An Interdisciplinary Proposition', *Diversity: Design/Humanities*, Proceedings of Fourth International Forum of Design as a Process, 240–8, Belo Horizonte: EdUEMG.

Anastassakis, Z. (2013), 'Laboratório de Design e Antropologia: Preâmbulos Teóricos e Práticos', *Arcos Design*, 7 (1): 178–93.

Bakhtin, M. (2003), *A Estética da Criação Verbal*, São Paulo: Martins Fontes.

Binder, T., De Michelis G., Ehn P., Jacucci G., Linde, P. and Wagner, I. (2011), *Design Things*, Cambridge, MA: The MIT Press.

Brandt, E., Redstrom, J., Eriksen, M. and Binder, T. (2011), *XLAB*, Copenhagen: The Danish Design School Press.

De Certeau, M. (1990), *L'invention au Quotidien*, Paris: Gallimard.

Dewey, J. (1927), *The Public and Its Problems: An Essay in Political Inquiry*. New York: Holt.

DiSalvo, C. (2009), 'Design and the Construction of Publics', *Design Issues*, 25 (1): 48–63.

Foucault, M. (1997), *Sécurité, Territoire, Population. Cours au Collège de France (1977–78)*, Paris: Gallimard/Seuil.

Foucault, M. (1994), *Dits et Écrits*, 1954–88, Paris: Gallimard.

Gatt, C. and Ingold, T. (2013), 'From Description to Correspondence: Anthropology in Real

Time', in W. Gunn, T. Otto and R. C. Smith (eds.), *Design Anthropology: Theory and Practice*, 139–58, London and New York: Bloomsbury.

Gunn, W. and Donovan, J. (eds.) (2012), *Design and Anthropology*, 121–34, Farnham: Ashgate.

Gunn, W., Otto, T. and Smith, R. C. (eds.) (2013), *Design Anthropology: Theory and Practice*, London and New York: Bloomsbury.

Halse, J., Brandt, E., Clark, B. and Binder, T. (eds.) (2010), *Rehearsing the Future*, Copenhagen: The Danish Design School Press.

Heidegger, M. (2010), *A Origem de Obra de Rte*, São Paulo: Edições 70.

Hunt, J. (2011), 'Prototyping the Social: Temporality and Speculative Futures at the Intersection of Design and Culture', in A. J. Clarke (ed.), *Design Anthropology. Object Culture in the 21st Century,* 33–44, Vienna and New York: Springer.

Ingold, T. (2000), *The Perception of the Environment: Essays on Livelihood, Dwelling and Skill*, London and New York: Routledge.

Ingold, T. (2011), *Being Alive: Essays on Movement, Knowledge and Description*, London: Routledge.

Ingold, T. (2013), *Making: Anthropology, Archaeology, Art and Architecture*, London: Routledge.

Ingold, T. and Hallam, E. (eds.) (2007), *Creativity and Cultural Improvisation*, Oxford and New York: Berg.

Kjærsgaard, M. and Otto, T. (2012), 'Anthropological Fieldwork and Designing Potentials', in W. Gunn and J. Donovan (eds.), in *Design and Anthropology*, 177–91, Surrey and Burlington: Ashgate.

Latour, B. (2006), *Changer de Société – Refaire de la Sociologie*, Paris: La Découverte.

Latour, B. (2008), 'A Cautious Prometheus? A Few Steps Toward a Philosophy of Design (With Special Attention to Peter Sloterdijk)', *Proceedings of the international conference of the Design History Society*, 2–10.

Lazzarato, M. (2006), *As Revoluções do Capitalismo*, Rio de Janeiro: Record.

Lenskjold, T. U. (2011), 'Accounts for a Critical Artefacts Approach to Design Anthropology', *Proceedings of the Nordic Design Conference Nordes 4*, 85–93.

Marcus, G. E. and Rabinow, P. (2008), *Designs for an Anthropology of the Contemporary*, Durham, NC and London: Duke University Press.

Mogensen, P. (1991), 'Towards a Provotyping Approach in Systems Development', *Scandinavian Journal of Information Systems*, 3: 31–53.

Rabinow, P. and Marcus, G. E. (2008), *Designs for an Anthropology of the Contemporary*, Durham and London: Duke University Press.

Reyes, P. (2010), 'Construção de Cenários no Design: O Papel da Imagem e do Tempo', in *Anais do 9. Congresso Brasileiro de Pesquisa e Desenvolvimento em Design*, 1, 1–14, São Paulo: PPG em Design Anhembi Morumbi.

Szaniecki, B. and Anastassakis, Z. (2014), 'Entremeios: Ways of Living and Creative Practices in Rio de Janeiro', *Transnational Dialogues Journal 2014*, 34–7.

Tarde, G. (2007), *Monadologia e Sociologia – E Outros Ensaios*, São Paulo: CosacNaify.

Wasson, C. (2000), 'Ethnography in the Field of Design', *Human Organization*, 59 (4): 377–88.

9   The Irony of Drones for Foraging: Exploring the Work of Speculative Interventions

CARL DISALVO

The disciplinary encounter between design and anthropology may take different forms. While some are concerned with how engagements with design might affect the discipline of anthropology or the practices of ethnography (see for example Marcus, this volume), the purpose of this article is to explore how engagements with anthropology and ethnography might affect the discipline of design and its practices of scholarship. These are real concerns with implications for work and the production of knowledge, but they are not new concerns. Scholars in both anthropology and design have probed the overlap of the disciplines and their practices for several decades, spanning the contexts of academia and industry, schools of social science and schools of art. From this there has been, and continues to be, a productive exchange of ideas and methods. The most exciting cases result in a melding of anthropology and design to produce truly hybrid practices. Such practices include, for instance, the idea of 'design ethnography' as first discussed by Salvador, Bell and Anderson (1999) and more recently what Lury and Wakeford (2012) call 'inventive methods' that make use of conceptual and material devices in social and cultural research.

What seems to be distinctive about this current turn in the relationship between anthropology and design is an emphasis on the future, or futures. For instance, in already hybrid fields such as Human–Computer Interaction and Science and Technology Studies, Dourish and Bell (2011) have examined the 'ideas that animate' and 'the stories that motivate' the forever ongoing pursuit of a vision of ubiquitous computing, and Wilkie and Michael (2009) use literatures of expectations to understand how potential users of a system are enacted in the design process. Across design studies we find, repeatedly, the assertion that design is distinctively concerned with 'what does not yet exist' or with 'what might be'. This is a crucial point of differentiation between design and most other fields of study and methods of inquiry, including anthropology (Hunt 2011). Usually, this interest in futures in design serves instrumental ends – the objective is to engage the future in order to invent it and make it through useful and usable products and services that solve problems or fulfil desires. But within design anthropology we can find examples of a more exploratory engagement with futures, engagements that bring anthropological concerns with culture and anthropological techniques of description and interpretation to the design activities of invention and making (Halse 2013; Otto and Smith 2013).

Within design anthropology, the phrase *speculative intervention* has gained prominence. It is a useful phrase for expressing exploratory engagements with futures, which blend together designerly concerns with 'what might be', design techniques of invention and making, anthropological concerns for culture and anthropological techniques of description and interpretation. What results is a methodological mess that is not yet defined, which calls for our imagination and reflection to make sense of it. Speculative intervention, then, is a label we can apply to projects that inhabit this jumbled space of exploratory futures at the overlap of design and anthropology.

Whatever speculative interventions are, they are *not* simply speculative designs by another name. Certainly, there is an association with speculative design. To state the obvious, these interventions are usually 'designerly'. They draw conceptually and materially upon the practices and products of design to give a particular form and character to inquiry. But these interventions also strive to be something more than design as we commonly think of and do it. Although speculative interventions are done *through* design, they are not necessarily done *for* design. That is, the knowledge produced through speculative interventions does not, and should not be required to, have close or tactical value to the near-term making of goods or services.

In a recent seminar paper, George Marcus states that '[d]esign methods provide the legitimation, and most importantly, the craft and form to produce third spaces, studios and studies for collective or collaborative work within fieldwork' (2015:16). My approach to this chapter is to use a project to provide a bit of specificity regarding such design methods, while also reflecting more generally on speculative interventions as a mode of inquiry. In what follows I present a speculative intervention – one involving foraging and drones. I will not delve too much into the particulars of this project except to provide enough context and content so that I can use it to explore this broader notion of speculative interventions. In particular, if speculative interventions are a mode of designerly inquiry, then how do they work? And if their purpose is not simply to inform product development, then what is the work that they do? Answering these questions leads me to argue that one of the ways that speculative interventions work is by employing irony as an inventive mode of doing. In this context, irony is a tactic to construct a paradox and perform a kind of dialogic inquiry. The purpose of this dialogic inquiry, then, is not so much to innovate new products or services, but rather to collaboratively pursue conceptual thinking and making as a cooperative approach to basic design research.

Speculative Interventions in Foraging

Our standard notions of agriculture involve farms, on which crops are purposefully planted and cultivated, in ordered ways. Fields of lettuce, orchards of peaches, all in rows. Industrial agriculture has taken this orderliness to an extreme, producing methodical landscapes of yield. Small-scale agriculture may be more diverse in crops and their management, making different use of land, with greater care for product quality and ecological impact as opposed to per acre yield, but it is still usually farming as we know it. Indeed, it is the smaller farms functioning outside of industrial agriculture that express the quintessential, romantic notion of agriculture as a craft-like commitment to growing, tending and harvesting.

Foraging is another mode of agriculture altogether. One might even argue that foraging is not agriculture, that it constitutes some fundamentally different relationship to natural foodstuff. Foraging is the collection of produce – including fruits, vegetables, nuts and fungi – from places other than farms. This might be berries from bushes in parks, lettuce and other greens growing wild in roadside ditches, plums from trees in a neighbour's yard, or mushrooms found under a log in the woods. Foraging makes use of the abundance and excess of produce in the environment, recognizing it as consumable and free food. Unlike standard agriculture, these bushes, trees and vines are not purposefully planted and they are not cultivated. They are accidental, haphazard and harvesting them is an ad-hoc and opportunistic affair.

People forage for different reasons. Some forage for themselves, as a tradition of sorts, for instance collecting berries in the Spring and Summer to be enjoyed with family and friends. Others forage in order to sell their finds in batches; this is especially true of niche goods such as mushrooms. Still others forage to give away *en masse*, as a way of contributing to the food security of a community. In many cities there are groups committed to this mode of foraging, groups that forage in bulk and then distribute the goods to others, often those in need. This contribution can be significant. In cities such as Los Angeles (large and with favourable growing conditions), foraging at scale can amount to collections upwards of 10,000 kilos per year. Even then, however, foraging is not a replacement for agriculture. It is simply a supplement to the local food supply. But for those social service providers that give food to the needy, foraged goods can be a way to augment the more standard fare of donated food. Foraged apples, berries, lettuces and other greens are welcomed additions to the staples of boxed pasta and canned stew that line the shelves of the food pantries of social service providers.

Foraging at scale becomes, in large part, a logistics problem. Fruits and vegetables must be located, then watched, at some point collected and finally distributed. Farms and orchards are, in a sense, a technological solution to the challenges of foraging – farms and orchards co-locate trees, bushes and plants. On a farm there is no need to go looking for the apples because they are right there, in rows. If you want to know if the apples are ripe, you simply need to walk through the orchard to take stock of them. Not the case with foraging. Trees and bushes and plants can be separated by significant distances, and they are often in difficult or dangerous-to-reach locations. Foragers either have to spend significant time monitoring the trees, bushes and plants, or make educated estimations of when a particular tree, bush, or plant will be ready for picking. The estimations come with risk: miss the date and the fruit will fall to the ground and spoil, go too soon and the fruit will not be ready to pick and the effort to travel to the site will be wasted. Like many logistics problems, information is key to managing the process, and so foraging is, at least in part, a problem of data.

The Drones for Foraging project is part of an ongoing project exploring how to design tools – broadly construed – to support the practice of foraging at scale. Specifically, we are exploring how we might appropriate or re-design the logistics challenges of foraging by using technologies of precision agriculture, such as remote sensing, sensor networks, digital maps and unmanned aerial vehicles. The project is an example of a speculative intervention in that it works both to create design things to explore what the practices of foraging might be and, in the process, to manifest and articulate some of the factors and relations that constitute an issue. More broadly, as an endeavour of design anthropology, the project knowingly (if unsurely and awkwardly) oscillates between reaching towards understanding and gesturing towards action. There is no single question that motivates the project but rather a swirl of nested provocations. Can the technologies of contemporary industrial agriculture be used to support alternative (decidedly non-industrialized) agricultures? How do we scale down design or use design to shift between scales of technology and practice? Does the introduction of technologies of automation and monitoring fundamentally change a practice such as foraging?

Importantly, the Drones for Foraging project is not a speculative design project in the more familiar sense of designers taking an authorial stance towards a topic or technology and creating fantastic representations of futures or alternate presents. Dunne and Raby's work (2001; 2013) is an example of speculative design from an authorial stance. This is not meant as a critique against that approach, but to signal an important point of distinction. Instead of taking an authorial approach, the project is firmly grounded in the methods and theories of contemporary participatory and co-design. More than simply enrolling others into a design process, the project takes its cue from the notion of participatory design as a practice of collaboratively constructing design things: socio-material assemblages that work to articulate issues and express a range of possibilities without committing to singular solutions (Binder et al. 2011; Bjögvinsson 2012; Ehn 2008; Ericson et al. 2011; Halse et al. 2010). So, while the project strives towards workable tools, the broader agenda is to make a collective that works towards discovering and expressing the potentials of foraging.

The project is being conducted together with members of a foraging collective based in Atlanta, GA, USA, called Concrete Jungle. This collective is comprised of volunteers who give of their time to spot, collect and distribute fruit from public fruit trees and bushes to need-based food organizations in the metro Atlanta region. A small core of four to six volunteers take on the majority of the coordination – keeping track of fruit trees and bushes, scheduling picks and arranging deliveries to food pantries, churches and social service organizations. A larger group of volunteers are

Figure 9.1 Checking a tree for fruit with ladders and crew © Carl DiSalvo

mobilized at various points throughout the year for specific tasks, such as picking a particular tree or set of trees. One of the issues that the organization faces is knowing when to organize a pick – knowing when the fruit is ripe. This is the logistics problem previously mentioned. Concrete Jungle was interested in exploring technologies that might be designed to assist in monitoring the fruit trees and bushes, in order to mitigate the demands on volunteer labour and more accurately anticipate when picks should be organized (see Figure 9.1).

But What is Really is Done?

The idea of using hobbyist drones for remote fruit monitoring is not entirely ridiculous; unmanned aerial vehicles (UAVs) are an increasingly common component in precision agriculture. This term – precision agriculture – refers to an ecosystem of technologies and techniques designed to provide farmers with information with which to make a wide variety of farming decisions. Key to precision agriculture is the collection of data, which comes from a combination of sources including ground-based sensors for soil and air monitoring and remote imaging, often combined together in maps produced by sophisticated geographic information systems (GIS) that offer a variety of modes of data analysis. A farmer, then, might use these technologies to produce images that provide insight into the quality of soil and crops, and over time produce a rich corpus of information about developing growing conditions and patterns of yield, to inform such fundamental decisions as what to plant where and when. UAVs provide yet another vantage from which to collect data, usually in the form of imagery that can either be analysed through naked-eye techniques or by employing speciality cameras or image analysis software.

Curious about the application of UAVs to foraging, together with Concrete Jungle, we explored the potential of similar platforms for foraging. The question was simple: could we use inexpensive hobbyist drones for remote monitoring of fruit trees, in order to ascertain the general ripeness of the fruit? If so, this could greatly lessen the time and effort needed for fruit monitoring and take some of the risk out of sched-uling picks (when volunteers go to collect the produce). After comparing multiple drone models, we settled on a Parrot AR 2.0 drone. This model of hobbyist drone is one of the most widely accessible; it can be easily purchased at a number of retail outlets (including bookstores and consumer goods stores) at a reasonable price. The device is remote controlled via a tablet or phone, it can be outfitted with a global positioning system (GPS) for automated flights, it is equipped with two cameras, and it has a software developers kit (SDK) that enables customization of the software.

Over the course of two seasons we ran multiple test flights with the hobbyist drones, using them, or attempting to use them, to spot and monitor fruit around Atlanta. For the sake of simplicity we focused our attention on apple and pear trees, as the fruits are relatively large. In addition to the test flights we also developed custom flight software using the Parrot SDK in an attempt to enable more precise

Figure 9.2 Drone in flight, looking for fruit © Carl DiSalvo

positioning of the drone and its camera in orientation to the fruit, and we investigated the use of computer vision to detect shapes and colours from the images captured by the drone. We also developed the standard fare of interaction design materials, such as scenarios and low-fidelity user interfaces that provided representative conceptualizations of both the functionalities and experiences of use (see Figure 9.2).

But How is it Intervening?

As a speculative intervention, the Drones for Foraging project combines exploratory design and participation in a community of practice to probe questions about what foraging might be. Rather than treating intervention generically, as simply something that happened, it is worth briefly detailing what these interventions were and how they can be considered speculative. The interventions took place – they were performed – with every flight of the drone, as well as with the activities that took place in between the flights. It is important to recognize and appreciate that each drone flight was itself a moment of inquiry through experimental use. In each flight we progressively developed proficiency with the device and we were progressively able to explore how this particular device might affect this particular practice. Indeed, the subject of design in this project was less the drone itself and more the practice of foraging. The drone was not so much a device to be designed but rather a device through which to experiment with alternate configurations to the practices of foraging.

More specifically, within the project we can identify at least three modes of intervention: spatial, material and conceptual. Quite literally, each intervention was an intervention in space as the drone was flown through the city. The drone occupied space. It moved through space. And moreover, it did so in a manner that bordered on the spectacular. It is not common to see drones flying through city parks or in residential urban neighbourhoods; it is not common to see a drone hovering in front of a tree or bush, moving back and forth. In some contexts the spatial intervention carried a particular valance: as a nuisance or threat. The drone makes a whirring noise as it flies, it manoeuvres awkwardly, often appearing erratic and unstable. At times, the drone would collide with the tree or bush, damaging both the device and the object it was observing. So, for good reasons, the spectacle of the drone in public, the spatial intervention of the drone, was not always welcomed.

Each intervention was also a material intervention as we crafted design objects in service of the drone and the experiments in the practice of foraging with drones. Some of these were mundane in both content and format, such as scenarios and diagrams. Others were more sophisticated, such as the custom software. The software was a material intervention in that it was created based upon the existing code and frameworks made available through the SDK – our custom code interfaced with the existing code producing a new collection of capacities. These capacities were also material capacities, such as the ability to discern shapes and colours from the environment and the ability to specify navigation routes through the environment.

These material interventions, particularly the software, which is shared as open source, also provide scaffolding for others to build upon, ostensibly furthering the exploration of drones for foraging or other pursuits.

Finally, each intervention was a conceptual intervention as we reconfigured assumptions about, and expectations of, agricultural technologies. To a lesser extent this reconfiguration of assumptions or expectations also applies to drones more generally. Even though drones are increasingly used in a host of commercial contexts, for the general public drones are most commonly perceived as weapons of war or tools for intelligence. So, to envision drones for civil purposes may also have been a conceptual intervention. In a sense, the spatial and the material interventions hinge upon, or are articulated by, the conceptual intervention. It is the conceptual intervention that opens the space for invention, which is then manifested through the spatial and material inventions. This opening of the space for invention is not an accident but rather the outcome of a particular design tactic: the use of irony.

Designerly Irony

Exploring drones for foraging is an ironic endeavour because, as has been alluded to, foraging is anything but precise. Yes, data could assist the practice of foraging; for instance, data about the ripeness of fruits might make the endeavour of foraging more manageable. But there is no information solution that would *change* the conditions of foraging. The conditions – accidental, haphazard growth, and ad-hoc harvest – are what they are: they are the conditions that comprise foraging. It is not as if these experiments with drones (or experiments with other techniques of precision agriculture) will transform foraging into farming, nor would that be desired. The value of foraging is precisely in making use of excess and abundance, precisely in seizing the opportunity that uncultivated but accessible trees, bushes and vines provide for free food.

Let's pause to call attention to this irony, because it is a characteristic quality of many speculative interventions and, I claim, it is a design tactic of sorts that opens an imaginative and resourceful space for design anthropology. Irony here is not the caustic mockery and sarcasm of a jaded culture. Irony here is a trope – an inventive manner of thinking, and in the case of a speculative intervention, irony is an inventive manner of doing.

Without delving too far into literary theory, this mode of irony in the Drones for Foraging project is akin to what theorist Kenneth Burke (1941) terms 'irony of circumstance': the conditions of an event or site being counter to our expectations. Within the event of foraging one would not expect to encounter a drone. Similarly, within the site of precision agriculture one would not expect to encounter foraging. Irony of circumstance is but one form of irony and it seems particularly suited toward speculative interventions. By employing design methods, by using the objects and processes of design, we can craft props to purposefully stage an irony of circum-stance. Our speculative interventions become the performance of circumstances of irony, enabled by design. These speculative interventions are then both descriptive and generative. Or rather, they generate an event that we can ethnographically describe, and this event is an imaginative conjecture of a design future.

Consider that there is little research into technologies for small-scale agriculture. There is even less research into technologies for so-called alternative agricultures. Pursuing the question 'Can the technologies of contemporary industrial agriculture be used to support alternative agricultures' by exploring the design and use of drones, sensors and other components of precision agriculture for foraging is a calculated move for the purpose of opening a practice to inquiry, to attend to a practice that is otherwise not so attended to. The intentional juxtaposition of technologies and practices through design is an ironic act. It is also a particularly appropriate act, or method, for speculative interventions within design anthropology because irony can be a component of inquiry.

One aspect of irony is paradox. Inquiry is often grounded in paradox. When we find irony we may find inquiry to follow. When we *do* irony, we may perform inquiry. It is the perceived inconsistency of a situation, and the desire to engage, understand, express and appreciate the conflicting aspects of a situation or issue that undergird and motivate the investigation and experimentation that comprise inquiry. So, what we get from this particular inquiry – this speculative intervention – is insight into the interplay between the conditions of foraging and the conditions of contemporary agriculture technologies, and through that, an articulation of the needs and desires of foragers as they are and might be instantiated through the possible re-design of agriculture technologies. These insights range from the immediate to the abstract. With regards to the immediate, we can identify specific technical capabilities that would be needed in the hardware and software design. We can also identify policy issues that would need to be addressed now, in order to enable such activities in the near future. With regards to the abstract, we can begin to articulate design strategies and tactics for transforming technologies across scales, for instance for re-making industrial systems to fit and work in non-industrial contexts. We can also begin to theorize, through the ethnographic work, new modes of practice; in this case, new modes of agriculture and civics. In this formulation I want to emphasize that there is not necessarily a desire to *resolve* the conflicting, paradoxical aspects of a situation or issue. The factors may remain in tension. Or through the process of inquiry they may be articulated into new issues. But the impetus is not to problem solving, not to solutionism.

Burke (1941) identifies irony with dialectic – a dialogical encounter between multiple positions through which some understanding is arrived at that would have been impossible to grasp from any one perspective alone. If, as others have suggested (Halse 2013; Otto and Smith 2013; Smith and Otto, this volume), design anthropology is a distinctive way of knowing, perhaps one of its particular qualities is that it is a dialogic way of knowing. Irony is one way of enacting a productive tension between multiple positions. The objects and processes of design materialize those positions and allow us to experiment with and between them.

With the Drones for Foraging project we are able to experiment with and between the tools and techniques of precision agriculture and the practices of foraging. And through the dialogic encounter between these devices and practices, what was arrived at was an understanding of the design potentials at the overlap of those conditions. For instance, through the project we experimented with simple, low-fidelity techniques of computer vision to identify and isolate colours and shapes from the drone video feed, software for custom flight planning and techniques of image analysis, including object recognition and counting. Many such techniques are readily available in the software and service packages of precision agriculture; our design inquiry allowed us to manifest the potential of these techniques in decidedly non-precise practices. In addition we identified mundane issues of dealing with repair and maintenance, which were exacerbated by the conditions of foraging that often have drones flying in extremely close proximity to trees, powerlines and buildings, all of which, with the slightest slip in control or variation in wind, can quickly result in a damaged device – which is quite different from the standard conditions of precision agriculture in which drones fly relatively unobstructed over large swathes of land.

Fanciful but Not Fantastic Things: Speculation without the Spectacle

As Jamer Hunt points out: 'Two forms of speculative design thinking are familiar from design history: the utopian and the critical. Each of them, however, overemphasizes the designed over the lived' (2014: 12). As a speculative intervention, the Drones for Foraging project wavers between the utopian and the critical. With just a bit of a nudge, through its aesthetics or discursive framing, it could veer in either direction. But it stabilizes along a third position, in part because it *is* grounded in lived experience and current socio-technical conditions. The irony at play in the project is a product of the back-and-forth between the possible and the fictional. So while the work of the Drones for Foraging project is fanciful it is not fantastic in the ways that much speculative design is often fantastic: concerned with producing the extraordinary.

Instead, the exploration of drones in the practice of foraging is *almost* do-able, we can *almost* integrate these technologies into practice. The obstacles to making it 'really real' include both mundane concerns such as battery life (these drones can only fly for about 20 minutes, making them useful only for short distances) and more complex issues of public policy (such as regulations on the use of hobbyist drones in public space). But the capacities of the technology are just enough to make an inventive foray into the practice possible. The result is a speculative intervention that can be prototyped – performed and experienced – with only a modest bit of imaginative projection.

The Drones for Foraging prototypes are different from common notions of prototypes as steps towards a product. Instead, these prototypes might best be understood as engaging in what Binder et al. (2011) call 'thinging'. Drawing on

Bruno Latour's (2004) discussion of 'things' as objects that gather and express matters of concern, Binder et al. (2011) have developed the notions of design things and 'thinging' to describe the roles of design in this process of expressing matters of concern. 'Thinging' can be interpreted as a kind of prototyping, a way of constructing representations and performances of goods and services that brings to the fore the social, cultural and/or political potentials and consequences of the design in the potential use of the product. Form and function are still important in this process of 'thinging', but only to the extent they work to assemble and hold together the various factors of an issue (see also Lenskjold and Olander, this volume).

This notion of prototyping as 'thinging' opens yet another space for integrating design and anthropology. Marcus (this volume) points out that the conceptual thinking of anthropologists may function in a manner similar to a design prototype. As an example, he offers the concept of 'the gift'. Following from Marcus, we can understand 'the gift' and 'gifting' not as definitive labels, but rather as constructs with which to probe and interpret cultural phenomena. Much like a prototype then, the anthropological concept serves as an experimental device for encapsulating and expressing a complex concept.

Might we consider prototypes that do the work of thinging, that work to assemble and hold together the various factors of an issue, akin to conceptual thinking in anthropology? For the most part, these prototypes do not yet carry the same richness in idea and model as 'the gift', but could they? What would it take to make a design thing robust and durable enough to circulate through sites of engagement and interpretation? The durability, I would argue, is not a matter of material sturdiness, but rather of the malleability and resilience of the abstraction that undergirds the object. For instance, the notion of a 'drone for foraging' is too specific, thereby too brittle, likely to break upon transfer. But could it be abstracted to an idea of a 'public robot' that might travel across sites? Such conceptual things would become like 'the gift', subjects of inquiry, models used for the interpretation of phenomena and events. Perhaps the 'intervention' itself is the first of these conceptual-design-anthropology-things.

By Way of Conclusion: Who Constitutes the 'We' to Whom this Matters?

In this paper I have developed an argument that speculative interventions function as inquiry. Towards addressing the question of 'how', using the Drones for Foraging project, I have argued that irony can function as a tactic of inquiry in speculative interventions, as it works to set-up a dialectic between perspectives and conditions. Design materializes these perspectives and conditions and constructs situations in which we can experiment with new arrangements. This process enables us, as researchers, to come to explore and express 'what might be' in an informed manner, ideally grounded in lived experience, cultivated through a participatory approach. Along the way, I also suggested that the prototype of speculative interventions exemplify what Binder et al. (2011) refer to as design things, and that these things might come to function as conceptual devices in design anthropology, akin to conceptual categories such as 'the gift'. At least one tension persists: who is this work for? The very label 'design anthropology' confounds expectations and audiences.

As Ramia Mazé (2014) has posed the question, when we consider a commons of social innovation, who is included? Who is the 'We' that constitute these participatory endeavours? The Drones for Foraging project was grounded in the practices and commitments of participatory design, which includes an obligation that the project produce value for the participants, as well as for the designers and researchers. Throughout the project design researchers and foragers came together to explore collaboratively what the future of foraging might be. Efforts were made to blend roles – to varying extents design researchers engaged in foraging and foragers engaged in design (if not design research). Along the way discoveries were made about drones, about foraging, about the potentials for scaling down technologies of contemporary industrial agriculture to be used to support alternative agricultures. For instance, we were able to identify specific technical limitations in hobbyist drones and from these limitations enumerate desired features and alterations to the drone design, including both the hardware and software components. Moreover, these features and alterations would be useful beyond foraging; they would be useful for many public or civic environmental monitoring purposes, ranging from community ecological surveys to citizen journalism. In addition we developed insight into the values and motivations that undergird this particular foraging collective, as we worked together to explore what knowledge, actions and responsibilities might be delegated across systems. Finally, from the various test flights and software demos we created we were able to begin to outline a general user experience of hobbyist drones in civic contexts and how these experiences might fit into service models. It is fair to say that there is a desire to make the knowledge generated through the project matter. But herein lies a conundrum – to whom does this work really matter?

It does, in fact, matter to the foragers – they do comprise a component of the 'We'. But the project is not instrumental in the familiar ways of design: the immediate outcome of our working together is not a functional system. Indeed, what matters is not innovation or even invention. What matters is the collective effort of exploring a desired future. This desired future is not reducible to merely the use of drones for foraging. Rather, that concept, that design thing, is expressive of a desired future in which we recognize, appreciate and engage in diverse approaches to food systems and food justice. This is the future that we are speculating on – gesturing towards – together. This is how a more inclusive 'We' is constituted through the project: by joining in the commitments of an other, in this case, by joining in the commitments of the foragers.

What speculative interventions such as the Drones for Foraging project provide is the opportunity to experiment with possible futures, to play out, materially and experientially, what might be, to suggest conditions we might choose to work towards as well as factors we might have to contend with along the way. Projects such as these produce descriptions and interpretations, enabled by invention and making. But they are not roadmaps. A speculative intervention does not list a series of progressive milestones along a progressive trajectory toward a product. It is more akin to a kind of basic research than research that is either clinical or applied. By embracing the capacity of design anthropology to do basic research, we distance design from rote instrumentalism. Design becomes something other than problem solving and design research becomes something other than informing the concep-tualization and production of the products and services that do problem solving (see also Halse and Boffi; Lindström and Ståhl; Lenskjold and Olander, this volume). Perhaps, then, we might even consider that design anthropology itself is a kind of speculative intervention into the field of design research, a suggestion of what design might be.

References

Binder, T., De Michelis, G., Ehn, P., Jacucci, G., Linde, P. and Wagner, I. (2011), *Design Things*, Cambridge, MA: MIT Press.

Bjögvinsson, E., Ehn, P. and Hillgren, P. A. (2012), 'Design Things and Design Thinking: Contemporary Participatory Design Challenges', *Design Issues*, 28 (3): 101–16.

Burke, K. (1941), 'Four Master Tropes', *The Kenyon Review*, 3 (4): 421–38.

Dourish, P. and Bell, G. (2011), *Divining a Digital Future: Mess and Mythology in Ubiquitous Computing*, Cambridge, MA: MIT Press.

Dunne, A. and Raby, F. (2001), *Design Noir: The Secret Life of Electronic Objects*, London and Basel: Birkhäuser/August.

Dunne, A. and Raby, F. (2013), *Speculative Everything: Design, Fiction, and Social Dreaming*, Cambridge, MA: MIT Press.

Ehn, P. (2008), 'Participation in Design Things', in *Proceedings of the Tenth Anniversary Conference on Participatory Design*, 92–101, New York: ACM Press.

Ericson, M. and Mazé, R. (eds.) (2011), *Design Act: Socially and Politically Engaged Design Today – Critical Roles and Emerging Tactics*, Stockholm: Iaspis.

Halse, J. (2013), 'Ethnographies of the Possible', in W. Gunn, T. Otto and R. C. Smith (eds.), *Design Anthropology: Theory and Practice*, 180–96, London and New York: Bloomsbury.

Halse, J., Brandt, E., Clark, B. and Binder, T. (eds.) (2010), *Rehearsing the Future*, Copenhagen: Danish Design School Press.

Hunt, J. (2011), 'Prototyping the Social: Temporality and Speculative Futures at the Intersection of Design and Culture', in A. J. Clarke (ed.), *Design Anthropology: Object Culture in the 21st Century*, 33–44, Vienna and New York: Springer.

Hunt, J. (2014), 'What is a System and Why Can't You Touch It?', paper presented at *Seminar 2: Interventionist Speculation*, The Research Network for Design Anthropology, August 14–15, Copenhagen, Denmark.

Latour, B. (2004), 'Why Has Critique Run Out of Steam? From Matters of Fact to Matters of Concern', *Critical Inquiry* 30 (2): 225–48.

Lury, C. and Wakeford, N. (eds.), (2012), *Inventive Methods: The Happening of the Social*, New York and London: Routledge.

Marcus, G. E. (2015), 'Jostling Ethnography Between Design and Participatory Art Practices... And The Collaborative Relations That It Engenders', paper presented at *Seminar 3: Collaborative Formations of Issues*, The Research Network for Design Anthropology, January 22–23, Aarhus, Denmark.

Mazé, R. (2014), 'Our Common Future? Political Questions for Designing Social Innovation', in *Proceedings of the DRS Design Research Society Conference*, 560–71.

Otto, T. and Smith, R. C. (2013), 'Design Anthropology: A Distinct Style of Knowing', in W. Gunn, T. Otto and R. C. Smith (eds.), *Design Anthropology: Theory and Practice*, 1–29, London and New York: Bloomsbury.

Salvador, T., Bell, G. and Anderson, K. (1999), 'Design Ethnography', *Design Management Journal (Former Series)*, 10 (4): 35–41.

Wilkie, A. and Michael, M. (2009), 'Expectation and Mobilisation Enacting Future Users', *Science, Technology and Human Values*, 34 (4): 502–22.

Section III
Collaborative Formation of Issues

Resources informed us that, although the managers shared the same intentions and ambitions, they differed quite substantially in their ways of acting and communicating. While Gustav's observations could thus be said to simply replicate this pre-existing perception, the point is rather that his para-ethnographic field note neither adamantly declares nor explicitly evaluates how management unfolds in practice. Instead, it concretely *describes* it as viewed from his particular perspective. When the managers, a few weeks later, encourage the employees to write and submit more field notes, Gustav zooms in again on the management of the para-ethnographic experiment itself:

> Niels (standing up as always) asks how the experiment is going. He is pointing out that the anthropologists didn't receive many observations. Michael is sitting next to him and seems to agree. Christian is on the other side and seems to be staring at the floor [...] In the discussion, Niels and Michael are doing a good job as facilitators. Christian is still looking at the floor. At this point, the discussion starts to take a weird turn. Lots of people are talking, but no one is really paying attention. At this point, Christian stands up and begins to summarize the situation.

Again, Gustav here observes and describes how the managers act rather differently in terms of their enthusiasm, communication and social interactions. Indeed, this appears to be of critical importance to him as an observation or exploration of how management unfolds in the department. But it is also openly clear that this is management as viewed from Gustav's distinct perspective – a point which becomes even clearer when Thomas, another employee, writes a field note describing the exact same meeting:

> It quickly developed into a discussion about why it is so difficult to write field notes. This was a discussion characterized by the 'usual suspects': NVB, who mentioned the wish to write a whole thesis as a kind of showstopper; ESO, who always presents an intellectual analysis; JG, who thought our management is so unrealistic that it couldn't possibly be interesting to analyse; and myself, who thought an unanalytical observation must be the easiest thing to provide. During the meeting, there was traffic back and forth: one employee chose to leave the meeting to answer his phone at his desk (in the same open office space), after which he returned, and two employees chose to leave the meeting a few minutes early to resume work at their desks. Interestingly, the three local managers Niels, Michael and Christian decided to conclude the discussion, with Christian saying 'Should we just leave it here then,' Michael commenting 'And let people give it a few thoughts,' and Niels sarcastically concluding 'Okay, let's see, then, if Carsten writes to all of you that you MUST write some field notes'.

In these observations, the focus is not only on the managers but also on the employees, emphasizing a variety of actions which, from Thomas' point of view, influence how the situation is managed. In particular, the intricate dynamics between the managers, who seek to stake out a certain direction (i.e. to increase the production of field notes), and the employees, who seek to navigate the various demands placed on them (i.e. to attend a meeting, to answer the phone etc.), are the centre of attention. In this sense, the field note concretely describes the challenges of what Thomas and others emphasized as the importance of 'self-management'; that is, to be able to manage one's own working time and efforts while, at the same time, being subject to particular demands and directions.

Of course, not all field notes were concerned with the para-ethnographic project itself. While other notes placed the emphasis on more humdrum managerial practices – for instance, how a complaint from a client was taken care of, how a meeting unfolded in practice, or how the managers articulated a frustration with another department – they all provided different insights into the social dynamics of management as experienced and perceived from different positions and perspectives within the organization. In this respect, the point is not so much that the para-ethnographic approach generates entirely unprecedented issues and insights but that it prompts *concrete accounts and portraits* of a range of managerial situations. Thus, by distributing the perspective, the self as the instrument of exploration is clearly de-centred, as each field note constitutes a particular window into the proclaimed management 'complexity'; that is, into how management concretely unfolds in practice.

But where, then, does this leave the relationship between the para-ethnographers and the ethnographers? Importantly, the point is not that para-ethnography 2.0, with its focus on detailed descriptions, by any means reduces the complexity (Strathern 2004). Nor does it necessarily entail the idea that management is 'out there' as a singular object which is simply seen from different perspectives (Law 2004). Rather, as each para-ethnographic perspective represents a window into the complexity, concretely describing managerial situations, it is examined how management is *enacted* in different ways, to paraphrase Annemarie Mol (2002). The independent and interdependent relationship between the para-ethnographers and the ethnographers is thus characterized by the latter initiating and facilitating a collaborative exploration of the *multiplicity* of management through the former's descriptions and perspectives. In fact, this may be the most important task and responsibility of the ethnographers: to ensure that the multiple para-ethnographic perspectives are taken into account and brought into dialogue. Thomas's perspective is not entirely different from Gustav's viewpoint, but it is not altogether similar either. In this sense, the key point is to pursue an exploration that is grounded in, and attends to, a multitude of para-ethnographic perspectives.

Changing Perceptions

Perhaps it could be argued that none of the above is as new as we proclaim. Undeniably, ethnographers have for a long time involved their fieldwork subjects in their research endeavours by asking them to write diaries, take photos, serve as research assistants etc. As Tim Ingold contends, anthropology is not so much a study *of* as a study *with* people, as 'the world and its inhabitants, human and non-human, are our teachers, mentors and interlocutors' (2008: 83). In our experiment, however, the point was not merely to gain ethnographic insights through various participatory initiatives but more fundamentally to instigate a collaborative exploration based on a distributed yet shared ethnographic sensibility. While it is by now a truism that ethnographic practice does not constitute a disinterested observation but a situated intervention, this entails, as James Leach points out, that 'the ethnographer's presence produces events – micro-moments of replication and differentiation, ideas and suggestions, associations, and so forth which may well be innovations. But that these ... may or may not be events that matter, events that have an influence on the future trajectory of the social form or ethos' (2010: 202). By way of concluding this chapter, we argue that the production of a para-ethnographic sensibility proved to be precisely such an event that mattered beyond the particular experiment.

At first, however, this was not so evident. Since our plan was to engage in a process of collaborative analysis with the para-ethnographers, we organized a half-day workshop that ultimately turned out largely to reproduce debates and arguments, which were all too familiar to the managers and employees. Quite a few of them did not say anything at all, and, as facilitators, we did not succeed in conducting a constructive analysis of the descriptions and insights provided by the field notes – probably because we had been so preoccupied with how the managers and employees would respond to para-ethnography 2.0 that we had basically ignored what para-ethnography 2.0 would require from us. In addition to giving us certain insights into the everyday tensions and social dynamics in the department, the workshop made us worry that our intervention had in fact produced events that would contribute to the 'downward spiral' rather than changing it. Surely, it might not be unproblematic to work in a social environment in which everybody is potentially a para-ethnographer, observing while participating and then documenting the observations in detailed field notes.

But perhaps we did not have to think too much about this. The managers and employees consistently told us that the para-ethnographic experiment was not only the object of intense discussion in the department, but that many of them found it truly constructive to see both their own and their colleagues' practices and opinions from an ethnographic perspective; that is, to approach them with a sense of ethnographic curiosity rather than immediately engaging in debates about rights and wrongs. In this way, the ethnographic sensibility induced a change in perception among the managers and employees, as it entailed a degree of distance which counteracted their inclination to jump quickly to conclusions or see things from their own perspective only. As such, it was emphasized by more than a few of them that the ethnographic sensibility prompted them to have a more 'level-headed' (*nøgtern*) – or, in Leth's words, 'cool-headed' – approach to various situations and issues facing them every day. An approach which was, they stressed, highly productive in their tense and demanding work environment.

In this sense, the most significant contribution of the experiment might certainly be this general change in perception. As para-ethnography 2.0 instilled a reflexive ethnographic sensibility among the managers and employees, essentially grounding the collaborative issue formation in this sensibility, it also distributed the ethnographic perspective and reconceptualized conventional ideas about the relations between the fieldwork subjects and the ethnographer. Moreover, the ethnographic sensibility proved to elicit an awareness of the fact that to see or perceive a given object, practice or situation always takes place from a distinct point of view, and, by implication, that this viewpoint could in fact be different (Merleau-Ponty 2002 [1945]). Indeed, this goes to the very core of ethnographic practice and anthropological critique (Marcus and Fischer 1986), which seek to defamiliarize and disrupt the taken-for-granted by disclosing its socio-historical contingency; that is, by emphasizing that 'the world could be different' (Halse 2013: 191). For the managers and employees, the ethnographic sensibility induced precisely this change in perception: it allowed them to approach and see their current assumptions and practices in a new way and, by so doing, to realize and explore how things might be different. In this sense, para-ethnography 2.0 may be said to 'wedge' itself in between 'that which already is' and 'that which could be'.

Acknowledgements

We would like to thank the Danish Agency for Science, Technology and Innovation for funding our experiment with a so-called Innovation Voucher. Moreover, we are deeply grateful to both the engineering company and the two enthusiastic consultants – Jacob Christoffer Pedersen and Flemming Toft – with whom we have collaborated. It has been truly inspiring.

References

Beebe, R. and Myers, J. (2010), *Foundations of Paramedic Care*, Clifton Park, NY: Delmar.

Dourish, P. (2006), 'Implications for Design', in *Proceedings of the SIGCHI Conference on Human Factors in Computing Systems*, 541–50, New York: ACM Press.

Ehn, P. (1993), 'Scandinavian Design: On Participation and Skill', in D. Schuler and A. Namioka (eds.), *Participatory Design: Principles and Practices*, 41–77, Hillsdale, NJ: Lawrence Erlbaum Associates.

Gunn, W. and Donovan, J. (eds.) (2012), *Design and Anthropology*, Farnham: Ashgate.

Halse, J. (2008), *Design Anthropology: Borderland Experiments with Participation, Performance and Situated Intervention*, PhD dissertation, IT University of Copenhagen.

Halse, J. (2013), 'Ethnographies of the Possible', in W. Gunn, T. Otto and R. C. Smith (eds.), *Design Anthropology: Theory and Practice*, 180–96, London and New York: Bloomsbury.

Holmes, D. R. and Marcus, G. E. (2005), 'Cultures of Expertise and the Management of Globalization: Toward the Re-Functioning of Ethnography', in A. Ong and S. J.

Collier (eds.), *Global Assemblages: Technology, Politics, and Ethics as Anthropological Problems*, 235–52, Oxford: Blackwell.

Holmes, D. R. and Marcus, G. E. (2006), 'Fast Capitalism: Para-Ethnography and the Rise of the Symbolic Analyst', in M. S. Fisher and G. Downey (eds.), *Frontiers of Capital: Ethnographic Reflections on the New Economy*, 33–57, Durham, NC: Duke University Press.

Holmes, D. R. and Marcus, G. E. (2008), 'Collaboration Today and the Re-Imagination of the Classic Scene of Fieldwork Encounter', *Collaborative Anthropologies*, 1: 81–101.

Ingold, T. (2008), 'Anthropology is *Not* Ethnography', *Proceedings of the British Academy*, 154: 69–92.

Ingold, T. (2012), 'Introduction: The Perception of the User-Producer', in W. Gunn and J. Donovan (eds.), *Design and Anthropology*, 19–33, Farnham: Ashgate.

Kensing, F. and Blomberg, J. (1998), 'Participatory Design: Issues and Concerns', *Computer Supported Cooperative Work*, 7 (3): 167–85.

Kjærsgaard, M. (2013), 'Serendipity and Business Development – Design Anthropological Investigations at The Post', in *Proceedings of the Ethnographic Praxis in Industry Conference*, 365–76.

Kjærsgaard, M. and Otto, T. (2012), 'Anthropological Fieldwork and Designing Potentials', in W. Gunn and J. Donovan (eds.), *Design and Anthropology*, 177–91, Farnham: Ashgate.

Law, J. (2004), *After Method. Mess in Social Science Research*, London and New York: Routledge.

Leach, J. (2010), 'Intervening with the Social? Ethnographic Practice and Tarde's Image of Relations between Subjects', in M. Candea (ed.), *The Social after Gabriel Tarde: Debates and Assessments*, 191–207, London and New York: Routledge.

Leth, J. (2000), *Billedet Forestiller*, København: Gyldendal.

Malinowski, B. (1922), *Argonauts of the Western Pacific*, London: Routledge.

Marcus, G. E. (2010), 'Contemporary Fieldwork Aesthetics in Art and Anthropology: Experiments in Collaboration and Intervention', *Visual Anthropology*, 23 (4): 263–77.

Marcus, G. E. (2013), 'Experimental Forms for the Expression of Norms in the Ethnography of the Contemporary', *HAU Journal of Ethnographic Theory*, 3 (2): 197–217.

Marcus, G. E. and Fischer, M. M. J. (1986), *Anthropology as Cultural Critique: An Experimental Moment in the Human Sciences*, Chicago: University of Chicago Press.

Merleau-Ponty, M. (2002 [1945]), *Phenomenology of Perception*, London and New York: Routledge.

Mol, A. (2002), *The Body Multiple: Ontology in Medical Practice*, Durham, NC: Duke University Press.

Murphy, K. M. and Marcus, G. E. (2013), 'Epilogue: Ethnography and Design, Ethnography in Design … Ethnography by Design', in W. Gunn, T. Otto and R. C. Smith (eds.), *Design Anthropology: Theory and Practice*, 251–68, London and New York: Bloomsbury.

Nafus, D. and Anderson, K. (2009), 'Writing on Walls: The Materiality of Social Memory in Corporate Research', in M. Cefkin (ed.), *Ethnography and the Corporate Encounter: Reflections on Research in and of Corporations*, 137–57, New York and Oxford: Berghahn Books, 29 (1): 58–70.

Otto, T. (2016), 'History in and for Design', *Journal of Design History*, 29 (1): 58–70.

Otto, T. and Smith, R. C. (2013), 'Design Anthropology: A Distinct Style of Knowing', in

W. Gunn, T. Otto and R. C. Smith (eds.), *Design Anthropology: Theory and Practice*, 1–29, London and New York: Bloomsbury.

Rabinow, P. and Marcus, G. E. with Faubion, J. D. and Rees, T. (2008), *Designs for an Anthropology of the Contemporary*, Durham, NC: Duke University Press.

Smith, R. C. (2013), 'Designing Heritage for a Digital Culture', in W. Gunn, T. Otto and R. C. Smith (eds.), *Design Anthropology: Theory and Practice*, 117–35, London and New York: Bloomsbury.

Snowden, D. J. and Boone, M. E. (2007), 'A Leader's Framework for Decision Making', *Harvard Business Review*, (November): 1–9.

Strathern, M. (2004), *Partial Connections*, Walnut Creek, CA: Altamira Press.

Suchman, L. (2011), 'Anthropological Relocations and the Limits of Design', *Annual Review of Anthropology*, 40: 1–18.

Thouber, M. (2012), 'Jørgen Leths Sidste Rejse', Radio24syv, http://www.radio24syv.dk/programmer/24syv-dokumentar/4938124/jorgen-leths-sidste-rejse/ (accessed 5 January 2016)

Uhl-Bien, M., Marion, R. and McKelvey, B. (2007), 'Complexity Leadership Theory: Shifting Leadership from the Industrial Age to the Knowledge Era', *The Leadership Quarterly*, 18 (4): 298–318.

Wasson, C. (2000), 'Ethnography in the Field of Design', *Human Organization*, 59 (4): 377–88.

11 Design Anthropology On the Fly: Performative Spontaneity in Commercial Ethnographic Research

BRENDON CLARK AND MELISSA L. CALDWELL

Despite the different time frames, analytical scopes and ethical standards that distinguish academic ethnographers from their peers in the commercial sector (Evans 2015; Jackson 2015; Truninger 2015; Wasson and Metcalfe 2013), the richness of ethnographic research, with its emphasis on complexity, complications and the unexpected, provides creative possibilities for both business and scholarship. Not least when researchers move between, and collaborate across, academic and commercial spheres, new opportunities for the nature of ethnography and how it is understood and practised emerge.

It is this theme of ethnographic possibility brought about by collaboration across the academic/industry divide that we explore in this chapter. Inspired by our work together in 'innovation labs' for a global food corporation, we examine how the highly structured nature of the project and our respective roles were upended by the dynamic, contingent nature of ethnographic research. These 'innovation labs' were not permanent or stable spaces but rather an ever-shifting collection of methodological concepts and techniques drawn from multiple disciplines and professions. Participants in these 'labs' represented diverse constituencies, including managers and researchers from the hiring corporation, representatives from outside design, branding, marketing and research consultancies, local chefs and illustrators, and local consumers. Each lab was structured as a dynamic, emergent mode in which all participants performed continuously in the presence of, and in collaboration with, others. This explicitly spontaneous, performative dynamic shifted the nature of the project away from clearly defined and predetermined outcomes to emergent potentialities. Ultimately, the lab spaces and the forms of collaborative production that were engendered by these spaces were themselves institutionalized practices of making things new (see Nafus and anderson 2009; Suchman and Bishop 2000).

Our concern in this chapter addresses the value of ethnographic approaches for facilitating and responding to these spontaneous, emergent potentialities. As we illustrate, our interactions with one another and the other stakeholders revealed constant tensions between structure and spontaneity and between the need to produce business-appropriate insights and anthropological commitments to recognize and work with messy data. As ethnographers, we each had different roles in the process: Clark was a co-creation lead whose role was to sculpt the space and process of interaction in order to integrate the different people and pieces and lead to appropriate deliverables, while Caldwell was the academically based food and culture consultant whose charge was to provide deep cultural and historical expertise for the target field site (Russia) and to ensure that (Russian) customer-users' experiences and perspectives were appropriately captured and represented during the analysis and innovation phases. As our different roles evolved throughout the project, at times they produced conflicts, especially given the different scales, timelines and types of knowledge each one of us brought. Yet at other times, we discovered important points of convergence and synergies, as our ethnographic training supported trust building and shorthand communication around the value and purpose of what we were and were not doing.

Ultimately, it was our shared commitment to the inherently improvisational and emergent nature of ethnographic research that generated intriguing possibilities for considering design anthropology practices. Through a case study of a specific set of events that emerged during our interactions, we examine how the interdependent and performative nature of our collaboration supported a dynamic mode of collaborative research that transformed not only the insights generated through the project, but also the very nature of the project itself. While other chapters in this book focus on collaborative formations of issues between anthropologists, managers and employees (see Vangkilde and Rod, this volume) or between various agents in designerly public engagements (see Lindström and Ståhl, this volume), our emphasis is specifically directed towards our own design anthropological collaboration amidst a multitude of stakeholders.

Transforming Ethnographic Work: Innovating Collaboration

Accounts of ethnographic work for design and business purposes have described how research roles and activities are commonly delineated according to sequential and structured phases of work: first ethnographers or ethnographic teams conduct ethnographic research, and then designers or design teams turn research data, insights and explanatory frameworks into concepts and business decisions (Blomberg and Burrell 2003; Diggins and Tolmie 2003; Jones 2006). In practice, however, such roles and divisions are not always so sharply defined or experienced, as Françoise Brun-Cottan (2009) has demonstrated through her attention to anthropological fluidity and complexity. By highlighting how ethnographers in industrial projects craft their work for diverse audiences that often include informants, various stakeholders and colleagues, Brun-Cottan positions anthropologists as ontological choreographers who perform various 'dances' that are expressed through multiple interactions with various constituencies and audiences. For Brun-Cottan, the ethnographer's 'dance' expresses the challenges inherent in producing and communicating results to differently positioned participants.

Despite the contingency and fluidity suggested by Brun-Cottan, the types of ethnographic output she describes favour taken-for-granted modes of delivery in which the audience sits around a table while images, text, video and diagrams are projected onto a screen as the ethnographer speaks. As Nina Wakeford (2006) has argued, within corporate ethnography the normalization of software such as PowerPoint for representing data masks the analytic work of ethnographers. While Wakeford finds that ethnographic presentations using PowerPoint can be 'thick' socio-material events, the subsequent separation of the ethnographer and the material format of representation tend to turn PowerPoint presentations into 'thin' knowledge-transfer devices. Wakeford thus argues that ethnographers must find alternatives for enriching ethnographic materials and highlighting ethnographers' contributions.

In contrast, collaborative approaches often involve introducing ethnographic activities and ethnographic training for organizational stakeholders (see e.g. Vangkilde and Rod, this volume). Involving stakeholders in such activities as 'bridging workshops' (Karasti 2001) or participatory ethnography collaborations (Darrouzet, Wild and Wilkinson 2009) essentially re-frames the role of ethnographer and audience. These more porous and fluid forms of ethnographic delivery are, for instance, central to the work by Dawn Nafus and ken anderson (2009) at Intel. By focusing on the social dynamics of project rooms, methodological practices of writing on the walls and the use of visual material, Nafus and anderson argue that institutionalized modes of working anthropologically depart from the single-author model of knowledge production and dissemination: 'working through project rooms, rather than individually authored texts, de-centers the self as the technology of knowledge production' (2009: 142). As they show, the walls and materials of the project room introduce a collaborative form of engagement that puts ethnographic insights and authority up for grabs. Rather than acting as an authoritative source, a mediator of real-world facts or a carrier of insights about others, the ethnographer becomes one voice among many making claims of meaning, identifying connections and patterns and negotiating possibilities. Just as significant is that these methods privilege discovery and newness.

The fluid, dynamic and decentred nature of ethnographic collaboration also characterized our experiences working together in the 'Innovation Lab' project. We were part of a group of approximately one hundred participants who moved into and out of the project over a two-month period. While we are both professional anthropologists, we were hired to fulfil different roles. Hired as an expert in user-centred design, Clark co-organized and facilitated co-creation activities that blended the expertise of the diverse participants, including local consumers who participated as paid research subjects, in order to evoke insights and then capture those insights in material and visual formats. Caldwell's role was to provide scholarly expertise about the topic and the field site, specifically, food cultures in Russia. The project organizers did not plan in advance that we would work together or anticipate the possibilities that anthropological approaches could offer to the project more generally. Yet, as we detail below, the unplanned events of one particular set of activities within the project demonstrate how anthropological approaches could contribute significant value to corporate needs while also creating possibilities for new forms of design anthropology.

Co-Creating a Practical Metaphor

The goal of the 'innovation labs' was to develop healthy product and service concepts for 'the breakfast occasion' that could be added to the company's local and global innovation pipeline. It was structured so that a core research team first interviewed and observed consumers in Russia, the target field site, before taking preliminary results off-site for preliminary analysis. In the second phase of the project, the larger research team returned to Russia for a co-creation phase with consumers and stakeholders. In consultation with Caldwell, the core research team had collated and organized the preliminary research data according to several themes that the corporate directors had found intriguing and potentially fruitful for further development in order to inspire potential healthy food product and service prototypes. The company's project managers were optimistic that the co-creation activities would produce rough prototypes that could be introduced to product engineers, chefs and marketing professionals for refinement.

On the second day of the co-creation week, a team of researchers and designers engaged consumers in a series of activities meant to elicit local categories, rituals, needs and desires. These activities were followed by co-creation activities that invited consumers first to build metaphoric constructs representing their ideals about a particular sub-theme identified by the research team, and then to co-design new service concepts with stakeholders and experts. After these sessions, the consumers were dismissed and their work output was taken up by groups of stakeholders and experts for further analysis and development.

In these processes, Clark was responsible for the overall organization and schedule of activities, which included three simultaneous consumer workshops, as well as for facilitating a workshop specifically dedicated to the theme 'out-of-home breakfast'. During the later stages of this workshop, one session included two consumers, a local chef, an industrial designer, two company representatives and Caldwell. Caldwell's participation in this group was coincidental, as up to that point she had not yet been assigned a role beyond providing general ethnographic knowledge about Russian food and culture in response to questions from researchers and designers.

Herald, the corporate executive responsible for oversight of the Lab, joined the workshop for the afternoon session. Throughout the entire lab process, Herald was often the focal point of discussions, both because he frequently took charge of conversations, leading them in certain directions, and because other participants deferred to him and directed their presentations to him. One of Herald's key strengths was in asking questions that pushed researchers to develop and refine their ideas and to draw insights from seemingly unrelated pieces of evidence. Yet the generative results of Herald's interventions belied their potentially disruptive nature, as participants occasionally responded in ways that moved away from the immediate tasks and objectives, for instance, by referring to company goals or past company projects in other contexts. Consequently, despite Herald's insistence on tangible outcomes from the work sessions, concrete or feasible results were often elusive, a recurring challenge for Clark in developing, adjusting and facilitating collaborative activities.

During this discussion, Herald, Clark, Caldwell, two other researchers and two company representatives discussed the theme 'out-of-home breakfast' with reference to two objects created by consumers during the morning co-creation activity. One object was a picnic-mobile that installed a fully equipped mini-kitchen on a vehicle, allowing consumers to take their home with them anywhere they travelled, while the second was a flying carpet that delivered hot, home-made meals anywhere a consumer might desire. During this discussion, someone – probably Caldwell, but we cannot remember it exactly – said that it was like 'taking home with you'. After the phrase was uttered, Clark grabbed a Post-It note and quickly sketched an image of a body with a house as a head (see Figure 11.1), and stuck it to the theme document on the wall. Both the phrase and the sketch emerged spontaneously: none of us had discussed or planned the possibility of creating metaphors or giving them visual or material form. Importantly, Herald became

Figure 11.1 Sketch of body with house as a head © Brendon Clark

immediately captivated by the metaphor and image, a point he raised repeatedly for the remainder of the project. He subsequently attributed the identification of the metaphor and the value of the process for eliciting the metaphor to Clark's expertise in co-creation, suggesting that it was a purposeful outcome of this series of activities rather than a spontaneous consequence.

What seemed to be most exciting for Herald was that the combination of the metaphor and the iconic image enabled him to tell a coherent story that moved from consumer research to analysis and co-creation and then on to powerful metaphors and their accompanying design principles. The metaphor was powerful because it expressed more than just the particular ideas that had emerged in that particular conversation but also, as we explain below, encapsulated a much deeper and broader set of insights and values about Russian cultural trends more generally. As such, the metaphor was grounded ethnographically in ways that not only framed participants' ideas within the logic of local Russian practices and values, but also translated them into concepts that could travel cross-culturally and resonate with the perspectives of the corporate clients.

To consider the value of the metaphor only in terms of a spontaneous and individualized emergence is thus to misrecognize the significance of the other forms of collaboration and improvisation that were at play. Notably, while the concre-tization of the metaphor was Clark's unanticipated inspiration, it required a particular framing narrative grounded in Caldwell's deep cultural knowledge of Russia. As an ethnographer with almost twenty years of fieldwork experience in social life in Russia, Caldwell provided ethnographic details that grounded and illuminated the concept of 'taking home with you' and its importance in the Russian context. As she explained, in Russian social practice, meals simultaneously foster community and intimacy and trouble distinctions between public and private, and between safe and dangerous. Because Soviet-era officials viewed private spaces such as home kitchens as dangerous because they were out of the gaze – and reach – of the state, socialist planners tried to eliminate private dining and instead compel Soviet citizens to eat together in public spaces such as public canteens. While public dining solved social problems such as freeing women from the labours of shopping, cooking and cleaning, it created other problems, as citizens complained about the lack of privacy and poor food quality. Moreover, not all public dining spaces were created equally, as restaurants were more typically reserved for special occasions or the elite. At the same time, Russian cultural values privileged home-made foods as being healthier, safer and more flavourful than foods prepared in commercial settings, while practices of informal exchange that had arisen as survival strategies during times of scarcity had cultivated an ethical system of sharing with friends and family (see also Caldwell 2009).

This historical and cultural context made sense of the experiences reported by consumers during the research encounters and shed light on what the consumers in this specific working group envisioned as an ideal meal represented by the co-created picnic mobile and flying carpet: the experience of home-cooked food and domestic familiarity in any setting, either inside or outside the home. Consequently, the sketched metaphor did not simply convey a phrase, but symbolized visually a very particular historical and cultural context.

The actual enactment of that knowledge was spontaneous, however, as Caldwell responded on the spot to what participants and Clark materialized in fluid and emerging discussions. This type of unplanned, improvisational enactment continued at the end of the work session, when participants contributed to what Clark has termed a 'one-shot-video' that presented an impromptu coherent 'story' behind the metaphor and became part of the documentary record which informed other activities throughout the week and travelled back to the corporate headquarters. Caldwell provided the overarching narrative for the video, an assignment that for her was unplanned and occurred in the moment but which depended on her deep knowledge of the field and her experience engaging ethnographic materials in other contexts, such as a classroom.

Clark, however, had a different perspective on the spontaneous and improvisational qualities of these enactments. First, although his response to the phrase 'taking home with you' was an unplanned act of creating a visual representation, in a larger context it was a logical and ordinary way of engaging what seemed to be a potentially significant point. Second, the forms by which Clark organized and elicited performances by the various participants, including prompting Caldwell to perform a contextually Russian narrative around the metaphor, relied upon his established repertoire of professional experience, research and teaching – most notably in this case, his technique of creating short, semi-structured, uncut video recordings with live voice-overs to curate collaborative efforts and provide short but contextually rich documentation for further reference. Through this lens, Clark acted as a choreographer who facilitated Caldwell's improvisational performance of Russian cultural knowledge and anthropological background in concert with the actions of other participants and the materials in the room, thereby giving Caldwell an opportunity to further interrogate the assumptions present. Most importantly, the sketch provided a powerful visual output combining multiple perspectives and interests in a way that was historically consistent and could provide grounding for developing healthy food products and services alternatives.

In many respects, even as Caldwell's authoritative expertise formalized and legitimized the sketch, it also closed it off from being additionally fragmented by participants, which relieved Clark from further pursuing frames and roles for challenging or reinforcing loosely derived conclusions and explanations. Moreover, although the knowledge and expertise of each of us depended on many years of work, the performance and perceived value, as well as authority, of our respective skills and contributions emerged largely impromptu and in response to the changing dynamics and unexpected questions that arose in the session.

The larger set of events around the development of the 'taking home with you' metaphor produced several unexpected outcomes. On the one hand, Herald's enthusiasm for the potential of the metaphor inspired him to modify the research protocols to require visual metaphors as key components in the insight development and design brief phases. In fact, visual metaphors became a standard by which the progress and outcomes of the other workshop groups were measured, including levelling criticism toward other members of the research team who failed to produce comparable metaphors. On the other hand, Herald's recognition of the value of grounding the metaphor in ethnographic contexts coincided with an expansion of roles and responsibilities for each of us. While Clark subsequently played a more central role in organizing collaborative stakeholder activities in other stages of the lab, Caldwell's role expanded to provide framing explanations for emerging themes and metaphors, including explaining data and insights to senior stakeholders. Our different roles were thus incorporated more substantially into the project, including as specific analytical techniques for later phases.

The unanticipated successes and outcomes of the metaphor illuminate the extent to which spontaneity and contingency existed within the project, both as the practical reality of the give-and-take flows of the research and analysis processes, and as framing modes and techniques of critical inspiration for interpretation, insights and innovation. For both the generation of the metaphor and subsequent moments of improvised analysis, the unplanned and seemingly spontaneous nature of these actions disrupted the otherwise scripted nature of the format, methods and even roles of both the specific workshop discussion and the larger research project. In so doing, these events opened up possibilities for new, unanticipated directions in the research and analysis. In other words, the propensity for newness was not reserved for output, but became part of the very structure and process of the lab activities. At the same time, these improvisational, unplanned qualities belied the deep knowledge and expertise that not only made them possible but also made them appear effortless and spontaneous. Most notably, both Caldwell's role as an expert on Russian cultural practices and Clark's role as an expert on elicitation and facilitation techniques made possible the effectiveness of these activities. As a result, these interactions challenge more conventional participatory design approaches that privilege a framework in which all participants are presented as equals in the workshop setting and where each participant is an expert on their own lives and able to speak for themselves (e.g. Buur, Binder and Brandt 2000; Nafus and anderson 2009; cf. Flynn 2009). What the improvisational performative dynamic of this workshop highlighted, then, was that both equality and spontaneity may be more mythical than actual.

Structuring Spontaneity for Eliciting Possibility

How are we to make sense of the relationship between spontaneity and potentiality as it emerged in this project? In some respects, the propensity for discovery and the identification of newness appear to be intrinsic to the pressures of innovation within organizations, such as the case of Intel as described by Nafus and anderson (2009). However, their work raises questions about whether those working practices open up possibilities or might, in fact, limit them, especially when the interaction of multiple participants across and through multiple milieus diffuses any central authority and challenges the legitimacy of ethnographic materials and knowledge (2009). Moreover, at the same time that project settings and collaborative material props pull participants together into common threads, they also produce a narrowing of those threads and of the possibilities that might have emerged. As Nafus and anderson note, 'a contained world is still seen as a knowable world, and therefore can be managed' (2009: 148). What emerges is a potential paradox of both endless possibilities and contained sets of possibilities. Consequently, even the most deliberately experimental and open-ended modes of corporate ethnographic work can prevent the realization of potentiality.

In contrast to these limitations identified by Nafus and anderson, it was, in fact, the highly pressurized, ad hoc nature of our collaboration that generated possibilities for new formulations of content and process. In many respects, the lab's activities were governed by principles of 'adhocracy' in which seemingly contingent and spontaneous events generated new data, insights and practices (Dunn 2012). As we worked through the ideation and co-creation activities, the scripted portions of our work frequently gave way to improvisational activities as we moved quickly and fluidly between roles, materials and goals. The flexibility became a form of performance that required us to deploy skills of improvisation and persuasion. Importantly, however, this flexible adhocracy was not anti-structure. Rather, it produced and relied on a very different form of structured expectations and opportunities that we see as being supported greatly, perhaps even prompted, by our shared anthropological training in theory, method and pedagogy.

Ethnographic performances have been variously described as activities that privilege the kinetic aspects of ethnographic output for participants playing different parts, including that of the audience (Turner and Turner 1987), as means of inquiry for cultural understanding (Fabian 1990), and even as generative activities that explore future possibilities (Halse and Clark 2008; Halse and Boffi, this volume). The crux of performances is their uncontrollability and the openness of their outcome, as compared to other forms of inquiry and presentation. As Johannes Fabian has written in relation to performance as a form of ethnographic inquiry: 'Performances ... are not really responses to questions. The ethnographer's role, then, is no longer that of a questioner; he or she is but a provider of occasions, a catalyst in the weakest sense, and a producer (in the analogy of a theatrical producer) in the strongest' (1990: 7). While in many respects this perspective captures the nature of the lab activities described here, for Clark a theoretical and practical repertoire for organizing ethnographic performances provides a foundation for organizing activities that combine versions of field research, analysis, co-creation and prototyping future practices (Clark 2013).

This is not to say that the lab process overall, and the events of the co-creation week specifically, were a pre-determined set of activities geared toward providing ideal paths of interrelated performances. As a co-organizer, Clark was responsible for co-ordinating interrelated activities for participants, including accommodating those who arrived unexpectedly, and multiple streams of research, often initially prepared in the form of PowerPoint presentations. Although he attempted to introduce and continually improve the material and technological formats to support open-ended semi-structured performance processes, at times he was confronted aggressively by changing demands from the sponsors as well as the dynamic process itself, requiring him to respond relationally and spontaneously in order to generate forward momentum that was grounded, collaborative and meaningful.

The necessity and value of integrating multiple streams into productively dialogic interaction became especially apparent to Caldwell in the explicitly anthropological work of the project. After demonstrating her expertise in fielding unpredicted questions about the region and topic, Caldwell was frequently pulled into conversations to interpret and explain confusing data through insights about the cultural context. Initially those moments occurred when members of the research team were working through data, but they became more frequent during the 'share out' exercises that occurred at the end of sessions, often through Clark's facilitation and prompting. Thus, one of her roles became that of pulling together disparate ideas and reframing them into coherent narratives, often taking the creative metaphors and fleshing them out with ethnographic insights. In this respect, Caldwell did not so much retell vignettes as she provided a 'back story' rich in historical context, cultural significance and connections to larger theoretical issues. Perhaps more importantly, she supported Clark's efforts to prevent participants' attempts to simplify complex ethnographic data and force them into overly suggestive and restrictive models. The 'off the cuff' nature of these narrative encounters highlighted the precariousness and indeterminacy of the project.

In many ways, these encounters resembled Caldwell's professional experiences as a university professor. Through years of teaching and lecturing in public settings, she has gained considerable experience in responding to any kind of question or comment, no matter how vague, unclear or off topic. Pedagogically, her job is to take what students present, rework it, reinterpret it, neaten it up and return it to them in an accessible and authoritative way. Thus, without realizing it, she automatically went into what we jokingly called 'professor mode', which enabled her to respond to high-ranking corporate executives in ways that made them feel, as they told her later, that their contributions were meaningful and without her feeling constrained to adhere to their expectations. This 'professor mode' aligned with Clark's focus upon collaborative performance, as he often ended group activities with an improvised description that integrated materials and frameworks into coherent stories.

As we discovered, then, the lab was an intersubjective space, or, as Michael Jackson (2012) would put it, a state of being that exists 'between one and one another' marked by the interplay between the self and the other, between acting and being acted upon. At the same time, it was a space marked by indeterminacy in the sense described by Paul Friedrich (1986: 18) as 'the processes by which individuals integrate knowledge, perceptions, and emotions in some creative way ... in order that they may enter into new mental states or new relations with their milieus'. In other words, as much as the lab space was a scripted, over-determined space, it was also an immensely dynamic state of being; that is, a place of great opportunity (see also Binder, this volume).

This dynamic state of being produced possibilities, most notably open-ended, forward-moving insights. It also required new tools and techniques for apprehending data and insights, and interrogating assumptions on the move. The combination of our different anthropological approaches aligned well and was productive in these design endeavours precisely because they were inherently flexible and accommodated change. Especially in the early stages of engagement in the first of these labs, as demonstrated in the workshop, the research process contained an uncertainty akin to the early stages of fieldwork in an unknown place.

The Ethnographic Potentiality of Opportuneness and Timeliness

In this chapter, we have discussed how, in the context of a particular innovation project, we developed a design anthropological partnership with distinct characteristics. This partnership was neither pre-planned nor pre-plannable but emerged spontaneously out of fluid and dynamic circumstances that alternately privileged asking for performances and being asked to perform. Our very different orientations to anthropology and ethnographic fieldwork put on display a design anthropological practice that is grounded simultaneously in long-term single-authored fieldwork and in short-term, collaborative forms of transactional relationships. This duality troubles not only norms of both academic and commercial ethnographic research (Rabinow et al. 2008), but also the forms by which long-term anthropological knowledge can be performed in concert with other knowledge traditions in an action-based timely manner. While the value of our work depended upon our ability to put into play, and most significantly into repeated play, cultural nuance and qualified positionings, the relational nature of practice does not lay claims to rigid distinctions between academic and non-academic, or between single-author and collaborative. Rather, it raises questions about how new roles or modes of engagement can elicit different forms of knowledge and put them into working relationships with one another with a future-oriented gaze, how those relationships change the nature of the knowledge, and how these roles can emerge in practice.

Our experiences also highlight the inherently translational aspects of this type of collaborative ethnography and design anthropological work. In almost every instance and at every moment, we were both translating across languages, concepts, methods, data, modes of representation and professional standing. We each brought our own respective languages and expertise – terminological, representational, ethical – but through a shared sense of the ethnographic project, including both what ethnographic work has been in the past and what its potential might be, we were able to engage one another in a dialectic in which, through negotiation, we reached a shared understanding. This was not done through stable professional negotiation, but in the ongoing traffic of project work, on the fly.

The near-constant collaboration with others over long periods of time and the close proximity to people in a wide variety of roles, whether executives, consumers, researchers or competitors, produce many unanticipated encounters and, consequently, the opportunity or need to perform in often unscripted ways. This responsive orientation approximates the realities and demands of ethnographic participant observation, or observant participation (Gatt and Ingold 2013), by relying upon real-time willingness and ability to listen and draw on different aspects of one's repertoire, often in improvisational ways, to forge complementary partnerships with others. This requires a willingness to act within the window of time that can influence the output, what Donald Schön (1991 [1983]: 62) refers to as the action present; that is, actions that can have unchangeable and unforeseeable consequences. In many respects, we were engaged in an improvisational dynamic of taking another's work and moving it forward, with the intention of modifying it and then improving it, before handing it on to someone else.

Collectively, these experiences highlight the extent to which design anthropology as a method and repository of knowledge is fruitful for corporate-based research, not just in terms of providing a useful framework for rethinking culture and cultural processes, but also in terms of modelling forms of research, analysis and presentation that are oriented to emergent and dynamic streams of data and experience. Anthropology itself is a contingent exercise that is always in the mode of navigating difference, contradiction and the unexpected. Its scalar orientation also provides possibilities for navigating and contextualizing multiple layers of meaning, from the macroscopic to the microscopic, in order to identify and pull out cultural patterns that recur at multiple levels. Thus the fluid, dynamic nature of anthropology itself can respond quickly and efficiently to multiple streams of activity and meaning-making, even under compressed temporal circumstances.

At the same time, these experiences provide opportunities for rethinking the ways in which anthropology is taught and practised in more conventional academic settings, including the classroom. Cooperative engagements provide excellent models for collaborative research and interpretation, especially to encourage work that fully accommodates and benefits from partnerships, in contrast to models in which independent researchers either work alone or work alongside one another on a shared project. It also allows for new ways of developing roles and devising methods on the fly in response to changing circumstances, a useful skill for any field-working anthropologist, but one that is difficult to teach in conventional methods courses focused on rehearsing specific techniques that lead to predictable (and replicable) forms of data: interviewing, surveying and observation, most notably. The dynamic nature of this project, as well as the need to communicate data, concepts and interpretations in material form, is instructive for devising innovative pedagogies that take students out of a traditional lecturing–passive listening model and into more active engagements with materials.

Ultimately, these experiences suggest ways in which the constraints of our respective professional fields, and that of the corporate environment in which we worked, can be productively turned into possibilities. For the specific case of design anthropology, these encounters highlight the extent to which collaboration and spontaneity enable opportunities to be comfortable, and even creative, with limits and unknowns and transform them into new opportunities and possibilities. Yet, as our experiences demonstrate, what makes this flexible, spontaneous improvisation possible is our respective expertise, gained through extensive research and training. The successes of our improvisation derived from our own rich repertoires of experiences and knowledge, which provided structuring possibilities for our performances individually and collectively, even while disguising those rich fields of knowledge. Thus, what these experiences show is that even though design anthropology is grounded in an ethos of novelty and innovation, the practices and outcomes of design anthropology in fact rely on pre-existing experiences and forms. In this respect, both novelty and spontaneity are paradoxically only made possible by what has already come before.

References

Blomberg, J. and Burrell, M. (2003), 'An Ethnographic Approach to Design', in M. Sears and J. A. Jacko (eds.), *The Human Computer Interaction Handbook: Fundamentals Evolving Technologies and Emerging Applications*, 964–85, Mahwah, NJ: Lawrence Erlbaum Associates.

Brun-Cottan, F. (2009), 'The Anthropologist as Ontological Choreographer', in M. Cefkin (ed.), *Ethnography and the Corporate Encounter: Reflections on Research in and of Corporations*, 158–81, New York and Oxford: Berghahn Books.

Buur, J., Binder, T. and Brandt, E. (2000), 'Taking Video Beyond "Hard Data" in User Centred Design', in *Proceedings of the Participatory Design Conference*, 21–9, New York: ACM Press.

Caldwell, M. L. (2009), 'Introduction: Food and Everyday Life after State Socialism', in M. L. Caldwell (ed.), *Food & Everyday Life in the Postsocialist World*, 1–28, Bloomington, IN: Indiana University Press.

Cefkin, M., (ed.) (2009), *Ethnography and the Corporate Encounter: Reflections on Research in and of Corporations*, New York and Oxford: Berghahn Books.

Clark, B. (2013), 'Generating Publics through Design Activity', in W. Gunn, T. Otto and R. C. Smith (eds.), *Design Anthropology: Theory and Practice*, 199–215, London and New York: Bloomsbury.

Darrouzet, C., Wild, H. and Wilkinson, S. (2009), 'Participatory Ethnography At Work: Practicing in the Puzzle Palaces of a Large, Complex Healthcare Organization', in M. Cefkin (ed.), *Ethnography and the Corporate Encounter: Reflections on Research in and of Corporations*, 61–94, New York and Oxford: Berghahn Books.

Diggins, T. and Tolmie, P. (2003), 'The "Adequate" Design of Ethnographic Outputs for Practice: Some Explorations of the Characteristics of Design Resources', *Personal Ubiquitous Computing*, 7 (3–4): 147–58.

Dunn, E. C. (2012), 'The Chaos of Humanitarian Aid: Adhocracy in the Republic of Georgia', *Humanity*, 3 (1): 1–23.

Evans, D. (2015), 'Researching (with) Major Food Retailers: Leveling and Leveraging the Terms of Engagement', *Gastronomica: The Journal of Critical Food Studies*, 15 (3): 33–9.

Fabian, J. (1990), *Power and Performance*, Madison, WI and London: The University of Wisconsin Press.

Flynn, D. K. (2009), '"My Customers are Different!" Identity, Difference, and the Political Economy of Design', in M. Cefkin (ed.), *Ethnography and the Corporate Encounter: Reflections on Research in and of Corporations*, 41–57, New York and Oxford: Berghahn Books.

Friedrich, P. (1986), *The Language Parallax: Linguistic Relativism and Poetic Indeterminacy*, Austin, TX: University of Texas Press.

Gatt, C. and Ingold, T. (2013), 'From Description to Correspondence: Anthropology in Real Time', in W. Gunn, T. Otto and R. C. Smith (eds.), *Design Anthropology: Theory and Practice*, 139–58, London and New York: Bloomsbury.

Halse, J. and Clark, B. (2008), 'Design Rituals and Performative Ethnography', in *Proceedings of the Ethnographic Praxis in Industry Conference*, 128–45.

Jackson, M. (2012), *Between One and One Another*. Berkeley, CA: University of California Press.

Jackson, P. (2015), 'Commercial Collaboration and Critical Engagement in Food Research', *Gastronomica: The Journal of Critical Food Studies*, 15 (3): 28–32.

Jones, R. (2006), 'Experience Models: Where Ethnography and Design Meet', in *Proceedings of the Ethnographic Praxis in Industry Conference,* 91–102.

Karasti, H. (2001), 'Bridging Work Practice and System Design: Integrating Systemic Analysis, Appreciative Intervention and Practitioner Participation', *Computer Supported Cooperative Work*, 10 (2): 211–46.

Nafus, D. and anderson, k. (2009), 'Writing on Walls: The Materiality of Social Memory in Corporate Research', in M. Cefkin (ed.), *Ethnography and the Corporate Encounter: Reflections on Research in and of Corporations*, 137–57, New York and Oxford: Berghahn Books.

Rabinow, P., Marcus, G. E. with Faubion, J. D. and Reese, T. (2008), *Designs for an Anthropology of the Contemporary*, Durham, NC: Duke University Press.

Schön, D. A. (1991 [1983]), *The Reflective Practitioner: How Professionals Think in Action*. Farnham: Ashgate.

Suchman, L. and Bishop, L. (2000), 'Problematizing "Innovation" as a Critical Project', *Technology Analysis and Strategic Management*, 12 (3): 327–33.

Truninger, M. (2015), 'Engaging Science with Commercial Partners: The (Dating) Stages of a (Lasting) Relationship', *Gastronomica: The Journal of Critical Food Studies*, 15 (3): 40–6.

Turner, V. and Turner, E. (1987), 'Performing Ethnography', in V. Turner (ed.), *The Anthropology of Performance*, 139–55, New York: PAJ Publications.

Wakeford, N. (2006), 'PowerPoint and the Crafting of Social Data', in *Proceedings of the Ethnographic Praxis in Industry Conference,* 94–108.

Wasson, C. and Metcalf, C. (2013), 'Teaching Design Anthropology through University–Industry Partnerships', in W. Gunn, T. Otto and R. C. Smith (eds.), *Design Anthropology: Theory and Practice*, 216–31, London and New York: Bloomsbury.

12 Politics of Inviting: Co-Articulations of Issues in Designerly Public Engagement

KRISTINA LINDSTRÖM AND ÅSA STÅHL

A crucial but little-explored practice in design anthropology is the crafting of invitations: invitations to user studies, to interviews, to ethnographic fieldwork projects, to co-design workshops, to prototyping and to public engagement events. The reason for issuing these invitations is partly to widen the epistemological community, partly to democratize the development of new designs or technological systems. In this chapter we engage with the politics of inviting by proposing a shift in what we invite to, and when. Rather than inviting stakeholders to participate in design projects before use, we will argue for the value of inviting participants to take part in co-articulations of issues that arise in the course of the ongoing living with technologies. This, we argue, is an important shift, because the issues and potentialities that emerge as things are used can never be fully predicted in a design project, whether by designers or potential users. We have termed this practice of inviting to collaborative formations of issues connected to the ongoing living with technologies *designerly public engagements*.

Reconfiguring the Relationship Between Design and Use

In discussions of the emergent field of design anthropology, one difference between design and anthropology is often presented as having to do with temporality. Whereas anthropology is portrayed as being concerned with understanding the present through the past, design is interpreted as being more future- and change-oriented (Otto and Smith 2013; Gunn and Donovan 2012). This difference in temporality has, however, at times resulted in a rather linear mode of design anthropology in which anthropological knowledge about the present is used to inform designerly speculations about the future. Wendy Gunn and Jared Donovan (2012) propose three versions of design anthropology, which they have termed dA, Da and DA. The capital letter in the contraction indicates where the emphasis is placed. With reference to Mette Kjærsgaard (2011), they describe DA as characterized by 'a shift from informing design to re-framing social, cultural and environmental relations in both design and anthropology' (Gunn and Donovan 2012: 8). By this argument,

DA is thus about mutual transformation, rather than one discipline serving the other. As we see it, this mutual transformation also invites further kinds of temporal engagement over and above the rather linear version mentioned above. More specifically, it suggests re-framed relationships not only between designers and users, but also between design and use – an issue that is also central in design anthropology (see Gunn and Donovan 2012; Ingold 2012).

Another kind of temporal engagement can be identified if we turn to participatory design, which has both topical and methodological overlaps with design anthropology. Participatory design is a predominantly research-based design practice in which the relationships between designers and users have been re-framed by inviting potential users to take part in the design process (Robertson and Simonsen 2012; Kensing and Greenbaum 2012). This work is often done by multidisciplinary teams that include designers, anthropologists, sociologists, engineers and various other stakeholders. But perhaps most importantly, potential users are part of these teams, as participatory design largely emerged due to the recognition that new technologies and infrastructural systems have considerable influence on people's lives, for example in the workplace (e.g. Bjerknes and Bratteteig 1987; Ehn 1988). Workers were therefore invited to participate in the development of these technologies as a way of inviting users to democratize innovation and technology development and to enable mutual learning.

Nowadays, with technological systems less confined to a specific time, space and community, scholars within the field of participatory design have argued for strategies such as *design-after-design*. Compared to more traditional participatory design projects that primarily invite participants to engage during project-time, design-after-design as a design strategy suggests that participation is not restricted to making design decisions before use, but can also allow for some decisions to be taken during use (Binder et al. 2011; Ehn, Nilsson and Topgaard 2014), thus deferring some design decisions from project-time to use-time. In this respect, Johan Redström (2006), for instance, articulates the challenge of inviting for participation before use as twofold. To begin with, a design that does not yet exist but is in the making cannot yet have users, because it is not yet in use. And secondly, not even potential future users who have knowledge and experience of a potential context of use can fully predict issues that will emerge through, and in, use. To meet these challenges, Redström argues that we should design for questions to be answered in use rather than designing answers (2006: 136–7). In our view, this is one approach to support design-after-design.

To adopt the design strategy of design-after-design is, then, not only to re-frame designer and user by engaging users during project-time, but also to re-frame design and use by allowing for design decisions to be made in use-time. Moreover, these reconfigurations of the temporality of design work create new conditions for the encounter between design and anthropology. As described earlier, one common configuration of design anthropology is that anthropological studies are carried out in advance, so as to inform designers in their creation of objects. Design-after-design challenges this approach, by locating the participation during *use-time,* rather than *project-time*. While we sympathize with this approach, we also find that the focus on designing for open-endedness and for questions that are to be answered in use demands skilled and 'response-able' (Haraway 2013) users. If design is also made in use, another objective of design anthropological work could be to invite participants to co-articulations of issues in their own everyday life, and to foster skilled users who approach design-in-use with careful curiosity (Lindström and Ståhl 2014).

This brings us to the politics of inviting. In order to foster skilled users, we argue for a shift in when we invite, and to what. Rather than inviting participants to engage in the shaping of new technologies and design to be used in the future, or deferring some decisions to be made in use, another productive approach would be to invite participants to engage with designs and technologies that are already in use, and with the potential issues that arise through ongoing use. What we suggest thereby is that design anthropologists invite people not only to participate in design projects, but to participate in designerly public engagements.

Inviting to Designerly Public Engagement

To discuss how design practices and objects can be used to foster inventive problem making in everyday issues of living with technologies, we turned to Mike Michael (2012), who has described speculative design as a mode of designerly public engagement with science. Speculative and critical design, like participatory design, is a type of design that is often practised in multi- or transdisciplinary teams. These design practices do, however, differ in how and when they direct their invitation at various collectives or publics. Whereas scholars of participatory design often invite participation in the making of new design, scholars of critical and speculative design usually engage publics through evocative objects that are exhibited in galleries or circulated in media (e.g. Dunne and Raby 2013).

Public engagement in science (PES) is a term that, in the social-science context, is used primarily to describe various activities intended to inform or engage the public in new scientific findings. Like participatory design, this practice can be understood as an attempt to democratize science and technologies. Coming as he does from the social sciences, Michael (2012) argues that we need to ask ourselves what kind of techno-scientific citizens are produced through the formalized mechanism of voicing opinions on scientific development that is often set to work in PES activities. He describes social-scientific PES as a way of counteracting the presumed democratic deficit by inviting the public to join citizen panels and focus groups regarding the latest scientific findings and technological innovations, such as biotechnology. These gatherings thus represent opportunities for social scientists to facilitate an encounter between experts and laypeople, with the aim of channelling public opinion into the existing institutions in order to influence policymaking. The enactment of this form of public engagement is, however, rather linear and goal-oriented. It rests on an understanding of publics that are out there, that can be called into an assembly, and whose voices can be transported upstream in order to solve problems.

Michael's argument for speculative design as a mode of PES is based on the project 'Material Beliefs', which emerged from an interdisciplinary exploration of emerging biotechnology at Goldsmiths, University of London (Beaver et al. 2009). Unlike social-scientific PES envisioned in the abstract, this project lacked a single, well-defined issue to engage with or a specific target audience, and little effort was spent on collecting or packaging the public's responses for communication to policy-makers. Rather, the public were invited to encounter speculative objects, which opened up 'a space for a reframing of the issues, that is, inventive problem making' (Michael 2012: 539).

Coming back to the question of what kind of techno-scientific citizenship is enacted through various kinds of PES events, Michael describes designerly PES as an enactment of 'the public where its members suffer neither from intellectual deficit nor citizenly shortcomings – rather, it is a constituency whose role is not to be "citizenly" (whatever form that might take) within a context of policy making, but thoughtful within a context of complexity' (2012: 541). Thus designerly PES is not about scientists informing publics or publics informing policymakers. Rather, it collaboratively generates potential issues *between* scientists, designers, publics and materials. In this sense, this way of practising PES events rests, as we see it, on an understanding of publics as co-emerging with its objects (Latour 2005; Marres 2012). Designerly PES events using speculative design can be one forum that sparks these publics into being.

Allowing issues to emerge rather than dealing with issues that are pre-figured poses a challenge for how we invite. Mahmoud Keshavarz and Ramia Mazé (2013) argue that framing a design project, for example by articulating an invitation, inherently defines a problem or issue. To some extent this means that the initiators of any kind of participatory project have ruled out in advance the possibility for dissensus or for inventive problem-making. One way of understanding this argument is that an invitation, including the choice of who it is directed to, frames what the problem is, how to engage with it and who is to participate. We agree with Keshavarz and Mazé that issuing invitations is clearly a way of framing – and also that doing so is by no means innocent. However, it still needs to be kept in mind that the framing does not determine what issues are engaged with and articulated.

In our own collaborative practices during the past decade, we have found it generative to craft invitations that spark, and are built on, curiosity, rather than expressing a problem. We call this an *area of curiosity.* In broad terms, our invitations have addressed an area of curiosity that we term *ways of living with technologies.* When we use the term 'living with technologies', we mean the everyday use of computers and mobile phones, as well as living with technologies without explicitly using them but being in touch with them, for example through rag-picking and recycling e-waste. In the following sections, we will discuss two of our so-called PEST projects – public engagement in science and technology[1] – in which we invited people to engage with everyday socio-material entanglements in mobile telecommunication. Although the two projects differed in scope and structure, we will show how we and others, through the invitations and the responses to these invitations, co-articulate more specific issues within this area of curiosity. And, as we shall argue, these co-articulations can be inventive to a greater or lesser degree.

Co-Articulations of Issues: Two Projects

The two projects were entitled 'Threads – a Mobile Sewing Circle' and 'UNRAVEL/ REPEAT'. In the former, we invited participants to embroider an SMS by either hand or machine; in the latter, we acted as rag-pickers and invited to a relationship in which we signed a contract promising to take care of people's discarded mobile phones as responsibly as possible. Compared to critical and speculative design, these projects engaged not with technologies that are unfamiliar to most people, but technologies that are already entangled in the participants' everyday lives; that is, designs which are or have been in use. This is important because we need to recognize that issues of, for example, sustainability or health and other issues of living with technologies are, to quote Mazé:

> always and continually at stake, as forms and solutions continue to be negotiated in everyday life (and a range of other politics besides those of policy and design). Something that might be a solution for someone in some place at a given time may generate problems for others, elsewhere, or later on (2013: 109).

In neither of the projects did our invitations express a well-defined problem but enacts certain expectations of how participants live with technologies. In 'Threads', the invitation assumed that the participants use text messaging. In 'UNRAVEL/ REPEAT', the invitation assumed that the participants had a surplus of discarded mobile phones tucked away in a drawer.

Threads – A Mobile Sewing Circle

This project was a collaboration between the Swedish National Federation of Rural Community Centres, Swedish Travelling Exhibitions, the adult education association Studieförbundet Vuxenskolan and the youth organization Vi Unga and Malmö University, where we were based.[2] The project was initiated by the two authors when we sent a proposal for a travelling exhibition to Swedish Travelling Exhibitions, an institution with state funding for cultural projects with outreach to all parts of Sweden. The proposal was based on an already ongoing art project in which we invited participants to embroider an SMS in a sewing circle. When we brought the project into this larger collaboration, we also brought it into our doctoral research in which we dealt with public engagements in issues to do with living with technologies. Thus from 2009 to 2013, 'Threads' travelled not only to numerous rural community centres but also to rural and urban cultural centres in Sweden. In total, about 100 sewing circles were hosted.

All the collaborating partners had different points of entry into the project. For example, Swedish Travelling Exhibitions wanted to try out a small-scale, participatory exhibition that could reach beyond big cultural institutions. Studieförbundet Vuxenskolan was interested in exploring contemporary topics and forms for study circles. The National Federation of Rural Community Centres, with its vast network of meeting-places across Sweden, wanted to reactivate those. What these organizations had in common was that they all work with *folkbildning* – a Swedish term for informal learning that has much in common with the idea of public engagement. In this collaboration, public engagement was undertaken through the invitation to 'Threads', which was, in brief, 'Welcome to embroider an SMS'.

Each sewing circle lasted for about six hours including lunch. Usually a group of ten to twenty people gathered. The day started with the hosts introducing the participants to 'Threads' as both artwork and a research project through the materials in the room. Since not everyone knew each other, time was spent on a round of introductions. Some participants had a strong connection to the place, some were members of the collaborating organizations, and others were drawn to 'Threads' because of the invitation itself and the topics, practices and materials that it indicated. Over the years that 'Threads' has been travelling, big changes in mobile-phone design have taken place. In the beginning, the participants mostly had feature phones with little storage space for text messages. They therefore saw the embroidery as an opportunity for another kind of storage. As time passed, most participants had smartphones, with a radically increased capacity for storing text messages. Despite the changes in storage capacity, the invitation to 'Threads' has continued to spark curiosity and participation over the years.

Figure 12.1 Participants gathered in 'Threads' © Kristina Lindström

Figure 12.2 Invitations made through embroidered text messages hanging on clotheslines ©
Kristina Lindström

The materials that travelled with 'Threads' were, among other things, thread, needles, new and second-hand fabrics and additional durable goods. The tables in the room were set with tablecloths to embroider on, while clotheslines, pegged with embroidered text messages from previous sewing circles, hung across the room. On a separate table, an embroidery machine connected to a mobile phone made it possible for participants to have their messages embroidered by a machine, all with the same font and size – just as an SMS has a rather set format.

The invitation to embroider an SMS was communicated not only through words (although a lot of attention was paid to the words), but also carved out in several materials. Furthermore, it was not enacted only by us, but by the collaborating partners and participants as well. These multiple invitations were, for example, enacted through posters, the project website, phone calls and embroidered garments on a clothesline in the venue where the gathering would take place. During the gathering, the inviting continued through the introduction, the inspirational examples on the clotheslines, how the table was set and what could be seen on the tablecloth in the form of traces from previous sewing circles. While the connection to these previous circles was also established through anecdotes, the marks and traces on the tablecloths, indicating how others had understood and encountered other participants and materials in the sewing circle, proved to be a generative way of inviting to the project. On one occasion when we asked how participants would tell others about 'Threads', one specifically replied that she would show what she had embroidered. Inviting in the form of showing examples was similarly done on the website, where participants could upload pictures of their embroideries.

Once they were gathered in the sewing circle, participants responded to the invitations in various ways. Some participants knew already at the beginning what to embroider by hand or with the machine; others took some time to look carefully through their mobile-phone inboxes and outboxes. At times, these responses became co-articulations of issues of living with technologies. On one occasion, for instance, two young participants came to 'Threads' and responded to the invitation to embroider an SMS by making what they called a BFF pillow[3] made of two linen towels. In this way they made a new artefact, onto which they embroidered text messages they had sent to each other, as well as messages they had received from other friends. The embroidered messages were short sentences or a couple of words that were clearly part of an ongoing conversation. In being embroidered, they were taken out of the friendships' mundanity, ongoingness and documentation in digital media. Now the friendship was manifested in something tangible, something that could be shared in their home environments. Since they only made one pillow, they decided to take turns and have it every second week in their respective homes.

In this way our invitation, the selection of text messages sent between the two participants but also among and between other friends of theirs, and the making of the pillow, all in combination, became a co-articulation of how these two individuals, as best friends, live with technologies. This articulation suggests that their friendship is not only a relationship between the two of them but involves other friends as well. Text messaging is one important means of communication to sustain these relationships, but their response also proposed a new way of sustaining their relationship; that is, through sharing a pillow. Rather than altering or challenging our invitation to 'Threads', this response fits very well with the assumptions embedded in the invitation: for example, that text messaging is an important part of contemporary relationships.

Another kind of co-articulation emerged in another rural community centre, when one of the participants had no messages to embroider. For this reason, she had prepared herself before coming to 'Threads' by sending an SMS to her family members that said: 'Need a text before Saturday'. When she sent the message, she was in the same room as her husband, who responded with a message in which he expressed his love for her. The daughter also responded: 'Here is a message before Saturday.' While we were gathered in the sewing circle, the daughter sent another message: 'Why don't we call each other instead. Text messaging is so impersonal.' During the sewing circle, the woman embroidered this message and parts of the message from her husband with the machine, along with an additional embroidered heart by hand. While embroidering, she referred back to previous conversations concerning handwriting and embroidery by hand as something more nuanced than SMS and email. This understanding of technologies was later contradicted by another participating woman, who had received a message from her daughter. The daughter suggested that, in order to minimize fighting on the phone, they should communicate through text messaging rather than calling each other. Regardless of whether the participants changed their views of technologies and means of communication or not, these multiple responses to the invitation allowed diverging ways of living with technologies to emerge. These responses enact a co-articulation that is both dependent on and speaks back to the invitation.

Whereas the two participants who embroidered a BFF pillow had to choose between several messages stored in their inboxes, the first woman described above did not have a range of experience of living with SMS as a technology, which made it difficult for her to participate in 'Threads'. To gain experiences that could be part of her repertoire of living with technologies, she therefore had to initiate them. As a consequence, she also started a negotiation with her family members about how to practise and value this means of communication, which had been in her mobile phone all along, but not put to use. In this case, the invitation, her initiative in sending her family members a text message, their replies, her embroidery and the discussions in 'Threads' thus became a co-articulation of the coexistence of a technological push, as well as a curiosity about, and hesitancy towards, new technologies.

While both these examples involve complex relations between several engaged actors, the latter response did not fit as well with the expectations expressed through the invitation as did the girls' response with the embroidered BFF pillow. Importantly, however, rather than the absence of experience in text messaging being seen as a failure, this misfit in the second example, i.e. between assumptions and experiences, amounted to a more inventive co-articulation of ways of living with technologies. This was also evident in our second project, to which we turn now.

UNRAVEL / REPEAT

This project was a commissioned artwork for the art museum Konstmuseet i Norr, based in Kiruna at the very northern tip of Sweden. Our commission included being encouraged to engage with the whole of this geographical area, which is very sparsely populated and stretches over an extensive area, neighbouring Finland as well as Norway. Since neither of us live in this area of Sweden, we did not want to define a clear problem in advance, or solutions for that matter. Rather, we tried to craft an invitation that expressed an area of curiosity with which we and others could engage. This still involved *ways of living with technologies* – or, more specifically, telecommunication technologies. Compared with the invitation in 'Threads', which had invited participants to engage with the practice of text messaging, the invitation extended in 'UNRAVEL / REPEAT' was to engage with what makes mobile phones become obsolete or not.

To do this, we took on the role of contemporary rag-pickers (*lumpsamlare* in Swedish). While rag-pickers in Sweden traditionally travelled and collected discarded wool, we envisioned in this project that a contemporary form of rag would be discarded mobile phones, possibly tucked away in a drawer. Being curious about these processes, we invited people to donate their phones to us, so that we could work with and take care of the materials. We did this partly in the hope that we would be invited into people's homes, workplaces or other contexts.[4]

As with our work in 'Threads', we used multiple invitations to reach out to, and engage with, people living in this area. We used flyers, put ads in the newspapers, made envelopes so that people could send us their mobile phones, and set a table at a cultural centre where we invited people passing by. Thanks to our contacts at Konstmuseet i Norr, we were also able to direct our invitation to relevant actors. On this basis we visited, and spent some hours with, several people in their homes, as well as at a youth club, a home for the elderly, a recycling centre and a mining company. Some of the phones given to us had broken screens, some had no batteries, and some seemed to be working just fine but were no longer in use because of changes in infrastructure for telecommunications. For most of the time, the responses did not challenge the assumption, embedded in the invitation, that people have an excess of discarded mobile phones which they are willing to let us take care of.

However, there were other instances in which the invitation was challenged. For example, one elderly man refused to give us his discarded mobile phone. He got upset when he heard about our rag-picking, and said he kept his old mobile phone as a treasure. There was simply too much gold in it to give away without compensation. Another day, we went to a village with three households. Although the village

Figure 12.3 Discarded mobile phones collected at a youth club © Kristina Lindström

is very far north in such a sparsely populated area, in two out of the three households no one held a driving licence. For this reason, the landline phone had been a crucial means of communication. A woman who invited us into her home told us that due to the expansion of mobile telephony, it had been decided that the landline would be cut off. For her and the others living in the village, however, mobile telephony was a less reliable means of communication, since the reception was weak. This meant that batteries did not last very long, and that it was not always possible to make or receive phone calls. Therefore, to secure a more stable phone connection, she had spent a considerable amount of time, effort and money setting up a system that allowed her to get an Internet connection, through which she could have access to telephony (see Figure 12.4). Compared to the landline, this configuration demanded continuous updates and upgrades, which, to her, meant money, time and worry.

Even though the mobile-phone reception was unreliable, she did have a mobile phone that she considered giving us. The phone was a so-called feature phone, the same kind we had received from several others. After our more-than-two-hour conversation, however, she decided to keep it. She described how, for her, a new smartphone would not be an upgrade, since what she valued the most was battery time. In this way she altered the parameters of our invitation, and reconfigured the implicit assumption in our invitation that an excess of technological devices is the normal state of affairs. Her decision not to give us her phone, thereby rejecting our invitation, challenged technological progress as the desirable. As her family does

Figure 12.4 Technologies assembled to enable telecommunication through the Internet © Kristina Lindström

not have a cash-based way of life but lives off the land and animal husbandry, continuously buying new telephones and other devices to connect it to amounts to heavy expenses compared to the landline phone, which had lasted many years. As expressed by Mazé in the quote cited above (2013), technological change – in this case proliferation of mobile telecommunications – might generate a solution for some, but problems and labour for others.

Framing Invitations to More or Less Inventive Co-Articulations

The politics of inviting has been explored in this chapter through the two projects: 'Threads' and 'UNRAVEL / REPEAT'. Although they were quite different in their structure, scale, objectives and materials, the projects had in common that they both started out from some kind of invitation, one which makes possible various more or less inventive co-articulations of issues. Both projects might seem sweet and cuddly. Our argument, though, is that framing the invitation to an art, design or research project which invites for collaborative formations of issues is clearly not innocent. Indeed, it is a way of framing (Keshavarz and Mazé 2013), if not a problem, at least an area of interest or curiosity, which inevitably both includes and excludes. Potentially, it will only attract those who are already interested in the given matter, and potentially it may thereby shape a space for consensus.

If we think of these projects as public engagement projects, it is reasonable to ask: What kind of engagement? What is our role as researchers in relation to the public? And how are problems or issues articulated? As we have shown in our accounts, the engagement involved was not simply about us (as researchers) trans-ferring knowledge or new scientific findings to the public. Nor was it about the public transferring information to us (as researchers) for use in informing future design decisions. Rather, the invitations engendered issues *to be co-articulated*. And, as we have shown, these issues – for instance concerning how to live with technologies – are essentially articulated between our invitation, the materials that we bring to the table, what the participants bring and, crucially, how all these materialities are relationally reordered.

Rather than *representing* issues of living with technologies, as if these were already there to be represented, co-articulations mean, in other words, that issues in 'Threads' and 'UNRAVEL / REPEAT' *emerge* in the encounter between the multiple invitations and the participants' various responses. In line with Michael (2012), Noortje Marres (2012) and Bruno Latour (2005), we therefore consider issues to be co-emergent in different kinds of material engagements. In our projects, issues are made or enacted together as particular compositions of the participants' experiences, memories and materials and the stories of other partici-pants, as well as the technologies and materials brought both by us and by the participants, including mobile phones and text messages. In brief, the issues are collaboratively formed, in a distinctive engagement involving both humans and non-humans.

Important to note is, however, that these co-articulations can be more or less inventive. For the most part, participants respond according to the expectations embedded in the invitation: for example, to embroider an SMS reminding them of someone important to them. When the issue emerges more inventively is usually when the assumptions enacted through the invitations do not fit well with how participants live with technologies. Following Gabrys, Hawkins and Michael (2013: 7), we thus suggest that it can be generative to bring together 'mutually incompatible framings' that, precisely, do not align easily, as this allows us to pose issues more inventively. If our aim is to craft invitations that precisely make it possible for inventive co-articulations of issues to emerge, then the concern is not to create a perfect fit between the invitation and participants' ways of living with technologies. Rather, we need to find ways to allow actors, situations, experiences and actions to speak up and contradict what is taken for granted. Clearly the framing of invitations to co-articulation is important, but it does not determine the co-articulations.

As a crafting together of two disciplines, design anthropology can be enacted in different ways. In this chapter, we have adhered to an approach, which assumes mutual transformations of both disciplines. As such, we have tried not to reiterate a version in which design is focused on creating futures and change, while anthropology is concerned with understanding the present through the past. To reconfigure this relationship, we turned in part to recent literature within participatory design that argues for designing for design-in-use, or design-after-design. In our view, this approach reconfigures not merely the relationship between designers and users, as traditional participatory design has done, but also the relationship between design and use. This insight, i.e. the point that design takes place not only in projects but also in use, is also acknowledged in some of the literature on design anthropology (e.g. Gunn and Donovan 2012; Ingold 2012).

This understanding of the relation between design and use has various implications for how design anthropology is enacted. Here, we have focused in particular on how it implies a shift in when we invite, and to what. Instead of inviting participants to engage in the making of design to be used in the future, we have argued for inviting participants to engage in issues that emerge when things are already in use. In this way, participants are invited not to solve problems, but to co-articulate issues of, for instance, the ongoing living with technologies. Through our own accounts of empirical work with designerly public engagement, we have demonstrated that inventive co-articulations of issues primarily take place when there is friction between the invitation and the response to it.

Our reason for expanding the epistemological community is not merely to inform us as researchers, policymakers or designers, but to enable mutual learning between researchers and participants through more or less inventive co-articulations of issues. Thus the collaborative formations of issues are not necessarily roadmaps to a desirable future, as Carl DiSalvo (this volume) also contends. Rather, they amount to a distinctive design anthropological exploration of a particular phenomenon (see also Lenskjold and Olander, this volume). Importantly, however, the potential inventiveness may not be the same for all involved. What may be inventive for those doing the inviting may not be inventive for those responding – and vice versa. The politics of inviting embedded in every designerly public engagement therefore begs the question: for whom is it inventive, how, when and why?

Notes

1   With PEST, we build on Michael's idea of designerly PES but add a T for technology to indicate that the public engagement involves not only science but also technology. See chapter four in Lindström and Ståhl (2014) for our elaborations on designerly public engagement.
2   At the time of conducting this research, we were PhD students at the School of Arts and Communication, Malmö University, Sweden. For a more extensive account of 'Threads', see Lindström and Ståhl (2014).
3   BFF is short for Best Friends Forever.
4   In a second phase of the project, we created an SMS novel that was based on recompositions of the collected material, stories and phones. In this chapter, however, we focus only on the rag-picking phase (see Ståhl, Lindström and Snodgrass 2014 for an account of the second phase).

References

Beaver, J., Pennington, S. and Kerridge, T. (eds.) (2009), *Material Beliefs,* London: Goldsmiths, University of London/Interaction Research Studio.
Binder, T., De Michelis, G., Ehn, P., Jacucci, G., Linde, P. and Wagner, I. (2011), *Design Things,* Cambridge, MA: MIT Press.
Bjerknes, G. and Bratteteig, T. (1987), 'Florence in Wonderland: System Development with Nurses', in G. Bjerknes, P. Ehn and M. Kyng (eds.), *Computers and Democracy: A Scandinavian Challenge,* 279–95, Brookfield, VT: Gower.
Dunne, A. and Raby, F. (2013), *Speculative Everything: Design, Fiction, and Social Dreaming,* Cambridge, MA: MIT Press.
Ehn, P. (1988), *Work-Oriented Design of Computer Artifacts.* Stockholm: Arbetslivscentrum.
Ehn, P., Nilsson, E. M. and Topgaard, R. (eds.) (2014), 'Introduction', in P. Ehn, E. M. Nilsson, and R. Topgaard (eds.), *Making Futures: Marginal Notes on Innovation, Design, and Democracy,* 1–13, Cambridge, MA: MIT Press.
Gabrys, J., Hawkins, G. and Michael, M. (2013), 'Introduction: From Materiality to Plasticity', in J. Gabrys, G. Hawkins and M. Michael (eds.), *Accumulation: The Material Politics of Plastic,* 1–14, New York and London: Routledge.
Gunn, W. and Donovan, J. (2012), 'Design Anthropology: An Introduction', in W. Gunn and J. Donovan (eds.), *Design and Anthropology,* 1–16, Farnham: Ashgate.
Haraway, D. (2013), 'SF: Science Fiction, Speculative Fabulation, String Figures, So Far', *Ada: A Journal of Gender, New Media, and Technology,* 3.
Ingold, T. (2012), 'Introduction: The Perception of the User-Producer', in W. Gunn and J. Donovan (eds.), *Design and Anthropology,* 19–33, Farnham: Ashgate.

Kensing, F. and Greenbaum, J. (2012), 'Heritage: Having a Say', in J. Simonsen and T. Robertson (eds.), *Routledge International Handbook of Participatory Design*, 21–36, New York: Routledge.

Keshavarz, M. and Mazé, R. (2013), 'Design and Dissensus: Framing and Staging Participation in Design Research', *Design Philosophy Papers*, 11 (1): 7–29.

Kjærsgaard, M. G. (2011), *Between the Actual and the Potential: The Challenges of Design Anthropology*, PhD dissertation, Faculty of Arts, University of Aarhus.

Latour, B. (2005), 'From Realpolitik to Dingpolitik or How to Make Things Public', in B. Latour and P. Weibel (eds.), *Making Things Public*: *Atmospheres of Democracy*, 14–41, Cambridge, MA: MIT Press.

Lindström, K. and Ståhl, Å. (2014), *Patchworking Publics-in-the-Making*: *Design, Media and Public Engagement,* PhD dissertation, Malmö University.

Marres, N. (2012), *Material Participation: Technology, the Environment and Everyday Publics*, Basingstoke and New York: Palgrave Macmillan.

Mazé, R. (2013), 'Who is Sustainable? Querying the Politics of Sustainable Design Practices', in R. Mazé, L. Olausson, M. Plöjel, J. Redström and C. Zetterlund (eds.), *Share this Book: Critical Perspectives and Dialogues about Design and Sustainability*, 83–124, Stockholm: Axl Books.

Michael, M. (2012), '"What Are We Busy Doing?": Engaging the Idiot', *Science, Technology and Human Values,* 37 (5): 528–54.

Otto, T. and Smith, R. C. (2013), 'Design Anthropology: A Distinct Style of Knowing', in W. Gunn, T. Otto and R. C. Smith (eds.), *Design Anthropology: Theory and Practice*, 1–29, London and New York: Bloomsbury.

Redström, J. (2006), 'Towards User Design? On the Shift from Object to User as the Subject of Design', *Design Studies,* 27 (2): 123–39.

Robertson, T. and Simonsen, J. (2012), 'Participatory Design. An Introduction', in J. Simonsen and T. Robertson (eds.), *Routledge International Handbook of Participatory Design*, 1–19, New York: Routledge.

Ståhl, Å., Lindström, K. and Snodgrass, E. (2014), 'Staying With, Working Through and Performing Obsolescence', *Acoustic Space; TECHNO-ECOLOGIES,* 2 (12): 243–53.

13 Collaboratively Cleaning, Archiving and Curating the Heritage of the Future

ADAM DRAZIN, ROBERT KNOWLES, ISABEL BREDENBRÖKER AND ANAIS BLOCH

Introducing Bauhaus Cleaning

In the anthropological project which we outline here, an installation called 'Cleaning Up After Gropius', we examined cultures of cleaning and archiving at the Bauhaus in Dessau, and the legacy of that site's extraordinary design heritage for contemporary work.[1] Design work always happens in the wake of previous design, and we ask how it is that people work everyday with a pre-designed world to manipulate change, transformation and stasis. We suggest that anthropology can contribute to the formation and clarification of design issues through critical ethnographies of design politics in which futures do not belong exclusively to design and designers (Suchman 2011). This can help designers to wrestle with what we will call the 'problems of the future', meaning confronting the problematic 'otherness' of futures, to locate their own approach to design futures among multiple approaches, and to identify with modes of change.

The Bauhaus in Dessau is one of the sites of the very origins of modernist design. In the 1920s, the professors at the Bauhaus in Dessau made a film, *How We Live in a Healthy and Economical Way*, which showcased their household designs and enacted the kind of modern lifestyle they envisaged. In the film, a maid, and Walter and Ise Gropius, demonstrate cooking, cleaning, relaxing and entertaining using a range of new household equipment. During periods of the film, the maid mops, does washing up and tidies throughout the striking modernist rooms of their new houses, the *Meisterhäuser*. In 2015, the Bauhaus Dessau Foundation re-evoked the theme of the household in the *Haushaltsmesse 2015* (Household Exhibition), entitled *On the Art of Housekeeping in the Twenty-First Century* and curated by Regina Bittner and Elke Krasny. The curators invited a range of designers, artists, architects and anthropologists (ourselves) to present work in the grounds of the *Meisterhäuser*, considering the question 'how can we live in a healthy and economical way?' In the intervening period, between 1927 and 2015, many of the designs in the film have become globally common, indicative of a normative conception of a modernist lifestyle, while the houses themselves have become a UNESCO World Heritage monument to celebrate their archetypal contribution to human culture through design.

As anthropologists, with a particular interest in material culture, we set out to develop site-based ethnographic work, with a view to observing and interpreting the cultural dimensions and tensions of the household. Spending time in the *Meisterhäuser* and related buildings, we quickly observed that this is a wonderful place to research cleaning, which is frequent, regular and careful. This being a heritage site, cleaning and tourism are at the heart of daily activity while many other activities (such as cooking) are constrained or forbidden. Research into cleaning made us aware that, in order to understand how it was being done, we also had to understand the wider heritage environment. How these sites are treated has been the subject of intense political debate in the past, and cleaning practices and skills also happen in parallel with the management and archiving of heritage objects and materials. We use the word archiving to refer to the management of collections, involving acquisition, research, preservation, storage and some display work. By contrast, we are using the word curation to refer to the assemblage of material (some from collections) for display. Following the ethnographic research, we developed an installation using the data gathered. The installation aimed to confront designers with the creativity of cleaning in making heritage, and to present a range of ways in which people every day in the Bauhaus sites work with the material world with one eye on the future. A design-interested audience might then locate themselves within this cultural ecosystem of futures.

Our argument draws on several ideas. In the Dessau Bauhaus, people who clean feel powerfully engaged in a project of value-creation, and are a part of wider design debates about how to mobilize the Bauhaus traditions for a better future through design. Cleaning happens as a part of multiple paradigms of action to shape and socialize the material world (including archiving, curating and design). It involves imagination, value-creation and social commitment to a collective project.

Dessau, however, also illustrates multiple futures. The town is littered with past materializations of visions of the future, and these gradually decaying concrete forms (decaying unless preserved through cleaning and archiving work) are humanized and socialized. They carry with them the accretive traces of human life and inhabitation, as Øye (2007) calls it, a homeliness in the 'feeling for grey'. The tensions in Dessau, in which people in many different positions and vocations must consider what is to be removed (i.e. is dirt), what is to be actively cleaned (i.e. is heritage) and what is to be left, involve the negotiation of multiple materializations and projects of futures. When we talk about the 'otherness' of futures, we mean how working collaboratively comprises a situation which itself has implications for the cultural conception of futures: that is, other people have previously materialized or objectified futures; they have done so with multiple purposes, skills and modes of behaviour; and there is a palpable issue in this heritage situation of when one feels able to physically engage with material forms and substances. Otherness can here be thought of as concerning the ways that conceptualizations of culture and of self involve objectification (Miller 1987), and also the politics of futures as the experience of sameness and difference (Appadurai 2013). One of the points of comparison between cleaning and design is the sense of working with sameness and difference to produce new arrangements of meaning; another is the ways in which a person feels equipped to engage. In cleaning, the categorization of parts of the world as 'dirt' is convergent with an embodied legitimation and compulsion to act on physical matter.

Artistic installations and re-presentations of ethnographic work, for design-interested audiences, should aim to help designers locate themselves within multiple site-based paradigms of change; and also help designers to think about their own bodily understandings of legitimately working with the material world, through evoking a sense of contextual immersion in a site (Wright 2010).

We argue then for more anthropological approaches, which consider futures in terms of encounters with externalized problems or otherness (Rosenberg and Harding 2005; Suchman 2011) rather than as expressionism (i.e. futures as made or imagined; see Ingold 2012; Yelavich and Adams 2014), and which present these problems and encounters to design audiences. This is an argument that is especially appropriate for heritage design, but may also be appropriate elsewhere.

This chapter proceeds with a brief description of the final installation, followed by two key parts. We outline Dessau as a site, the thinking, which led us towards material cultures, and cleaning, and some moments from our ethnographic work. Secondly, we consider the thinking behind the resulting installation. The chapter finishes with some comments on the implications for collaborative issue formation in design anthropology.

'Cleaning Up After Gropius': A Brief Description

The installation 'Cleaning Up After Gropius' was exhibited in several parts, each one making use of data and media in slightly different ways. The first part of the exhibit was sound-based, using three different soundtracks to explore cultures of cleaning. On entry to the house, standing on the staircase, one hears the sound of the mopping of Bauhaus spaces, with the distinctive echo of the concrete interiors. Intercut with these sounds are extracts of interviews with a cleaner, who outlines the techniques, materials and planning of what is involved. The intention is that the audience gains a sense of the collective work which has produced this particular banal environment; a staircase which otherwise remains unquestioned and self-evident. As such, the recordings make present in the imagination an absent cleaner.

Moving downstairs, the audience enters those basement spaces where cleaning and laundry work were once done out of sight of the main residential part of the house. In one relatively bare room, with steel pipes tracking across the ceiling, a much wider range of sounds of cleaning can be heard, including people talking about and organizing cleaning. An absence of things to look at forces attention to the sounds of people elsewhere discussing what to use, instructing one another or agreeing on a course of action. This soundtrack is intended to help the audience to imagine cleaning as a social event, and comprising a variety of cultures of household cleaning.

Entering the largest room in the basement, the audience encounters two other parts to the installation; a video and a display of 'dirt for auction'. In the corner, a massive, original concrete and steel washtub is built into the fabric of the house. On the walls are the hooks from which drying laundry lines could criss-cross the room. Here, a video plays on a loop. It presents people cleaning and washing in a modernist-style kitchen, doing the washing up, wiping down surfaces, sweeping the floor, and it sets these clips to repetitive classical music (rather than using research recordings, like the sound installations). The bodily actions of cleaning are often repeated, in time with the musical rhythms, going over spots and surfaces again and again, wiping then wiping again as if honing with a cloth the already-cleaned surface. As someone scrubs a pan with circular swipes, we hear the sawing of a violin, as if they are playing the pan. These bodily repetitions are supposed to evoke the embodied knowledges and craft of cleaning. After each twenty or thirty seconds of balletic musical cleaning, the audience then sees a video shot of *Meisterhäuser* interiors or exteriors, dwelling on the surfaces of the walls, windows and shelves. The cleaning sequences become faster and build towards a crescendo. Ultimately, the video ends fading to a black and white 1920s image of this *Meisterhaus*: Gropius' own vision of it.

Figure 13.1 The Video Installation in 'Cleaning Up After Gropius' © Adam Drazin

If this video does its intended job, by the end a viewer may begin to see the surfaces of the *Meisterhaus* differently. Even the view from a window is not 'given', but has largely been produced by cleaning. We may thus begin to see the glass which facilitates the view, and we may recognize how the image of our 'heritage' has itself been created by accretive cleaning. In this way, this video concerns the idea of cleaning as a creative act, which involves not only the disposal of dirt but the making of form, and potentially of value.

The last part of the installation consists of a display of Bauhaus dirt (*Bauhaus Schmutzes*), with associated notices saying it is to be auctioned. The dirt hangs in small sealed plastic bags from washing lines, selected by colour and form, and presented under lights. Some of the dirt is produced by the cleaning of the *Meisterhaus*, some is sourced from the site of the Bauhaus archives where the collections are kept and where archivists must often decide what objects or materials are to be preserved, cleaned or (sometimes) thrown away. Some of the dirt (the cheaper pieces) has been mixed with material from less important Dessau sites. These bags represent material categorized as unvalued 'dirt' by cleaners or archivists, consciously or unconsciously.

As a whole, these three parts of the installation – audio, video and collected dirt – explore different cultural dimensions of ways in which people on the Bauhaus site engage with futures, by re-presenting mostly contextual data from anthropological research. In the remainder of this chapter, we talk through the work process and thinking that underlies it. We will proceed by examining different approaches to the collaborative formation of issues, and what Dessau as a site can contribute to them.

Collaborative Approaches to Design Futures in Dessau

In recent years, the question of the formation of issues in user-centred design has been closely linked to cultural discussions of futures (e.g. Ehn, Nilsson and Topgaard 2014). Earlier debates around whether design work may be problem-focused or a reflexive learning process (Bannon and Ehn 2013), have been superseded by debates about the clear constitution of design issues, and how material things manifest or represent them. Design anthropological work has firstly problematized the clear separation of design questions from solutions, which often appear convergently (Binder et al. 2011), such that to address design issues, one must often pay more attention to design futures. Secondly, the idea that design provides a material response to an absence or gap, such as a need or demand, has also been challenged. Instead of dialogues of material and immaterial phenomena, design anthropology increasingly sees itself as conducting work through transformations of concrete material forms or artefacts (e.g. Halse 2013; Wallace 2012; Drazin 2013). As a site, Dessau has a particular contribution to make here because it is itself a grand proposal for a design solution, a future and a reinvention of modern living.

One powerful expression of the paradoxes of issue-formation is the concept of 'design things' (Binder et al. 2011), which characterizes the specific materialities of design work (used for conceptualizing, prototyping and demonstrating design) as particular kinds of emergent things. Thomas Binder et al. here develop the observation that the word 'thing' across Northern Europe used to mean a gathering of people or meeting, often of a political kind, but has come to also mean a physical object. Likewise, the meaning of the word 'matter' is binaristic, implying both what is (politically) significant – for example, a problem – but also meaning physical substance.

> How can we as designers work, live and act in a public that involves a heterogeneity of perspectives and actors to engage in alignments of their conflicting objects of design? How can we gather and participate around design things? These things themselves modify the space of interactions and performance, and will be explored as sociomaterial frames for controversies, ready for unexpected use and opening up new ways of thinking and behaving (Binder et al. 2011: 1).

Design problems are generally 'wicked problems' (Buchanan 1992) involving multiple social purposes, perspectives and understandings. It follows that to bring together a gathering of concerned parties may also be a manifestation itself of key design issues, expressed in the spaces and differences between them. Participation in such 'design things' traces the boundary between issue and response, because the conversation about what to do must necessarily involve learning about problems and action from other people's perspectives. As we outline later, this notion is crucial to understanding Dessau, where interaction (and friction) between a multitude of interested parties identifying closely with the site has been productive of emergent design pathways.

When it comes to the anthropological literature on futures and futurity, a different set of tensions emerge. There are many different kinds of anthropological approaches to futures, some design-related (Appadurai 2013; Yelavich and Adams 2014; Faubion, Marcus and Rabinow 2008; Suchman 2011) and some not (Wallman 1992; Fischer 2009). A common consideration of design futures is, however, to see futures as culturally existing through a combination of 'imagination' (Ingold 2012) and 'making' (Yelavich and Adams 2014). As Ingold (2012: 29) comments, although not in precise terms but more as a guideline: 'Let us allow then that design is about imagining the future.'

While both imagination and making are highly significant, we suggest futures necessarily manifest themselves in heterogeneous ways. Dessau, in particular, illustrates how existing material things and places constitute futures, and mobilize consciousness and collaboration. We consider that such material objectifications should be seen as important for cultural consciousness itself (Miller 1987).

The *Meisterhäuser* site manifests a number of design paradoxes, and its emergent form has been the result of the participatory engagement over many years of diverse stakeholders. Since German re-unification in 1989, it has re-emerged as a hugely symbolic site of national and international design interest. The Bauhaus Dessau Foundation, which controls the site, is committed, within the terms of its remit as a foundation, to heritage archiving and design education, and works to negotiate the space between the two. Its approach to the site and its running of the *Haushaltsmesse* have been important parts of how it conducts this negotiation.

Under intense media and public interest and debate for much of the last 25 years about the material details of how to treat its buildings, the site has been pulled between two alternative, and potentially conflicting, directions. One alternative has been to focus on restoration as a 1920s site. The thinking behind this approach would argue that the buildings may be seen as in themselves expressions of principles of design, and that by manifesting these principles one can celebrate, inspire and stimulate design action. The way forward for the site, in this conception, involves material preservation of the *Meisterhäuser* as heritage.

On the other hand, the material heritage of the late 1920s might be seen as more of a burden than a benefit for design action, since what is important for action are principles and values which can be adapted and applied in new, different circumstances. Dessau is itself considered a city which needs design attention, having lost its industrial base and experiencing unemployment and emigration. Arguments in this vein have, over the years, emphasized the importance of re-establishing a lively design school in Dessau, and building, changing or re-building using contemporary methods, in order to not only represent design but to practise it. Strong arguments were put forward that the *Meisterhäuser* should not be renovated, but appreciated effectively as preserved ruins, so as not to risk any confusion with contemporary design, which faces new and different issues and requires new design spaces and forms, not old ones.

The question of how materially to treat the Bauhaus sites and buildings was connected to questions of how to work for a better future for Dessau, and for Germany, through design. The physical buildings have catalysed these questions, representing and demonstrating the ability to envisage, imagine, collaboratively organize and shape the material world in wholly original ways.

After years of stalemate, what has eventually happened is, to an extent, a reconciliation of the two possible alternative modes of action. It was, however, the first argument, the site as heritage, which blazed the trail, which enabled collaborative design work to follow. The site was declared a UNESCO World Heritage Site in 1996, but while the Bauhaus building was preserved, among the Master houses only the Fringier House had been restored at this stage. As the extensive factories in Dessau and the surrounding region closed, and the consequences of the emigration of so many young and middle-aged adults became clear, money was ploughed into engaged social projects in the area. Two more of the buildings were renovated in 1999–2000, and the area was landscaped in 2002. This left the Walter Gropius House, which was perhaps the most symbolic of them but which had been destroyed, to be considered for rebuilding. Long after 2000, as it became clear that social investment was not going to reverse emigration or industrial decline, it was decided that the site should be an architectural park or museum for the public, and this was finally launched in 2014. Having established this site as a heritage park, the

Bauhaus Dessau Foundation then began to undertake public design exhibitions, and also build the educational capacities of the school. Two of the restored houses were planned as exhibitionary spaces for contemporary design, and design courses began to be expanded in the Bauhaus.

We believe that this site not only stands as a design history icon, but also epitomizes some paradoxical contemporary issues for design practice and its materiality. These include, in particular, the recurring tensions between working to presence and to erase design. When faced with a materialized design vision for the future, does one leave it, preserve it, modify it or erase it? Even if it is possible to express an opinion on this, a significant question remains: under what circumstances can a set of designers actually feel permitted to do something, to be allowed to engage materially?

Our own approach to futures was more informed by material culture than by imagination and making. In this approach, the future is not only being materialized now, but it always has been, producing multiple referents:

> This is the paradox of modern futurity: while we are taught to believe in the emptiness of the future, we live in a world saturated by future-consciousness as rich and as full as our consciousness of the past (Rosenberg and Harding 2005: 9).

For us, the study of the future is frequently archaeological, involving attention to material things, which invariably emerge from the past. The world may be littered with material anticipations of futures. The temporal framework of 'past-present-future' is inadequate here because, to compare change to a journey, one frequently traces where one has been in order to consider what comes next. Various anthropologists have addressed futures as commonly manifested, encountered, deployed and performing social roles. Wallman (1992) initiated such approaches, while Appadurai (2013) considers 'the future as cultural fact, that is, as a form of difference' (2013: 285). Suchman (2011) presents us with a major critical vision of some of the implications of this pervasiveness of futures. Because some professional groups, including designers, may present themselves as closer to, or owners of, manifest futures, consequently the study of futures can trace lines of power and inequality. In a world of futures, certain people, ideas, practices, groups and material forms become consigned to the past.

In our research, we asked not so much how people in their everyday lives express ideas of the future, but rather how they react to and confront problematic and ubiquitous potential futures. We focused on the material sites of the Dessau Bauhaus, considering how people work with these material sites, creating and removing matter and forms, negotiating the gradients of professional and everyday knowledges and skills. Our focus, then, became not so much how people make futures in response to problems, but how they deal with the problems of the future. We thought of such problems as having at least three interrelated aspects: the issue of the material legacy of past manifestations of possible futures as heritage; the question of how design change can happen in a site pervaded by prior design; and, lastly, how designers can achieve an engaged stance where they feel enabled to engage with the unfolding archaeology of futures.

Cleaning, Archiving and Value Creation

As previously mentioned, cleaning and archiving were the main ways in which we observed hands-on engagements with the *Meisterhäuser*. In a heritage environment, the drive to preserve or erase materialized futures is dealt with on an everyday level by cleaning.

One of our first impressions of the *Meisterhäuser*, especially the rebuilt Gropius house (by Berlin-based BFM Architects), was that no actual house could really be this clean. The unreal opalescent windows, half like windows, and half like walls, and the stark white walls are intended to communicate the house as a concept as much as a building. These square, concrete surfaces are echoed in familiar buildings in many parts of the world. Severe cleanliness of the exteriors then assists in the recognition both of design, incorporating thing as concept, and of heritage. The buildings are, however, simultaneously special and extremely banal (as familiar forms). Standing in one of the upstairs bathrooms, one could be anywhere in the world, in any house, apartment, hotel or institution. There are white walls, an enclosed bathtub beneath a window, a pedestal sink with mixer taps and a swivelling spout. It takes an act of imagination to remember that this bathroom is the original manifestation of this form, and it is partly *because* we could be anywhere that cleaning and preservation of *this* bathroom is so important.

The cleaning of each house, room and location is highly regulated, with careful attention to space, materials and public access. Different schedules (daily, weekly, monthly) may apply, as well as different intensities of cleaning apply (for example, floors might be mopped daily, while skirting boards are wiped only once a month). Contact with surfaces is sometimes regulated, as it is, for instance, forbidden to attach things to walls.

There is, then, something puzzling about the way cleaning mediates the special and the typical on this site. One might have expected cleaning of modernist houses to be globally uniform. A house is a house, the materials are mostly familiar, and there are measurable, quantifiable dimensions to cleaning. But not every modernist house is the same, apparently. These houses are cleaned by a professional company, whose manager details something of their trade, when we asked about a particular house:

> Anthropologist: How long does the cleaning take?
> Cleaner: About two hours. There are two women who do these houses together and clean them within this timeframe. There's an estimate for the objects and a norm, and then my colleagues are given the expected time.
> Anthropologist: What does estimate and norm mean?

Cleaner: We measure the square metres, then there's a norm per square metre. We estimate how much our colleague is able to finish within the time, and the square metres and norm combined then produce that time.

…

Cleaner: You can calculate this. It's just that our norm is our – I don't want to say 'business secret' – but they are different from cleaning firm to cleaning firm, so it means we don't reveal the norm.

The cleaning activity is evidently very like a craft. The actions of the cleaners are learned, embodied, repetitive movements with specific tools. The cleaner applies particular pressure, leans into the task to a certain degree, and moves the mop, cloth, vacuum or brush in repeated sweeps of a certain dimension, which cover the surface cleaned over a period of time. 'This is a craft, yes (*Gebäuderreinigerhandwerk*)', reports the cleaning manager.

Most importantly, many cleaners understand their work as a creative process, which maintains or creates value ('*den Wert der Objekte zu erhalten*'). In the Bauhaus buildings, value and preservation seem more significant than hygiene or tidiness per se. There is an evident pride in involvement with the site. Cleaning is generally officially a concealed activity, and while it was easy for us to witness cleaning, it was difficult to formally interview cleaners themselves, which indicated boundaries and control around cleaning knowledge. The manager comments, '"Clean" means not just washing floors but also preservation of value. This is actually very important… That's where the effort lies in cleaning.'

Figure 13.2 Cleaning equipment on a staircase in the Bauhaus building © Adam Drazin

Figure 13.3 Heritage materials in bags in the archive of the Bauhaus collection © Adam Drazin

The more we spoke with different people involved in Bauhaus properties, the more comments such as this one began to challenge the paper walls between different professional groups. For example, archivists and cleaners may have very different training, are differently appreciated, but both feel bound up in the bigger project of care for this site, and are actively making decisions about the material heritage. Cleaning and archiving can thus be thought of as parts in a political economy of knowledges in the Bauhaus Dessau Foundation properties.

In the extensive Bauhaus storage facilities, housed in an old disused factory, archivists are faced with two key kinds of decision about their collection. First, they have to decide what to keep or throw away, what is valuable heritage and what is better seen as rubbish. Second, they must decide how things can be preserved. Cleaning might be destructive, for which reason it is better to just leave and store some things so their slow decay is minimized. In this respect, archiving is ascribed a much higher 'pro-active' long-term decision-making value than cleaning, which by contrast is seen as more reactive and immediate in its decision-making.

Re-Presentation, Sensation and Change

As has been discussed, in Dessau it was wholly unclear whether the 'household of the future' already existed, was being designed, or is yet to be designed. After studying cleaning, we might think of it as the work of stasis, keeping things the same, or an ongoing work of change. To put this another way, there was the experience of a tension between the purposes of design heritage and of design practice as modes of social amelioration. We also observed multiple paradigms of action in reaction to these household futures.

These tensions were important for how an installation based on ethnography might be received by a design-interested audience, between a validation of the status quo and a call to redesign cleaning. As design is the 'science of the artificial' (see Cross 1982; Bannon and Ehn 2013), designed objects are, in their essence, collaborative humanized objects. These must entail consideration of prior experiences, knowledges and practices. Our installation aimed to help a design audience to locate themselves and operate within a politicized economy of plural cultural paradigms of material change, including cleaning and archiving. This exercise contains a sense of problematic 'otherness', confronting design with problems of the future in the three senses we have described: the prior material legacy of futures, other paradigms of change and the feeling of an ability to legitimately engage.

How might an audience identify with a sense of material change? The work of anthropologist Inger-Elin Øye in Shwerin, eastern Germany, is helpful here. She talks about the 'feeling for gray', and how senses of dirtiness and cleanliness are about appropriate change. In the 1990s, her informants compared their perceptions of different parts of Germany: 'Despite its less attractive appearance, the eastern environment was described as being more honest, modest, natural, human and *innerlich*. It was in the east that these people felt *zu Hause* (at home)' (2007: 114, emphasis in original). At first, Øye herself saw the slightly decaying, concrete facades of the blocks of Shwerin as being concerned with conformity and sterility. And yet, she writes, 'I came to see how gray walls, with their earth-like colours and their state of deterioration, resembled organic life processes: the development of individual differences, coming of age, and decay. I developed a better feeling for gray' (2007: 121).

Cleanliness and dirtiness, preservation and decay are perceptually relative, and here they are about how change happens and how we identify with it. Either can be seen as more or less about conformity or creativity, sterility or life. Øye's conceptualization of 'feeling for' suggests a personal identification by an anthropologist with senses of change, experienced in an aesthetic encounter with material surfaces. It parallels Wright's (2010) argument that when anthropologists use artistic methods, they can aim to achieve a sense of 'immersion' rather than the conceptual distance of most anthropological texts: 'Why would an artist attempt to immerse you, and an anthropologist attempt to largely extricate you from that experience?' (Wright 2010: 71).

Following the work of these anthropologists, we considered the artistic re-presentation of our ethnographic work on cleaning and archiving as an immersive critical re-location (Suchman 2011) of the design audience. Therefore, the installations we developed comprise exploratory questions, expressed in material form. Sensory variation is an especially important vehicle for doing this.

Our initial sound-based installations are perhaps the most simple. They unpack the work of cleaning and show its value by revealing the difficulties and efforts of cleaning. Counterpoised to the stillness of the grey walls, the sounds and descriptions are in essence a work of de-fetishization of value as manifested in the *Meisterhäuser*, revealing it to be created by labour. Because the sound comprises conversations, the installation also communicates how cleaning work necessitates collaboration.

As the audience moves to other parts of the installation, the contrasts with the sound installation are intended to open up the range of problems of dealing with futures for designers. In the sound installations, one should feel a bodily reaction and empathy: listening to echoing cleaning sounds, one almost feels the water, senses in one's own body the strokes of the mop and repetitive wiping. By contrast, when interviews with archivists are played in the final part of the installation, there is no feeling of embodiment, as one is simply listening to a set of cerebral decisions.

The video part of our installation poses the problem of different forms of temporality and evaluation in cleaning, and bridges notions of cleaning and heritage. It effectively illustrates the transformation of many, small, quantified moments of skilled cleaning work, to produce transcendent, eternal, Bauhaus heritage. At the same time, it considers some of the contradictions of the visibility of cleaning work. Cleaning eliminates and conceals matter, which is dirt, but also creates surfaces rendered as-new which are perceived as clean. Acts of evaluation are more explicit in the auction of *Bauhaus Schmutzes,* which present the audience very directly with the question of how they would evaluate individual remnants of past activity and work.

Thus, throughout the exhibition, there is an exploration of which people, and groups of people, have both the legitimate capacity and the collective motivation to clean. While conceptualization of matter as 'dirt' legitimizes physical intervention,

Figure 13.4 Dirt for auction (*Bauhaus Schmutzes*) in the 'Cleaning Up After Gropius' installation
© Adam Drazin

categorization as 'heritage' produces a barrier between matter and audience which may prevent legitimate physical engagement.

Audiences are in effect, we hope, being asked questions by these materialized problems of the future. What paradigms of change do they identify with? How do they evaluate cleaning? And how can they perceive or sense cleaning and dirt in material terms? In our attempt to break up the activities observed into multiple problematics of the future, we anticipate the possibility of multiple kinds of design projects, in which different designers find different 'feelings' for Bauhaus concrete, and try to establish how a project resonates with the different communities in Dessau who are engaging with futures.

The Challenges of Other Futures as Heritage and Dirt

We argue for collaborative issue formation in design anthropology which re-presents ethnographic work, to confront designers with the different kinds of projects and plural futures in which people are engaged in their own lives, and which seeks to draw designers into paradigms of action. Futures are not the preserve of designers, but are pervasive. While any social context involves imaginations, discourses, routines and practices, it is by researching futures through material culture that we can identify interesting key issues through which people experience problematizations of culture (Miller 1987). Convergently with being problematic, material design heritage in a place such as Dessau is a prime motivator of collaborative work, enabling many professional groups and stakeholders to come together and engage in mutual projects. This collaborative focus is possible largely because this material heritage exists as a manifestation of prior knowledges and practices of futures. The material landscape of Dessau should not be dismissed as the past of design (as dirt), but is part of ongoing processual materializations that enable engagements with future possibilities.

To be able to work on this site is an extraordinary opportunity. As we have outlined, the Bauhaus Dessau Foundation has faced a particular, persistent sense of having to choose between 'preservation of the designed past' and 'working for a newly designed future', but has moved to transcend this tension in a range of ways, including using exhibitionary techniques and spaces.

To re-present ethnographic data in design anthropology work is partly to try to evoke similar problems of the future, confronting design work with its potential to become either untouchable heritage or unrooted praxis, and need to recognize existing modes of engagement with futures. Design anthropology can itself be understood as knowledge which is 'situated' (Suchman 2011: 14, citing Haraway 1988), which needs to locate its own project in relation to other situated knowledges through acts of ethnographic re-presentation. The designer's perspective is often raised above others in its validity, yet this can be simultaneously a benefit and a burden. How do we both validate designerly perspectives as potentially progressive, and authorize them in relation to other ways of knowing? An appreciation of values is a necessary element of contemporary design work (Buchanan 2010), and yet values are expressed not so much in fixed knowledges as in process and transactionality, and we have here shown how value creation is a collaborative project, not the preserve of design paradigms only. An example of legitimate and authorized action would be when the material world is seen as 'dirt', valueless by definition and something to be cleaned; and yet the residue of one person's life and action risks being seen as dirt by another person. Design should collaboratively resonate with many people's perspectives and lives, and hence needs to try to negotiate this difficult territory of living dirt, of value-creation and change, through for example the mutual re-presentation of 'other' projects.

In *Cleaning Up After Gropius*, we therefore moved from asking about what the design issues of the future household are, to asking how change happens in this site, and how design is created and formed. The evocation of futures inevitably involves senses of fixity and change. Design anthropology's productions appear both to evoke senses of spaces where change may happen, but also to materialize propositions for new futures, which are already beginning to acquire fixity, and will become the heritage of the future, rigorously and professionally preserved and cleaned.

Note

1   The project title refers to Walter Gropius, the famous architect and pioneer of modernism, who was director of the Bauhaus school from 1919–33.

References

Appadurai, A. (2013), *The Future as Cultural Fact,* London: Verso.

Bannon, L. and Ehn, P. (2013), 'Design: Design Matters in Participatory Design', in J. Simonsen and T. Robertson (eds.), *Routledge Handbook of Participatory Design*, 37–63, London: Routledge.

Binder, T., Ehn, P., De Michelis, G., Jaccuci, G., Linde, P. and Wagner, I. (2011), *Design Things*, Cambridge, MA: MIT Press.

Buchanan, R. (1992), 'Wicked Problems in Design Thinking', *Design Issues* 8 (2): 5–21.

Buchanan, R. (2010 [1995]), 'Branzi's Dilemma: Design in Contemporary Culture', in R. Buchanan, D. Doordan and V. Margolin (eds.), *The Designed World: Images, Objects, Environments*, 13–27, Oxford: Berg.

Cross, N. (1982), 'Designerly Ways of Knowing', *Design Studies* 3 (4): 221–7.

Drazin, A. (2013), 'The Social Life of Concepts in Design Anthropology', in W. Gunn, T. Otto and R. C. Smith (eds.), *Design Anthropology: Theory and Practice*, 33–50, London and New York: Bloomsbury.

Ehn, P., Nilsson, E. and Topgaard, R. (eds.) (2014), *Making Futures: Marginal Notes on Innovation, Design and Democracy*, Cambridge, MA: MIT Press.

Faubion, J., Marcus, G. and Rabinow, P. (2008), *Designs for an Anthropology of the Contemporary,* Durham, NC: Duke University Press.

Fischer, M. (2009), *Anthropological Futures,* Durham, NC: Duke University Press.

Halse, J. (2013), 'Ethnographies of the Possible', in W. Gunn, T. Otto and R. C. Smith (eds.), *Design Anthropology: Theory and Practice*, 180–96, London and New York: Bloomsbury.

Haraway, D. (1988), 'Situated Knowledges: The Science Question in Feminism and the Privilege of Partial Perspective', *Feminist Studies* 14: 575–99.

Ingold, T. (2012), 'Introduction: The Perception of the User-Producer', in J. Donovan and W. Gunn (eds.), *Design and Anthropology*, 19–33, Farnham: Ashgate.

Miller, D. (1987), *Material Culture and Mass Consumption*, London: Routledge.

Øye, I.-E. (2007), 'The Feeling for Gray: Aesthetics, Politics, and Shifting German Regimes', *Social Analysis,* 51 (1): 112–34.

Rosenberg, D. and Harding, S. (eds.) (2005), *Histories of the Future,* Durham, NC: Duke University Press.

Suchman, L. (2011), 'Anthropological Relocations and the Limits of Design', *Annual Review of Anthropology,* 40: 1–18.

Wallace, J. (2012), 'Emergent Artefacts of Ethnography and Processual Engagements of Design', in W. Gunn and J. Donovan (eds.), *Design and Anthropology*, 207–18, Farnham: Ashgate.

Wallman, S. (ed.) (1992), *Contemporary Futures*, London: Routledge.

Wright, C. (2010), 'In the Thick of It: Notes on Observation and Context', in A. Schneider and C. Wright (eds.), *Between Art and Anthropology: Contemporary Ethnographic Practice*, 67–74, Oxford: Berg.

Yelavich, S. and Adams, B. (eds.) (2014), *Design as Future-Making*, London: Bloomsbury.

Section IV
Engaging Things

ways in which speculative and critical objects might engage with particular people, places, and practices 'in the field'. These design objects were not commentaries from afar, but situated objects that could graft onto, and interact with, concrete practices and images of futures 'out there' in the fields and in the design studio, sparking reflections, changing conversations, shifting perspectives and influencing practices. Rather than something intrinsic to or embedded within the design object itself, critique here was played out in situated encounters within particular contexts over time.

Our experiment succeeded in getting the students to reflect critically on possible understandings of futures, future-making, and the role of design within it. Some interesting and thought-provoking attempts resulted, which created situated critical objects that might also challenge perspectives on and practices of future making outside the design studio. Even if the student projects cannot be taken at face value as examples of design anthropology, critical design, or even a mix of the two, they point towards potentials and challenges in combining design and research approaches in these fields, and in bringing design 'fiction' into productive friction with real-world issues and settings.

Critical design and anthropology share a preoccupation with distant, unfamiliar and alternative worlds – whether these worlds are fictional or non-fictional, speculative or real, and whether they are distant in time or in space. Both critical design and anthropology tend to work from a liminal position between different kinds of realities, using this position between the strange and the familiar to question what we take for granted and to speculate about alternatives (Dunne and Raby 2013; Marcus and Fisher 1986). Hence, we see potentials for developing a more speculative, critical, and materially engaged design anthropology inspired by critical design, along with a more situated and anthropologically inspired form of critical design. Such an approach does several things. First, it takes design anthropology beyond ethnography, 'user studies', participatory design and applied anthropology in the direction of a more critical material engagement with potentials and alternatives. Second, it moves speculative design beyond the production of critical objects serving as conversation pieces for intellectual debates in showrooms (or one-off encounters with stakeholders), towards a more situated engagement with mundane practices of future-making in which critique is not intrinsic to the design object, but unfolds through encounters within particular contexts. Last, it explores how speculative practices and products of design may graft onto, and engage with, situated mundane practices of everyday life in order to provoke reflections, challenge assumptions, change conversations and influence (future-making) practices in 'the field' as well as in design projects.

Notes

1   Whether trained as a sociologist, an anthropologist or a designer.
2   See Kjærsgaard (2011) and Kjærsgaard and Otto (2012) for more elaborate descriptions of this move from ethnography to design anthropology.

References

Anderson, R. J. (1994), 'Representations and Requirements: the Value of Ethnography in System Design', *Human-Computer Interaction*, 9: 151–82.

Auger, J. (2013), 'Speculative Design: Crafting the Speculation', *Digital Creativity*, 24 (1): 11–35.

Auger, J. (2014), 'Living With Robots: A Speculative Design Approach', *Journal of Human-Robot Interaction,* 3 (1): 20–42.

Bardzell, J. and Bardzell, S. (2013), 'What is Critical about Critical Design?', in *Proceedings of the Conference on Human Factors in Computing Systems*, 3297–306, New York: ACM Press.

Bardzell, J., Bardzell, S. and Stolterman, E. (2014), 'Reading Critical Designs: Supporting Reasoned Interpretations of Critical Design', in *Proceedings of the Conference on Human Factors in Computing Systems*, 1951–60, New York: ACM Press.

Bardzell, S., Bardzell, J., Forlizzi, J., Zimmerman, J. and Antanitis, J. (2012), 'Critical Design and Critical Theory: the Challenge of Designing for Provocation', in *Proceedings of Designing Interactive Systems Conference*, 288–97, New York: ACM Press.

Bell, G., Blythe, M. and Sengers, P. (2005), 'Making by Making Strange: Defamiliarization and the Design of Domestic Technologies', *ACM Transactions on Computer–Human Interaction*, 12 (2): 149–73.

Bell, G. and Dourish, P. (2007), 'Yesterday's Tomorrows: Notes on Ubiquitous Computing's Dominant Vision', *Personal and Ubiquitous Computing*, 11 (2): 133–43.

Binder, T., De Michelis, G., Ehn, P., Jacucci, G., Linde, P. and Wagner, I. (2011), *Design Things,* Cambridge, MA: MIT Press.

Blomberg, J., Burrell, M. and Guest, G. (2003), 'An Ethnographic Approach to Design', in J. A. Jacko and A. Sears (eds.), *The Human-Computer Interaction Handbook: Fundamentals, Evolving Technologies and Emerging Applications*, 964–86, Mahwah, NJ: Lawrence Erlbaum Associates.

Boer, L. and Donovan, J. (2012), 'Prototypes for Participatory Innovation', in *Proceedings of Designing Interactive Systems Conference,* 388–97, New York: ACM Press.

Bowen, S. (2008), 'Getting it Right: Lessons Learned in Applying a Critical Artefact Approach', in *Undisciplined! Design Research Society Conference 2008 (DRS'08)*.

Button, G. (2000), 'The Ethnographic Tradition and Design', *Design Studies*, 21 (4): 319–32.

Buur, J., Binder, T. and Brandt, E. (2000), 'Taking Video Beyond "Hard Data" in User-Centred Design', in *Proceedings of the Participatory Design Conference*, 21–9, New York: ACM Press.

Buur, J. and Sitorus, L. (2007), 'Ethnography as Design Provocation', in *Proceedings of the Ethnographic Praxis in Industry Conference*, 146–57.

Clark, B. (2007), *Design as Socio-Political Navigation: A Performative Framework for Action-Oriented Design*, PhD dissertation, University of Southern Denmark.

Dourish, P. (2006), 'Implications for Design', in *Proceedings of the SIGCHI Conference on Human Factors in Computing Systems*, 541–50, New York: ACM Press.

Dourish, P. (2007), 'Responsibilities and Implications: Further Thoughts on Ethnography and Design', in *Proceedings of the Conference on Designing for User Experience*, 2–16.

Dunne, A. and Raby, F. (2001), *Design Noir: The Secret Life of Electronic Objects*, London and Basel: Birkhäuser Verlag/August Media.

Dunne, A. and Raby, F. (2013), *Speculative Everything: Design, Fiction, and Social Dreaming,* Cambridge, MA: MIT Press.

Gunn, W. and Donovan, J. (eds.) (2012), *Design and Anthropology*, Farnham: Ashgate.

Gunn, W., Otto, T. and Smith, R. C. (eds.) (2013), *Design Anthropology: Theory and Practice*, London and New York: Bloomsbury.

Halse, J. (2008), *Design Anthropology: Borderline Experiments with Participation, Performance and Situated Intervention*, PhD dissertation, IT University Copenhagen.

Halse, J., Brandt, E., Clark, B. and Binder, T. (eds.) (2010), *Rehearsing the Future*, Copenhagen: Danish Design School Press.

Heath, C. and Luff, P. (2000), 'Technology and Social Action', in C. Heath and P. Luff (eds.), *Technology in Action*, 1–45, Cambridge: Cambridge University Press.

Hunt, J. (2011), 'Prototyping the Social: Temporality and Speculative Futures at the Intersection of Design and Culture', in A. J. Clarke (ed.), *Design Anthropology: Object Culture in the 21st Century,* 33–44, Vienna and New York: Springer.

Ingold, T. and Hallam, E. (eds.) (2007), *Creativity and Cultural Improvisation*, Oxford: Berg.

Kjærsgaard, M. G. (2011), *Between the Actual and the Potential: The Challenges of Design Anthropology*, PhD dissertation, Faculty of Arts, Aarhus University.

Kjærsgaard, M. G. and Otto, T. (2012), 'Anthropological Fieldwork and Designing Potentials', in W. Gunn and J. Donovan (eds.), *Design and Anthropology*, 177–91, Farnham: Ashgate.

Kjærsgaard, M. G. and Smith, R. C. (2014), 'Valuable Connections: Design Anthropology and Co-Creation in Digital Innovation', in *Proceedings of the Ethnographic Praxis in Industry Conference*, 267–81.

Koskinen, I., Zimmerman, J., Binder, T., Redström, J. and Wensveen, S. (2011), *Design Research Through Practice: From the Lab, Field and Showroom*, Waltham, MA: Morgan Kaufmann/Elsevier.

Lindley, J., Sharma, D. and Potts, R. (2014), 'Anticipatory Ethnography: Design Fiction as an Input to Design Ethnography', in *Proceedings of the Ethnographic Praxis in Industry Conference*, 237–53.

Marcus, G. E. and Fisher, M. M. J. (1986), *Anthropology as Cultural Critique: an Experimental Moment in the Human Sciences*, Chicago: University of Chicago Press.

Markussen, T. and Knutz, E. (2013), 'The Poetics of Design Fiction', in *Proceedings of the International Conference on Designing Pleasurable Products and Interfaces*, 231–40, New York: ACM.

Mogensen, P. (1992), 'Towards a Provotyping Approach in Systems Development', *Scandinavian Journal of Information Systems,* 4 (1): 31–53.

Otto, T. and Smith, R. C. (2013), 'Design Anthropology: A Distinct Style of Knowing', in W. Gunn, T. Otto and R. C. Smith (eds.), *Design Anthropology: Theory and Practice*, 1–29, London and New York: Bloomsbury.

Pierce, J., Sengers, P., Hirsch, T., Jenkins, T., Gaver, W. and DiSalvo, C. (2015), 'Expanding and Refining Design and Criticality in HCI', in *Proceedings of the Conference on Human Factors in Computing Systems*, 2083–92, New York: ACM.

Smith, R. C. (2013). *Designing Digital Cultural Futures: Design Anthropological Sites of Transformation*, PhD dissertation, Faculty of Arts, Aarhus University.

Smith, R. C. and Kjærsgaard, M. G. (2015), 'Design Anthropology in Participatory Design', *Interaction Design and Architecture(s) Journal*, 26: 73–80.

Suchman, L. A. (1987), *Plans and Situated Actions: The Problem of Human-Machine Communication*, Cambridge: Cambridge University Press.

Suchman, L., Trigg, R. and Blomberg, J. (2002), 'Working Artefacts: Ethnomethods of the Prototype', *The British Journal of Sociology*, 53 (2): 163–79.

Tsing, A. L. (2005), *Friction: An Ethnography of Global Connection,* Princeton, NJ: Princeton University Press.

Watts, L. (2008), 'The Future is Boring: Stories from the Landscapes of the Mobile Telecoms Industry', *The 21st Century Society: Journal of the Academy of Social Sciences,* 3 (2): 187–98.

15 Things as Co-Ethnographers: Implications of a Thing Perspective for Design and Anthropology

ELISA GIACCARDI, CHRIS SPEED, NAZLI CILA AND
MELISSA L. CALDWELL

As humans, we have complex and intertwined relationships with the objects around us. We shape objects; and objects shape and transform our practices and us in return. Acknowledging this ongoing interaction among people and objects calls for approaches in both design and anthropology that give both parties an equal role.

In the current design research agenda however, humans take a central place in methodology with the tools and methods of user-centred design (Greenbaum and Kyng 1991) and participatory design (Schuler and Namioka 1993).[1] This focus on the human is essential for investigating the subjective experience of everyday practice, but assumes that possibilities for creativity and innovation are bounded only by human imagination and capabilities. In this arrangement, the relationship between humans and objects is unidirectional: humans are actants that 'make' objects with a clear encoded function.

But what happens if we shift the focus to objects that break down, get dirty, contest their original function and even begin to perform autonomously? What if we try to understand the world from the perspective of a 'thing' that is situated within relationships with other entities and that has the potential to influence the existence of those other entities? For instance, what would the world look like from the perspective of a kettle, and how might a kettle inspire the existence of other entities? What kind of anthropological insights and design opportunities would this approach provide?

Our argument in this chapter is that a thing perspective can bring unique insights about the relationships between objects and human practices, and ultimately present new ways of framing and solving problems collaboratively with things, which have different skills and purposes from humans.[2]

Drawing from materials gathered during the Thing Tank research project, a collaborative platform for design inquiry in the Internet of Things, this chapter examines the potential that a thing perspective holds for design and anthropology, and for design anthropology specifically, as it challenges anthropocentric assumptions about the world and opens up new ways of understanding objects, people and use practices.

In particular, the chapter is concerned with what a methodological and analytical focus on things as actants, and perhaps even social actors, may reveal about the types of social relations and power dynamics that inhere between things, and between things and people. Based on these considerations, we argue that things may serve as co-ethnographers. Equipped with software and sensors, they can have access to fields, data and perspectives that we, as human ethnographers, do not, and therefore may help us 'see' what was previously invisible to humans.

Thing Tank as Critical Inquiry in the Internet of Things

Thing Tank is an Internet of Things[3] (IoT) research project that uses a combination of field studies, object instrumentation and machine learning to 'listen' to what things have to tell us about their use, reuse and deviant repurposing. It uses this data to inspire idea generation, fabrication, rapid prototyping and business development generation.[4]

In the past, many Internet of Things projects have used the network connection of physical objects to identify cost saving and process efficiencies (e.g. vehicle manufacturers), to track goods within large networks (e.g. logistics companies), or to monitor the health and safety of systems (e.g. aircraft manufacturers) within a streamlined process of production. But as objects connected to the Internet become more common and able to collect massive amounts of data, they may begin to reveal patterns that were previously invisible to humans, and contest what we usually take for granted.

Within a user-centred design approach, the role of objects is usually to support people to imagine, discuss and shape future practices at project time (Donovan and Gunn 2012). By extension, design becomes a kind of stabilizing process through which future practice(s) are imagined and realized (ibid.: 122). Instead, in Thing Tank we take a design orientation according to which we consider every situation of use as a potential design situation. We approach the Internet of Things as an infrastructure that has the potential to support ways of understanding and designing that take place *after*, *with* and *beyond* the design work at project time (Giaccardi 2005; Ehn 2008; Binder et al. 2011; Redström 2012).

The Thing Tank approach requires anthropological engagement.[5] It assumes that one will 'spend time' with objects and 'work together with' them in order to elict and manifest forms of practice they partake in, which may have emerged 'after design'. As argued by Gunn and Donovan (2012), engagement in design approaches sensitive to anthropological concerns requires developing capacities to offer people different ways of understanding what they know and do. These different ways of understanding allow for reframing and reconfiguring social and material relations, and are inherently performative and transformative. By 'listening' to objects for an extended period of time, and reflecting on what we usually take for granted, we open up and articulate design spaces that were previously inconceivable. To understand the humans, we are asking the 'thing'.

In this chapter, we reflect on the Thing Tank pilot study to develop a conceptual framing about the role that things may play as co-ethnographers in both design and anthropology. As co-ethnographers, things contribute a different perspective and unique insights on human practices that enhance, complicate and perhaps even challenge those of human ethnographers.

Rethinking Practice From a Material Objects' Perspective

By suggesting an ontological symmetry between people and things, where objects too form networks, communicate and even perform tasks (Kuijer and Giaccardi 2015), Thing Tank troubles distinctions between subjects and objects (Law 1991), and between ideality and materiality (Engeström and Blackler 2005). These ontological reworkings are especially relevant for the emerging field of networked objects that belong to the Internet of Things, since these objects acquire perspective and agency through the data they collect, the stories they reveal, and the interventions they make in the lives of the people that use them (e.g. McVeigh-Schultz et al. 2012). But because the focus of IoT research has, to date, been exclusively human-centred, so that designed products and services are meant to answer the needs of people only, little attention has been given to how objects and their users are engaged in a 'dialogue' of mutual interaction that might produce new relationships and value. These were the themes that inspired the Thing Tank project.

Focusing on everyday home practices, the Thing Tank pilot study selected three mundane objects: a kettle, a fridge and a cup. Because these objects are often in proximity, it was thought that together they would reveal insights not just about themselves but also about their relationships with each other – that is, about unexpected horizontal arrangements of various practices. Data were collected through interviews and information gathered by intelligent cameras (Autographers) that were attached to three key material objects in the home (kettle, cup and refrigerator), as well as to four individuals who participated in home-based activities (see Figure 15.1).

Data collected from the Autographers (small cameras equipped with sensors and worn on a neck strap or clipped to an object) provided detailed information about the use patterns of particular objects and their trajectories throughout space and time, as well as data on parallel activities and objects. What was especially important was that the Autographers were intended to capture the experiences of objects from the perspective of those objects. As a form of 'intelligent' technology, Autographers automatically take pictures and capture data via five sensors (e.g. accelerometer to determine movement, colour sensor, magnetometer, thermometer and PIR proximity sensor). Autographers lack shutter buttons, and photographs are taken automatically by the camera, rather than according to deliberate choices or intervention by the photographer. As such, these images were not positioned from the perspective of the researcher and instead captured events and vantage points that might have evaded the researcher. The Autographers collected 3000+ photographs, which were then combined in a timeline (see Figure 15.2).

Figure 15.1 Autographers attached to a kettle and a cup © Connected Everyday Lab, Delft University of Technology

Whereas in-depth interviews conducted with the four participants documented how they described and subjectively valued their activities, the Autographers' data revealed additional objects that were related to those activities, besides the key objects initially selected: other dishes, cutlery, towels, papers and pet food, among many other things. The Autographers' data illuminated unexpected and otherwise

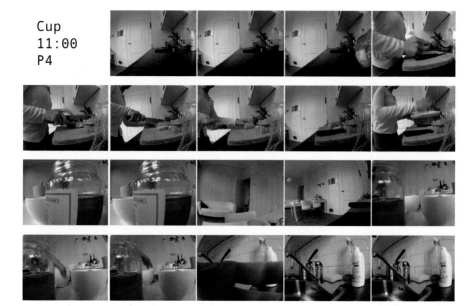

Cup
11:00
P4

Figure 15.2 Format of the photographs taken by Autographers (from a cup's perspective) © Connected Everyday Lab, Delft University of Technology.

invisible relationships among objects – that is, the bundles or ecosystems inhabited horizontally by objects. Such data about the wider ecosystems of objects and practices are productive for creating a topographic landscape of the environment in which objects as 'things' reside and the relationalities that exist between these things and their 'worlds' – a perspective that would have been difficult to elicit through traditional observations and interviews alone (see Figure 15.2).

Insights About the Implications of a Thing Perspective

The pilot study revealed a number of intriguing insights, both about the implications of a thing perspective and about the methods used to capture this approach. For instance, the preliminary data provided details for mapping out the landscapes that are occupied by things and the ways in which things – and the three key objects in particular (kettle, fridge and cup) – inhabit and move through those spaces. As the data showed, the things that inhabited our participants' kitchens and dining rooms demonstrated different degrees of dynamism and emplacement. There are differences between things that move and those that stay in one place or remain within a narrowly defined area of space. Over the course of an ordinary day, numerous things moved into and out of the spaces under observation: cups, fresh produce, plastic bags, cutlery, kitchen towels, particular items of clothing. Things travelled with participants from their kitchens and into other home spaces (dining rooms, bedrooms) and then out of their homes into cars and on to work. These travels brought things into contact with other things – cars, radios, telephones, computers, books, papers, cigarettes, among others – and even into other settings such as kitchens in workplaces. As a result, these things moved through networks of spaces, times and relationships, thereby not only occupying multiple ecosystems but also being the connector between these ecosystems.

Yet not all things move. As the data also revealed, some things remained in place, or within a confined area: refrigerators, kettles that were plugged into walls, sinks and food items remained within a narrow band of movement. While this lack of movement suggests stasis that is only a spatial stasis as those same objects are subject to movement through time. There is thus a paradoxical quality to things: while they may be 'substances-in-becoming' filled with potentialities (Ingold 2013: 31), they are also entities with distinct life cycles and potential finalities, even as those post-use phases may have life cycles of their own (Evans, Campbell and Murcott 2013). A simple teacup is simultaneously a thing with a predefined use that is actualized in a moment of praxis (i.e., when it is used as a vessel for tea or another beverage) and a thing that has possibilities for other practices and futures beyond those for which it was intended, such as when it is turned into a pencil cup, a measuring cup, or a prop to hold open a window. Or even when, as in the case of one of our participants, the cup is carried around for companionship, like a pet. At the same time, as a teacup moves through its own unique life cycle, its nature, identity and value may change: from useful object to waste to recycled object and so on. Thus, paying attention to movement illuminates distinctions between things that are located and things that are locational. They exist in relationships with one another, but they also inhabit separate, albeit occasionally overlapping, communities of things and practices, a distinction that invites questions about the boundaries and internal dimensions of things, ecosystems and the webs of relationality in which they are embedded.

The spatial parameters of the communities in which these things exist and circulate are further defined by temporal dimensions. While the things under view in the pilot study can be located in discrete temporal moments – for instance, the particular moments in which their existence and movements are captured discursively, visually, or with other sensors – these things also enjoy their own, unique temporal rhythms. For instance, while a cup, kettle, refrigerator, boiling water, coffee and sugar may exist at the same moment, they are moving through time in different ways, such that the cup warms up, the boiling water cools down and the coffee and sugar become transformed into different states. In addition, even as they interact with one another, at the same time, individual things do not have the same experience of time. A revealing finding was that while people were waiting for water to boil in the kettle and for their tea or coffee to be ready, they engaged in other activities: washing dishes, reading the paper, making a telephone call (see Figure 15.3). Hence even as things occupy time and take up time, they also make time. In some cases, things fill time, and in other cases they create empty time that needs to be filled by others, as with participants finding other tasks to complete while they waited.

Figure 15.3 Things done while waiting for the water to boil (from a kettle's perspective) © Connected Everyday Lab, Delft University of Technology

More than providing evidence of contemporary practices of simultaneity, or multitasking, the different temporalities that unite and separate things from one another and from their human partners present opportunities to consider what it is about the nature of things that enables them to create particular temporalities or make particular temporalities apparent or even visible. More generally, the effects of things' influence on time raise questions about the nature of filled time versus empty time. Paying attention to the ways in which both people and things create, fill and experience time in very different ways offers new insights for thinking about the extent to which temporal structures are products of human activity or may exist outside an exclusively human-centric framework (Munn 1992). Similarly, although 'empty' time might feel like anxiety, boredom, or another affective response from the perspective of a person (see Löfgren and Ehn 2010), considering the experience of time from the perspective of an inanimate thing troubles phenomenological approaches centred on the human only. A thing perspective to time invites us to reconsider the relationships between human and non-human partners and how each provokes the other to respond to these relationships. When participants elect to read a book or wash dishes while they are waiting for their tea to steep, it seems as if it is the inanimate thing that is controlling the relationship and compelling the human to respond.

Ultimately these are concerns with the nature of agency within things (Barad 2003; Bennett 2010; Latour 1988; 1992; Murphy 2013). If we take seriously the idea that things are actants, an idea that is supported by preliminary data from this pilot study, this shifts our understandings of how things move through time and space. While things may be mobile in the sense that they can be moved as the consequence of action by another, either human or non-human, a thing perspective also reveals that things possess qualities of motility and can move on their own, thereby changing the states, spaces and times of their own existence and of other entities with which they come into contact. As such, these qualities of motility and activity provoke intriguing questions about the nature of the agency that inheres in them. In these social relationships among things, where is power located? In a model of social action informed by a thing perspective, does power exist as a pulsing web of shifting relationalities (Foucault 1990), or is it a relationality of directed force and response (Gramsci 1994; Scott 1986)? Can agency be external, or is it always internal to the thing itself? And lastly, how do we need to rethink the troubling issue of motivation and desire that are presumed to inhere in human actions? How does a thing perspective on agency and effect open up spaces for rethinking not just how and where potentialities emerge, but whether there are dynamics of both spontaneity and purposefulness outside a subjective human experience?

Beyond these ethnographic and theoretical implications, the pilot study data also pointed to intriguing and challenging issues about the methods used to capture a thing perspective. For instance, Autographers were useful for capturing moments that were not mentioned by respondents during the interviews or in their diaries but were key moments in the daily routines of objects. Because many practices and encounters in everyday life are so mundane and taken for granted as to be unremarkable and invisible (Rosaldo 1993), they are often outside the scope of awareness of participants. Yet things that are unremarkable are actually made so through a 'politics of mereness' (Herzfeld 2005: 132) that disguises their meaningfulness within multiple relationalities and practices (Rosaldo 1993). Nothingness is, however, full of something (Löfgren and Ehn 2010; Ritzer 2003). Because Autographers automatically take pictures without input from the photographer, and are thus presumed to be outside the cultural values and perspectives of the observer, they capture images that might otherwise seem unremarkable and unmeaningful to a researcher or the participant. Thus, they are crucial for filling in the gaps and revealing to humans unexpected meaningful moments. A good example of these unmarked moments came in the series of photographs that showed participants engaged in multiple activities simultaneously (e.g. talking on the phone while preparing food), a detail that was not captured in the interviews.

While specific details about the significance of these activities and co-occurrence of these events are not available, Autographer data revealed events that were not expected and that could be investigated further. In other instances, the Autographer data revealed contradictions between participants' self-reporting in interviews and diaries and the captured images, such as the case of a participant who did not identify any other residents in the home yet the pictures showed pet food. In another case, the respondent framed answers only in terms of a single person, but images showed her interacting with another person and sharing a meal with that other person. Thus there were multiple persons and multiple things interacting simultaneously that were not otherwise documented and had been downplayed or forgotten by the participant.

Such types of data captured, in this case, by photographic equipment that is not dependent on the choices made by the photographer raise intriguing questions for visual anthropology, design anthropology, and other fields both about when and where 'meaningful' events and practices occur, and the role of humans and non-human things in demarcating social worlds and the relationships within those worlds.[6] A thing perspective opens up possibilities for understanding the limits of human action on time and space and the ways in which non-human things are directly informing and creating the everyday realities in which people live. For both anthropology and design, these are concerns that are simultaneously methodological, theoretical, ethnographic and even ethical.

Considering Things as Co-Ethnographers

According to Binder et al. (2011), the creation of a design space is the creation of a 'field work' that does not exist but is possible. Intended as a possibility, this speculative space emerges out of the ongoing interaction among participants in design. The Thing Tank pilot study suggests that things may have access to fields, data and 'perspectives' that we, as humans, do not. Considering things as co-ethnographers presents additional opportunities for design anthropological approaches concerned with opening up perspectives on the emergent (Smith and Otto, this volume), as things can help us 'see' what is not immediately apparent in human practices.

Of particular concern to anthropology is the use of ethnographic approaches to investigate the motivations, beliefs and values that inform people's practices and the objects they use in these practices, especially in terms of understanding discrepancies between reported and actual practice. The forte of ethnography is contextualization, holistic explanation and cultural interpretation through cross-cultural comparison and the development of theoretical concepts (Otto and Smith 2013). Data gathered through ethnographic research can help identify gaps and contradictions, and ultimately initiate critical inquiry into issues of generality and specificity, routine patterns and deviations from norms. However, as advocated by Kjærsgaard and Otto: 'the role of fieldwork and anthropology within design cannot simply be to provide designers with descriptions of users and use practices as in the tradition of ethnomethodologically informed design; nor can it simply be to supply methods and techniques for enrolling users and their knowledge directly within the design process as in the tradition of participatory design' (2012: 179).

A thing perspective challenges anthropocentric assumptions about the world and opens up new ways of understanding objects, people and use practices. Paying attention to the immanent dynamism inherent in things invites intriguing questions about how objects, practices and other things exist in the world and the qualities of their agentive capacities. Like humans, objects, practices and things never exist in a vacuum but are always situated in particular temporal and spatial contexts. As such, things themselves are positional and relational, and their uses, values and meanings may change significantly from context to context (Appadurai 1986; Herrmann 1997; Kopytoff 1986). On the other hand, objects, practices and things may themselves have their own temporal and spatial systems and rhythms that, in turn, affect and shape other elements in the world around them (Bachelard 1994; Amato 2013). Things are thoroughly imbricated within ecosystems that are populated by other things, both human and non-human, and both human-produced and non-human-produced. These insights about the mutually constituting life-worlds of things are helpful for thinking through the preliminary data from our pilot study, especially as possibilities for making sense of different perspectives about the nature and positionality of things.

Attributing agency to objects is not a new concept. Actor network theorists discuss the ontological symmetry of humans and non-humans, in which material forms take on the characteristics of humans: they judge, form networks, speak and work performatively (Engeström and Blackler, 2005). Developmental psychology has demonstrated that people ascribe intentionality and consciousness to inanimate things (Piaget, 1959), and the psychodynamic tradition in psychoanalysis points out striking similarities in how people relate to the animate and the inanimate (Turkle 2011). More recently, object-oriented philosophy posits that things do not exist just for us (Bogost 2012). They can be many and various (Bryant 2011), but no matter their size, scale, or order, they enjoy equal being (Harman 2009). And certainly anthropologists concerned with materialities have suggested that objects are dynamic and emergent entities that contain their own life forces, energies and histories (e.g. Appadurai 1986; Ingold 2013; Mauss 1990).

A thing perspective offers design nuanced ways of thinking about and intervening in agency and social arrangements, most notably those between producer and produced, and between subject and object, such that there is an understanding that these are never fully discrete roles or nodes, but rather emergent states of being (Anusas and Ingold 2013). Enlisting things as co-ethnographers provides unique insights about the temporality, movement and relationships of objects, and thus a new perspective to think about human practice. Imagining the time perception of objects (e.g. what would empty or filled time look like from the perspective of an inanimate thing? what are the multiple routines and rhythms that exist between and across the things that are in relationships with one another?) or speculating about how their social dynamics (e.g. how does the nature of the relationships change when an object moves among different users or the same user moves among different objects from the same category?) can bring novel insights about the role of objects in human practices, and thus open up design opportunities that we may not be able to foresee with traditional methods of user research.[7]

In the 'designerly' tradition (Cross 2007), a thing perspective aims to offer a possible, arguably more desirable, design alternative that is based on a fundamentally different relationship between humans and non-humans. In particular, it harbours different ideas about expertise and skills and redistributes ideation, design and control between professional design and everyday use practices. The patterns revealed through a thing perspective on human practices emerge at the intersection of the data and trajectories that things give access to and the theoretically informed analysis that humans bring to it. This is not done simply to provide anthropologists with different and unique information about use practices, or to offer designers inspiration for creative solutions. The aim of a thing perspective is fundamentally to enable the exploration of practices and objects of design that are not constituted yet but emerge in response to non-human ethnographies, or rather 'correspond' (Gatt and Ingold 2013) to their ongoing analysis.

For design anthropology, a thing perspective does not just expose and describe forms of practice that are difficult to express in terms of just design or use, but it reveals 'kinds of things' and 'states of being' as well (Redström 2012: 95). As opposed to a human-centred perspective, a thing perspective brings unique insights about the relationships between objects and human practices, and ultimately presents new ways of framing and solving problems collaboratively with 'things', which have skills and purposes different from those of humans.

Acknowledgements

The authors would like to thank Neil Rubens and Fionn Tynan-O'Mahony for their invaluable contributions to Thing Tank. Sincere gratitude also goes to the editors and to the reviewers of this text for helping the authors crafting this contribution with tireless dedication. The Thing Tank project was originally funded by the MIT Skoltech Initiative (2014–2015).

Notes

1. Cf. also the ISO standard Human-Centred Design for Interactive Systems (ISO 9241–210, 2010): http://www.iso.org/iso/catalogue_detail.htm?csnumber=52075
2. In this text, we use the term 'object' as a synonym for material artefact. We use instead the term 'thing' to emphasize the situated relationships of the object with other entities and its potential to influence the existence of those other entities. In that sense, equipped with software and sensors and connected to online databases, a fridge for example is unavoidably a 'thing': not just an object in its straight materiality, but a gathering of data, connections and interactions.
3. The phrase Internet of Things is attributed to the Auto-ID research group at MIT in 1999 (Ashton 2009) and refers to the emerging technical system of objects and materials that are becoming connected to the Internet. The specific reference to 'things' refers to the principle that physical objects will be part of this extended Internet, each with its own associated data cloud concerning where the object has been and how it has been used.
4. Thing Tank (http://www.thingtank.org/) operates as an international research platform coordinated by Delft University of Technology in collaboration with the Centre for Design Informatics, University of Edinburgh. The project was originally funded by the MIT Skoltech Initiative (2014–15).
5. The approach also requires sensitivity to the role of machine learning. The discussion, however, is beyond the scope of this chapter. For insights on the integration of ethnographic data and machine learning data, see Cila et al. (2015a).
6. A further layer to the Thing Tank study that extends the ability to capture data that is not dependent on a human, is the quantitative data that is captured through the sensors that record the use of the kettle, cup and fridge. Although the study did not go into depth using Machine Learning (ML) to interrogate the quantitative data captured from the accelerometers, magnetometers and proximity sensors, the use of ML offers a further method of enquiry with which to identify patterns that are beyond the 'vision' of the human.
7. On the development of thing-centred design methods see Giaccardi et al. (2016) on 'thing ethnography' and Cila et al. (2015b) on 'object personas'.

References

Amato, J. A. (2013), *Surfaces: A History*, Berkeley: University of California Press.

Anusas, M. and Ingold, T. (2013), 'Designing Environmental Relations: From Opacity to Textility', *Design Issues*, 29 (4): 58–69.

Appadurai, A. (1986), 'Introduction: Commodities and the Politics of Value', in A. Appadurai (ed.), *The Social Life of Things: Commodities in Cultural Perspective*, 3–63, Cambridge: Cambridge University Press.

Ashton, K. (2009), 'That "Internet of Things" Thing', *RFID Journal*: 22 June, December, 2011, http://www. rfidjournal.com/article/view/4986 (accessed 5 January 2016).

Bachelard, G. (1994), *The Poetics of Space*, Boston: Beacon Press.

Barad, K. (2003), 'Posthumanist Performativity: Toward an Understanding of How Matter Comes to Matter', *Signs: Journal of Women in Culture and Society*, 28 (3): 801–31.

Bennett, J. (2010), *Vibrant Matter: A Political Ecology of Things*. Durham, NC: Duke University Press.

Binder, T., De Michelis, G., Ehn, P., Jacucci, G., Linde, P. and Wagner, I. (2011), *Design Things*, Cambridge, MA: MIT Press.

Bogost, I. (2012), *Alien Phenomenology, or, What It's Like to Be a Thing,* Minneapolis, MN: University of Minnesota Press.

Bryant, L. R. (2011), *The Democracy of Objects*, Ann Arbor: Open Humanities Press.

Cila, N., Giaccardi, E., Caldwell, M., Tynan-O'Mahony, F., Speed, C. and Rubens, N. (2015a), 'Listening to an Everyday Kettle: How Can the Data Objects Collect Be Useful for Design Research?', in *Proceedings of the Participatory Innovation Conference*, 500–6.

Cila, N., Giaccardi, E., Tynan-O'Mahony, F., Speed, C. and Caldwell, M. (2015b), 'Thing-Centered Narratives: A Study of Object Personas', paper presented at *Seminar 3: Collaborative Formations of Issues*, The Research Network for Design Anthropology, January 22–23, Aarhus, Denmark.

Cross, N. (2007), *Designerly Ways of Knowing*, Basel: Birkhäuser.

Donovan, J. and Gunn, W. (2012), 'Moving from Objects to Possibilities', in W. Gunn and J. Donovan (eds.), *Design and Anthropology*, 121–34, Farnham: Ashgate.

Ehn, P. (2008), 'Participation in Design Things', in *Proceedings of the Tenth Anniversary Conference on Participatory Design*, 92–101.

Engeström, Y. and Blackler, F. (2005), 'On the Life of the Object', *Organization*, 12 (3): 307–30.

Evans, D., Campbell, H. and Murcott, A. (eds.) (2013), *Waste Matters: New Perspectives on Food and Society*, Malden, MA: Wiley-Blackwell/The Sociological Review.

Foucault, M. (1990), *The History of Sexuality*, New York: Vintage Books.

Gatt, C. and Ingold, T. (2013), 'From Description to Correspondence: Anthropology in Real Time', in W. Gunn, T. Otto and R. C. Smith (eds.), *Design Anthropology: Theory and Practice*, 139–58, London and New York: Bloomsbury.

Giaccardi, E. (2005), 'Metadesign as an Emergent Design Culture', *Leonardo*, 8 (4): 342–9.

Giaccardi, E., Cila, N., Speed, C. and Caldwell, M. (2016), 'Thing Ethnography: Doing Design Research with Non-Humans', in *Proceedings of the Conference on Designing Interactive Systems* (in press).

Gramsci, A. (1994), *Letters from Prison*, New York: Columbia University Press.

Greenbaum, J. and Kyng, M. (1991), *Design at Work: Cooperative Design of Computer Systems*, Hillsdale, NJ: Lawrence Erlbaum Associates.

Gunn, W. and Donovan, J. (2012), 'Design Anthropology: An Introduction', in W. Gunn and J. Donovan (eds.), *Design and Anthropology*, 1–16, Farnham: Ashgate.

Harman, G. (2009), *Prince of Networks: Bruno Latour and Metaphysics*, Prahran: Re.press.

Herrmann, G. (1997), 'Gift or Commodity: What Changes Hands in the U.S. Garage Sale?', *American Ethnologist*, 24 (4): 910–30.

Herzfeld, M. (2005), *Cultural Poetics: Social Intimacy in the Nation-State*, New York: Routledge.

Ingold, T. (2013), *Making: Anthropology, Archaeology, Art and Architecture*, London: Routledge.

Kjærsgaard, M. and Otto, T. (2012), 'Anthropological Fieldwork and Designing Potentials', in W. Gunn and J. Donovan (eds.), *Design and Anthropology*, 177–91, Farnham: Ashgate.

Kopytoff, I. (1986), 'The Cultural Biography of Things: Commoditization as Process', in A. Appadurai (ed.), *The Social Life of Things: Commodities in Cultural Perspective*, 64–91, Cambridge: Cambridge University Press.

Kuijer, L. and Giaccardi, E. (2015), 'Considering Artifacts as Co-performers', in Strengers, Y. and Maller, C. (eds.) *Animals, Automated Devices and Ecosystems: A Symposium on the Agencies of Dynamic Non-Humans in Theories of Practice*, October 9–10, Barcelona, Spain.

Latour, B. (1988), *Science in Action: How to Follow Scientists and Engineers through Society*, Cambridge, MA: Harvard University Press.

Latour, B. (1992), 'Where are the Missing Masses? The Sociology of a Few Mundane Artifacts', in W. Bijker and J. Law (eds.), *Shaping Technology/Building Society: Studies in Sociotechnical Change*, 225–8, Cambridge, MA: MIT Press.

Law, J. (1991), 'Introduction: Monsters, Machines and Sociotechnical Relations', in J. Law (ed.), *A Sociology of Monsters: Essays on Power, Technology and Domination*, London: Routledge.

Löfgren, O. and Ehn, P. (2010), *The Secret World of Doing Nothing*, Berkeley, CA: University of California Press.

Mauss, M. (1990), *The Gift: The Form and Reason for Exchange in Archaic Societies*, London: Routledge.

McVeigh-Schultz, J., Stein, J., Watson, J. and Fisher, S. (2012), 'Extending the Lifelog to Non-human Subjects: Ambient Storytelling for Human-Object Relationships', in *Proceedings of the ACM International Conference on Multimedia*, 1205–8, New York: ACM Press.

Munn, N. D. (1992), 'The Cultural Anthropology of Time: A Critical Essay', *Annual Review of Anthropology*, 21: 93–123.

Murphy, K. M. (2013), 'A Cultural Geometry: Designing Political Things in Sweden', *American Ethnologist,* 40 (1): 118–31.

Otto, T. and Smith, R. C. (2013), 'Design Anthropology: A Distinct Style of Knowing', in W. Gunn, T. Otto and R. C. Smith (eds.), *Design Anthropology: Theory and Practice*, 1–29, London and New York: Bloomsbury.

Piaget, J. (1959), *The Language and Thought of the Child,* London: Routledge and Kegan Paul.

Redström, J. (2012), 'Introduction: Defining Moments', in W. Gunn and J. Donovan (eds.), *Design and Anthropology*, 83–99, Farnham: Ashgate.

Ritzer, G. (2003), *The Globalization of Nothing*, Thousand Oaks, CA: Pine Forge Press.

Rosaldo, R. (1993), *Culture & Truth: The Remaking of Social Analysis*, Boston, MA: Beacon Press.

Schuler, D. and Namioka, A. (1993), *Participatory Design: Principles and Practices*, Hillsdale, NJ: Lawrence Erlbaum Associates.

Scott, J. C. (1986), *Weapons of the Weak: Everyday Forms of Peasant Resistance*, New Haven, CT: Yale University Press.

Turkle, S. (ed.) (2011), *Evocative Objects: Things We Think With*, Cambridge, MA: MIT Press.

16 Design Anthropology as Ontological Exploration and Inter-Species Engagement

TAU ULV LENSKJOLD AND SISSEL OLANDER[1]

In this chapter, we discuss the potential for a design anthropology that, while firmly grounded in a material-experimental practice, is also informed by, and explorative of, those ideas in contemporary anthropology that are related to what is commonly referred to as the ontological turn.

To detail this argument, we stage a discussion around an experimental design project carried out by one of the authors in which speculative prototypes were deployed at a care home in the Danish city of Elsinore. The purpose of this deployment was to experiment with, and possibly enable, new kinds of inter-species relations, in this case between the senior citizens of the care home and the wild birds in the surrounding area. The objective – to build and explore inter-species relations – along with the character and style of the experiment described here may seem foreign to the primarily human-centred field of design anthropology. However, a central concern in design anthropology is simultaneously to understand and reconfigure the very collectives that humans are continually both being formed by and giving form to. In this chapter we will show that material-speculative approaches that address non-humans are capable of generating questions-not-yet-posed that have relevance for contemporary design anthropology – questions that may expand the scope of this transdisciplinary field to such an extent that we may focus not only on the human capacity for change, but also on the capacity of others, including non-humans, to perform and configure both humans and the collectives of which humans form a part in ways that we are perhaps not yet capable of imagining.

We begin by briefly mapping some of the current positions in design anthropology in order to situate our approach in relation to them. This is followed by a condensed account of how we understand and are interested in the so-called ontological turn in anthropology. That will lead us to a presentation and analysis of the experimental project, which will fuel a discussion of the differences involved in attending ethnographically or experimentally to a series of other-than-human encounters.

Constructive Design Research in Design Anthropology

Although design anthropology is quite a young area of scholarship with many of its boundaries yet to be explored, some positions within this emerging field have already established themselves quite convincingly. These positions, for the most part, have placed human relations centre stage – whether examined through anthropological projects seeking to expand the tools and approaches of fieldwork, or through human-centred participatory design projects that aspire to integrate critical and reflexive traditions from the social sciences.

In their introduction to the publication *Design Anthropology: Theory and Practice* (Gunn, Otto and Smith 2013), Otto and Smith argue that design anthropology is coming of age as a distinct sub-discipline. Prompted by the challenges of our contemporary world, this new area of scholarship emphasizes how the production of knowledge in the present day must involve more than thinking and reasoning. Knowing in contemporary society cannot disregard practices of action that generate specific forms of knowledge (Otto and Smith 2013: 11). Otto and Smith argue for a possible new paradigm that accentuates the human capacity for change through interventionist fieldwork and design. Along the same lines, Gatt and Ingold (2013: 148) introduce the concept of correspondence to highlight the importance of the field encounter. What is produced during fieldwork, they argue, is of equal value to, if not greater than, what is produced after fieldwork. This fosters the idea of an 'anthropology by means of design': that is, an anthropology that is less concerned with ethnographic description and more with the field encounter. Reflecting on these attempts to forge a new design anthropology, Murphy and Marcus note that they provide a 'much needed rebalancing of the lopsided relationship' (2013: 253) 'with anthropology almost exclusively subordinated to the needs of design' (2013: 252).

While we thoroughly agree that the inventive recalibration of anthropology and design is an important step in the exploration of a hybrid design-anthropological stance, we also want to point to a different kind of imbalance lurking beneath. Murphy and Marcus outline an array of constitutive similarities between design and ethnography. Among other things, they note that *'design and ethnography are reflexive'* (emphasis in original), but importantly, 'that most designers do not count reflexivity among their core qualities' (2013: 259). This is perhaps true for design at large but, in our view, this take on design anthropology also masks what we perceive to be an important distinction between design and design research. Scholars in the field of design anthropology may need to reconsider how distinctions are made (or not) between design and design research; evidently these are highly interdependent yet not completely identical practices. When Murphy and Marcus claim that 'the most significant leverage point between design and *anthropology* is with *ethnography* itself, the complex mode of engagement that sits at anthropology's core' (emphasis added, 2013: 254), we will point to material-experimental modes of enquiry and to theoretical perspectives (e.g. of exploring inter-species relations) as equally significant leverage points between the two domains of design and anthropology. More specifically, we suggest that a symmetrical relation between, on the one hand, design *and* design research, and, on the other hand, anthropology *and* ethnography, will enable a richer exploration of a contemporary design anthropology. Such a move, we believe, has the potential to go beyond a skewed choice between the two supposed alternatives of a 'design by means of anthropology' or an 'anthropology by means of design'.

Our entry point into the field of design anthropology is that of constructive design research (Koskinen et al. 2011). Constructive design research, as we employ the term here, refers to research in which the work of constructing an object or a process becomes the main way of constructing knowledge (Koskinen et al. 2011). This kind of research presupposes in its very constitution an engagement that does not rely exclusively on the production of a text to render visible the object of research. The field of design anthropology, as it has emerged over the last decade, has appealed to constructive design researchers coming from traditions of participatory design. Focusing on design as a shared material and social process of future-making, this community of researchers, to which we ourselves belong, has paid special attention to certain branches of the constructivist social sciences such as science and technology studies, and actor-network theory. This has sparked an interest in complex issues over designed products and bounded objects (Lenskjold, Olander and Halse 2015; Lindström and Ståhl 2014; DiSalvo 2009; DiSalvo 2012). This work is sometimes presented as the work of staging and experimenting with design things (Ehn 2008; Binder et al. 2011).

Both within constructive design research and in the field of design anthropology, this movement has stimulated, we argue, an increased self-awareness among constructive design researchers. As concepts and ideas from the constructivist social sciences have merged with experimental approaches that explore inventive research practices, the speculative critical and epistemic potential inherent in design as material practice have been continuously elicited. The present authors consider ourselves a part of this push in constructive design research, and it is from this position that we, in this chapter, engage with a discussion that is currently taking place in a rather different corner of anthropology than the more classical landscape commonly associated with the field of design anthropology.

Design Anthropology and the Ontological Turn

The so-called turn to ontology in anthropology involves several different theoretical positions and methodological projects. This becomes evident, for example, as one explores a series of position papers made available online from a round-table discussion entitled 'The Politics of Ontology', held at the 2013 annual meeting of the American Anthropological Association. Here, a collection of prominent scholars debating under the umbrella of the ontological turn[2] (e.g. Holbraad, Pedersen and Viveiros de Castro 2014; Holbraad and Pedersen 2014; Kohn 2014; Jensen 2014) reflect on the political implications of employing ontology in the service of anthropology. Without pretending to be able to account for the many interesting nuances and idiosyncrasies of these discussions, let alone exhaust what is referred to when anthropologists talk of the ontological turn, we may say that the ontological turn is a critical response to traditional ideas of representation in anthropology. It refutes the idea that the anthropologist works as an interpreter of culture, or indeed, that the anthropologist, through the textual representation of cultural practices, is representing 'someone' or is speaking on someone's behalf. Anthropological 'ontographers' problematize the idea of the anthropologist as someone who is studying 'differing perspectives' on a given reality. Instead, they subscribe to ideas and concepts of multiple worlds or multiple ontologies, arguing that difference is the product of participation and existence in alternative, multiple realities. Ontology, Holbraad, Pedersen and Viveiros de Castro argue (2014), is not summoned to evoke essence, nor in an attempt simply to replace the concept of culture with something new. On the contrary, the anthropology of ontology, they state, is anthropology *as* ontology.

From a constructivist design research position, what is particularly compelling about this ontologically inclined project in anthropology is the explicit experimental ambition inherent in the venture. The ontological turn, Holbraad, Pedersen and Viveiros de Castro (2014) assert, is a technology of description designed in the optimistic, non-sceptical hope that the 'otherwise' can be made visible by experimenting with conceptual affordances. Elsewhere, Pedersen (2012) characterizes the turn to ontology as a sustained theoretical experiment. Neither a movement nor a school, it is rather, he contends, the ambition to devise a new analytical method which can enable anthropologists to make sense of their ethnographic material in experimental ways, in order to pose ethnographic questions anew. Appropriately, Pedersen (ibid.) and Holbraad (2009; 2012) call the practice of *doing* ontology 'ontography' – stressing its opposition to fixed theoretical frameworks in favour of producing new methodologies.

This position, which stresses ethnographic work as the practice of doing ontology, resembles a radical commitment to what we might call *research as eventuation* (Rheinberger 1997). The ethnographic engagement – the fieldwork and the writing up of the ethnographic account – is treated as an event with the potential to produce concepts and understandings that are not yet visible or known. There is no formula that can ensure a given outcome, only the possibility that a following experimental attempt may eventuate new insights. The intense focus on devising a new analytical method, combined with a certain reluctance or inability to subscribe to some generalized methods, is in some ways close to our own experience in conducting experimental design research. In our own practice we are always preoccupied with staging a workable set-up for conducting design experiments. This is a very practical and material process that involves a great deal of tinkering and feeling one's way, and questions, concepts and ideas that cannot be known in advance.

Attempting to Reopen the Category of the Human

While we share with ontologically inclined anthropologists an interest in questions that relate to the 'how' of doing research, we also share an interest in some of the themes that this particular area of anthropology is currently exploring. In the following account of how we have worked to explore and stage inter-species relations, we engage with a theme which has entered constructive design research primarily from science and technology studies and actor-network theory. Bruno Latour, through his sustained proposal for tracing and building relations between humans and non-humans, has popularized a kind of symmetrical approach (Latour 2005) which ascribes agency to other-than-humans. But whereas symmetrical approaches work to tease out how humans and non-humans relate and build networks, ontologically inclined anthropologists strive to reopen and rearticulate the culture-nature and human-non-human categories from within, so to speak. Ontological anthropologists, as Holbraad, Pedersen and Viveiros de Castro point out, are less interested in differences between things than in those within them. They strive to reach past assumptions and taken-for-granted ideas about the real, as they attempt to *pass through* what they study, to render ethnographically manifest shapes and forces that offer access to 'the dark side of things' (2014), understood as that which is deemed invisible or ungraspable. For example, Eduardo Kohn (2013) recently set out to explore what may seem both very strange and paradoxical, namely the phenomenon of 'how forests think'. Kohn's project, he explains (2013), is not about how the Runa people of Amazonian Ecuador think forests think, which would perhaps be a classical human-centred anthropological project. What Kohn (2014) tries to do is rather to instigate an engagement with Runa thinking and its relation to the thinking forest in a way that enables this hybrid – a Runa way of thinking and the thinking forest – to think *itself,* through us.[3] What colonizes human thinking, Kohn argues, is language, precisely because language is a form of thinking specific to humans. In response, Kohn proposes an ontological engagement in which the way that humans represent non-humans, for example jaguars, and how jaguars represent humans are understood as integral parts of a single, yet open-ended story (Kohn 2013: 9).

Our own experiment with staging inter-species relations between the residents at the care home and doves in many ways pursues the same ambition. The becoming together of seniors and urban animals, as we shall see, is indeed an open-ended story, although perhaps not a single one. On the one hand it is intentionally forged by the design research team, and on the other, it remains a story that is unpredictable and never fully controlled. But for us, as constructive design researchers, there is a significant difference, a difference from within, between attending *ethnographically* to a series of other-than-human encounters (Kohn 2013) and instead, as we propose, attending *experimentally* to a series of other-than-human encounters. As Latour has pointed out, there is a difference between being experienced and being an experimenter: namely, the difference between incorporation and *excorporation* (Latour

1990: 56). The difference may seem small or insignificant, but it is this particular difference that a contemporary design anthropology must become sensitive to, with the attendant implication, we suggest, that the relationship between design and anthropology must be recalibrated.

Urban Animals and Us: Design Experiments and Inter-Species Relations

Let us now turn to a more detailed investigation of the experimental practice that came to constitute the design research project 'Urban Animals and Us' (a research project conceived and executed by Tau Ulv Lenskjold and fellow design researcher Li Jönsson in 2013; see also Jönsson 2014, Jönsson and Lenskjold, 2014; 2015). The project unfolded over a period of eight months during which the main site of the project was the care home Grønnehave in the Danish city of Elsinore, Zealand.

As suggested by its title, the project was not solely directed towards life among the elderly residents of Grønnehave. The project itself began well before the collaboration with the care home. It started with curiosity about the prevailing and almost exclusive focus on human actors within the domain of collaborative and participatory design research. This curiosity was, in part, prompted by some of the ideas related to the ontological turn in anthropology described earlier in this chapter. Equally important to the theoretical scaffolding and interest, however, was the fact that this research project was conceived and developed within the disciplinary bounds of collaborative design. The curiosity about other-than-humans and about inter-species relations was approached through particular practices and methods related to co-design. Yet, at the same time, the work of designing prototypes drew heavily on methodologies associated with 'non-rational design' or 'design for ambiguity' (Gaver, Beaver and Benford 2003; Gaver, Hooker and Dunne 2001).

Documenting the pre-project influences is important because it illustrates, albeit superficially, the amalgamation of questions, agendas, disciplinary affiliations and material practices onto which the programmatic starting-point of the project's experimental and constructive research practice is composed (Binder & Redström 2006). It is not only methods and available material language, but also ideas about how designed prototypes can be put to use and for what purpose that inherently precondition any experimental or ontological proposition. Urban Animals and Us is no exception. In the process of designing a workable set-up, as pointed out by Rheinberger, the experimenter finds herself in the middle of an irreducible experimental situation in which concepts and materials are so intertwined that their sensible separation is only really possible in hindsight (1997).

In the case of Urban Animals and Us, the blend of concepts, materials and practices took the project in two directions simultaneously. One of these directions was the introduction to, and subsequent collaboration with, the care home Grønnehave; the other was that of conceptually developing and building – in short, designing – the three prototypes that were later deployed in the care home. In what follows, we will concentrate on the first and second deployment of prototypes.

The deputy manager of Grønnehave gave us permission to work in and around the home, and introduced us to the staff and residents of B1 Ward and the activity centre. They quickly became our most important collaborators in the first part of the process. Our initial visits to Grønnehave allowed us to explore the surrounding areas to see what kinds of urban animals we could 'invite' into the project. As it turned out, the surrounding parkland had a large population of gulls, doves, crows and magpies, so birds became the concretization of the category 'urban animals' towards which we would develop the project.

Dividing their time between a small office-turned-fabrication-space and a wood workshop, the design research team[4] conceptualized, built and tested three different prototypes prior to deployment. In this process, the development of the design concept (designing for inter-species relations) induced a 'borderline moment' between the interiorized thought and the exteriorized object (Drazin 2013: 41): that is, the inter-species design concept enabled the design research team collectively to negotiate a way of materializing the speculative idea of possible new inter-species relations into a workable prototype. At the same time, visualizations of the concept also served as a persuasive device with which to enrol various gatekeepers to support and endorse the project (see Figure 16.1). Notably, the efficacy of the design concept did not extend to the main actors of the project – the birds and seniors. Our use of design concepts was not markedly different from that in conventional design practices. Design concepts in most cases, because of their discursive and representational character, require a capacity for abstract reasoning and verbalization: and this is one element that fundamentally distinguishes such concepts from the experimental prototype, as we shall see.

A Bird's-Eye View Perspective

The first prototype of the series 'Bird's-eye view perspective' was modelled on the trope 'message in a bottle'. It comprised a small plastic container holding a miniature spy-cam, a written 'return-to-sender' request and a rubber-band for attaching a piece of bird food. It was deployed as the centrepiece of a performance we did in conjunction with a workshop in the activity centre, where seniors made fat-balls for birds (see Figure 16.1). The general aim here was to evoke a sense of interest and *co-conditioning* of the agenda: exploring the not-yet-existing senior-bird relations. By co-conditioning we refer to our attempt to assemble seniors and staff around the project as a 'socio-material gathering' (Binder et al. 2011), but also the way our programmatic intentions would become re-articulated in accordance with concretized experiences of the event among the seniors.

We would subsequently use these experiences to precondition and prepare the next experimental set-up. One such experience establishing the contours of the experiments that followed was of the many ways in which the seniors would address

Figure 16.1 Images of design experiments at Grønnehave. (Top left) The Head of the municipal volunteer centre has taken the prototype apart and reads out the 'return-to-sender' message. (Top right) The off-the-shelf spy cam that fits into the puck-sized prototypes. (Middle left) Seniors participating in the workshop are busy making bird fat-balls and attaching bits of food to the prototype. (Middle right) Seniors and staff are watching the bird's-view perspective event unfold. (Bottom left) The prototypes lying on the ground attached with bits of raw fish are waiting for a bird to pick them up. (Bottom right) Gulls are fighting over the food attached to the prototypes © Tau Lenskjold and Li Jönsson

the past rather than the present, as they recollected relationships with long-lost pets, or expressed strong feelings about particular animal encounters. One woman exclaimed: 'I've hated gulls ever since I was frightened by one as a child.'

Prior to the experiment, our time spent with seniors and staff on a number of extended visits had made us aware that the general state of cognitive health among the vast majority of resident seniors was considerably poorer than we had expected.

This proved a challenge to the collaborative intervention we had envisioned, because the workshop format presupposed at least some degree of verbalization and dialogic exchange. In collaboration with the staff of the activity centre, we decided to approach questions of the seniors' relations to the birds through the sensory simulation of mixing coconut oil with seeds and grain to form the fat-balls. The effect was an almost immediate change of mood and atmosphere. At first, most of the seniors were docile and withdrawn. After they mixed the seeds and the grains with the coconut oil, they appeared much more uplifted and engaged. We used the change of atmosphere as a prelude to our performance of the 'birds-view perspective' experiment, with the seniors as spectators (see Figure 16.1).

In itself, the experiment was not a huge success. None of the gulls would carry the boxed spy-cam far enough for someone else to find it. Yet we may say that the experiment succeeded as a transformation of the project's somewhat abstract objective into a collective experience – 'a design thing' – directed towards wild birds. We would subsequently take the sharedness of this experience as a starting-point for inviting those seniors from B1 Ward who had attended the workshop to participate in our next experiment.

The Talk-Into Prototype

The second experiment was developed around the deployment of a prototype entitled the 'Talk-Into'. The 'Talk-Into' consisted of two parts constructed in plywood: a gadget aptly named the Birdflute (a reassembled wind instrument) and a weather-proof loudspeaker. The idea was to place the prototype outside the care home. Like the 'Bird's-view perspective', the 'Talk-Into' is modelled on an existing communication device, namely the duck-caller used by hunters to attract wildfowl. By turning a couple of knobs on the side of the Birdflute and at the same time blowing into the protruding mouthpiece, much as one blows into a recorder, the seniors could choose between three types of bird calls belonging to either a crow, magpie or a blackbird. The variation in available calls was made to resemble a crude vocabulary of sorts by which communication with birds could be initiated (see Figure 16.2).

After a short period of testing the 'Talk-Into' in front of the activity centre, the Birdflute was moved to B1 Ward, where it was placed in the seniors' communal living room. The speaker was tested in various locations adjacent to the ward. After a while, we moved the speaker to the living-room balcony, as we learned that the lack of a visual connection made the experiment too difficult to comprehend for the seniors who took part.

During one of our visits, a dove suddenly appeared on the balcony. This event was greeted with much exhilaration among seniors, staff and ourselves no less. When Inge, one of the seniors, grabbed the Birdflute and sent off a couple of calls, it was hard to tell if the dove responded, but at the very least it did not seem to be scared off. Over the coming weeks, this dove began to take up permanent residence on the balcony. In the following weeks, plates with crumbs and water began to appear

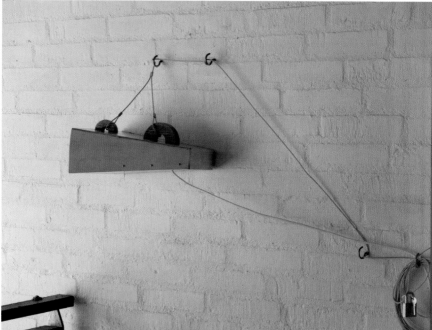

Figure 16.2 A resident is trying out the Talk-Into prototype. (Left) Inge, a resident at Grønnehave, is trying to lure birds with the different bird calls, as Ove, in the background, watches for birds. (Right) The outdoor speaker is placed on the balcony to enable visible contact through the seniors' living room window © Tau Lenskjold and Li Jönsson

Figure 16.3 A resident is feeding the dove on the balcony. Photos taken with a disposable camera handed out to members of the staff and residents at Grønnehave. (Top) Ove is feeding the dove on the balcony with leftovers. (Bottom) The dove became increasingly tame and daring in its pursuit of food © Tau Lenskjold and Li Jönsson

on the balcony (see Figure 16.3). A few of the more able-bodied seniors, among them one man in particular, Ove, started to keep back increasingly large portions of food from meals and bring it out on the balcony, much to the staff's dismay. The dove had apparently become emboldened to the point where it began to cross the balcony threshold and enter the living room. What had been initially instigated as a speculative intervention around the 'Talk-Into' prototype had now, over the course of a few weeks, developed into a series of daily events in which a few of the seniors, despite their frail state, sought to establish and extend an affective interest to form inter-species relations by means of food-sharing. However, by our next visit, the dove had suddenly disappeared. It was no longer to be seen on the balcony. Nor were the plates with the seniors' leftovers. The caretakers dutifully explained that the dove had been removed because the food-sharing practice, and the dove's subsequent attempt to enter the living room, did not comply with health and hygiene regulations. When we enquired into the seniors' reactions, we were told that Ove and his fellow dove-feeders had been given the euphemistic explanation that the dove had been relocated 'to a nice location in the countryside'.

The Autonomous Life of the Material-Speculative Experiment

These events in and of themselves, we might object, do not represent an exciting new example of inter-species relations, hitherto unknown. Perhaps, on the contrary, little could be more ordinary than elderly people feeding urban animals in the park, by the lake or on their balconies. Yet we argue that the events described in the foregoing precisely show how the design-experimental forging of inter-species relations, however precarious and fleeting, enables a situated differentiation between worlds or between ontologies to present itself. Such eventuation of a hybrid seniors–dove collective (Callon 2004) denotes one collective, or world, always in relation to others. As the ontological contours and internal power structures of the hybrid doves–seniors–institution collective are rendered visible, new questions about the nature of the institution, the seniors and the dove and how they could be otherwise, slowly begin to articulate themselves. One could ask, for example, would it not be fair to let the seniors care for the dove as their cognitive abilities decrease, rather than giving so much weight to generic hygienic regulations? Might it be possible to reintroduce the dove without violating the regulations, and, if so, how? One way of pursuing such questions from within design anthropology's arsenal of cultural interpretations and constructive experiments, we contend, would be to proceed by means of materialized speculation that at once restricts and enables the way our object of research takes form – a form that we ourselves are not able to reflect into being.

The practical circumstances, however, illustrate the often-slow endeavour of preparing an experimental set-up. The rigidity of the research programme furthermore did not allow resources or time to develop and execute a new material instantiation of the dove controversy to follow on from the 'Talk-Into'.[5]

The Politics of Generating Ontologies

The controversy, or perhaps the controversy *in potentia*, surrounding the dove and its removal by authority resulted from a slow-paced process of *excorporation* (Latour 1990) – specifically in the material unfolding of food-sharing. Importantly, the working-over of inter-species relations took place from within, but not solely from within the reflexivity of the researcher in charge of the experiment. Rather, experimentation which began as concepts, ideas and questions was *excorporated* and materialized so as to work as speculative and programmatic prompts, and was then formed into interactive prototypes and placed and displaced around Grønnehave, with the purpose of working out the not-yet-relations between the seniors and the doves, from within. And yet, as we have seen, what came out of it was in a certain sense that the enquiry itself was displaced from a concern with inter-species ontologies to a political concern. This exemplifies quite clearly the precariousness and difficulty of forging strong, lasting inter-species relations beyond whatever we are able to imagine.

The leap from an ontological commitment to a possible future political commitment calls for further elaboration. As we have argued, the forms and directions of a future activist engagement cannot be determined in advance, because such future engagement always necessitates a new experiment. The 'Talk-Into' in some ways echoes Eduardo Kohn's endeavour to move beyond the human by means of ethnography. Both enquiries are actively reaching for that which reaches beyond the human (as we know it), and both explorations are radical in their commitment to research as eventuation: that is, to research as a series of events that may or may not elicit what we hoped for. What is inherently different in these approaches is, however, that Kohn may be said to succeed in his experiential endeavour. He transforms his encounters with the Runa into a conceptual and disciplinary exegesis of an 'anthropology beyond the human'. And although it may be argued that the ethnographic mode of description – the fieldwork – and its conceptual framing become intertwined in the text (just as this chapter adds conceptual scaffoldings to the design experiments it recounts), the text is radically removed from the site of the engagement with the Runa. In this respect, it becomes at the very least more controllable and less contingent 'on the ground' than the excorporated materials and attempts to forge relations between doves and seniors allowed us to become. But it also foregrounds a designerly priority of affording change by intervention, in comparison with the body of the experiential-conceptual knowledge that an engagement with residents and doves, or with the Runa, may produce after the fact.

In this respect the design experiment carries an ontological commitment to the 'otherwise', understood as a possible derangement instilled in every arrangement (Provinelli 2014). In our case, the design interventions were specifically tailored to seek out derangements of the normative order: *in the care home, inter-species relations were restricted to highly domesticated animals.* In turn, such a move entails a 'practice of ethics' on the part of the experimenter, understood as an 'effort oriented to the formation of new existents and new planes of existence' (ibid.). Provinelli suggests, in other words, that we focus on establishing platforms for opening and inhabiting alternative worlds. Such worlds hold the potential 'of being raised to the level of politics' (ibid.), just like the experiment that started out as a speculative attempt to forge inter-species relations and ended up as a springboard for political questions about the institution's role in controlling inter-species relationships. The political implications of inter-species relations then would have been a precondition for any new experiment in the attempt to simultaneously unleash (by means of materialized speculations) and account for a *future otherwise*.

Design Anthropology as Material Experimentation

In this chapter we have discussed the consequences of framing design anthropology as a practice that encompasses ontological engagements and material speculations in an exploration of relations that hold the potential to reach beyond the human. Drawing upon the design research project Urban Animals and Us, as well as theoretical reflections in contemporary anthropology related to the ontological turn, we argue that material-speculative experimentation must be understood as a full-blown mode of enquiry in its own right. From a constructive design research position, the promise of ontological work opens for other-than-ethnographic events as potential sites for future-making and knowledge-making. We believe that the field of design anthropology is particularly well equipped to explore the forms of such events.

At the beginning of this chapter we argued briefly for a more symmetrical relation between, on the one hand, design *and* design research, and, on the other hand, anthropology *and* ethnography. This aspiration follows important attempts to reconfigure design anthropology by emphasizing, for example, collaboration, intervention and material speculation as sites of cross-disciplinary innovation.

Somewhat paradoxically, we suggest that for cross-disciplinary fertilization, or even hybridization, towards a distinct style of knowing to take even stronger hold, it is necessary also to acknowledge a distinction between design and design research – perhaps symmetrically positioned to the often-complicated distinction between ethnography and anthropology.[6] Such acknowledgement, we reckon, will constructively complicate, but also enrich, a transdisciplinary engagement and will stifle one-sided subordination to the needs of design or anthropology as disciplines proper. In their litany of semblance and dissemblance between anthropology and design, Murphy and Marcus suggest that anthropology's uneasiness with *making things* stems from the perception that it is 'unnervingly close to *making things up*' (2013: 260). In the project we have presented here, and especially in the way we emphasize the materialized speculation, the distinction between making and making things up is blurred. At the very least we may say that the making of material inter-species relations is not a straightforward matter that is easily constructed. But perhaps it is precisely in sites of disciplinary dissonance and material complication like these that we find the proving ground for new, hybrid modes of knowing in design anthropology.

Notes

1 Authors are listed alphabetically having made equal contribution to this chapter.
2 As noted by Casper Bruun Jensen (2014) the preoccupation with ontology is not confined to anthropology, as it has been discussed in science and technology studies (STS) since the mid-1990s. Likewise a concern with ontology is predominant in particular branches of philosophy; for example in object oriented ontology (OOO), see for example Bryant (2011).
3 In much social theory, Kohn argues, representation is conflated with language (Kohn 2013: 12). But encounters with other beings, for instance forests and jaguars, force us to recognize that seeing and representing, and perhaps even knowing and thinking, are not exclusively human affairs. What unites us with other beings, Kohn asserts, is the fact that how we represent the world is constitutive of our being. Therefore, according to Kohn, anthropology must become attentive to thoughts and forms of representations that do not work like culture and language.
4 Besides design researchers Li Jönsson and Tau Lenskjold, an interaction designer and an architect were employed to collaborate on the various and labour-intensive tasks of designing, crafting and deploying the prototypes.
5 Instead, and following the initial research programme, a final experiment was launched in connection with a new prototype (the Interfed) (Jönsson and Lenskjold 2014; 2015), developed to investigate reciprocally effected representations of species co-habitation.
6 We are well aware that such a dichotomy between anthropology and ethnography is contested in a contemporary context where many regard these terms as inter-changeable descriptors of the same practice. Ingold (2007) has argued against this view and stressed that ethnography and anthropology are not aligned by a 'one-way progression' of the former into the latter; from description into comparative analysis; from the singular event to the generalizable. This, for instance, enables the emergence of methods not related to fieldwork as a technology of description, but to other ways of *doing* anthropology. Holbraad's ontographic methodology (2012: 255–6) can be taken as an example.

References

Binder, T., De Michelis, G., Ehn, P., Jacucci, G., Linde, P. and Wagner, I. (2011), *Design Things,* Cambridge, MA: MIT Press.
Binder, T. and Redström, J. (2006), 'Programs, Experiments and Exemplary Design Research', paper presented at *Design Research Society International Conference*, Lisbon, Portugal.
Bryant, L. (2011), *The Democracy of Objects*, Ann Arbor, MI: MPublishing, University of Michigan Library.

Callon, M. (2004), 'The Role of Hybrid Communities and Socio-technical Arrangements in the Participatory Design Unities', *Journal of the Center for Information Studies*, 5 (3): 3–10.

DiSalvo, C. (2009), 'Design and the Construction of Publics', *Design Issues*, 25 (1): 48–63.

DiSalvo, C. (2012), *Adversarial Design*, Cambridge, MA: MIT Press.

Drazin, A. (2013), 'The Social Life of Concepts in Design Anthropology', in W. Gunn, T. Otto and R. C. Smith (eds.), *Design Anthropology: Theory and Practice*, 33–50, London and New York: Bloomsbury.

Ehn, P. (2008), 'Participation in Design Things: Theory and Practice', in *Proceedings of the Tenth Anniversary Conference on Participatory Design,* 92–101.

Gatt, C. and Ingold, T. (2013), 'From Description to Correspondence: Anthropology in Real Time', in W. Gunn, T. Otto and R. C. Smith (eds.), *Design Anthropology: Theory and Practice*, 139–58, London and New York: Bloomsbury.

Gaver, B., Beaver, J. and Benford, S. (2003), in *Proceedings of the SIGCHI Conference on Human Factors in Computing Systems*, 233–40, New York: ACM.

Gaver, B., Hooker, B. and Dunne, A. (2001), *The Presence Project*, London: RCA Computer Related Design Research Publications.

Gunn, W., Otto, T. and Smith, R. C. (eds.) (2013), *Design Anthropology: Theory and Practice*, London and New York: Bloomsbury.

Holbraad, M. (2009), 'Ontology, Ethnography, Archaeology: An Afterword on the Ontography of Things', *Cambridge Archaeological Journal*, 19 (3): 431–41.

Holbraad, M. (2012), *Truth in Motion: The Recursive Anthropology of Cuban Divination*, Chicago: University of Chicago Press.

Holbraad, M., Pedersen, M. A. and Viveiros de Castro, E. (2014). 'The Politics of Ontology: Anthropological Positions', Fieldsights – Theorizing the Contemporary, *Cultural Anthropology Online*, http://www.culanth.org/fieldsights/462-the-politics-of-ontology-anthropological-positions (accessed 5 January 2016).

Ingold, T. (2007). 'Materials against Materiality'. *Archaeological Dialogues* 14(1): 1–16.

Jensen, C. B. (2014), 'Practical Ontologies', Fieldsights – Theorizing the Contemporary, *Cultural Anthropology Online*, http://www.culanth.org/fieldsights/466-practical-ontologies (accessed 5 January 2016).

Jönsson, L. (2014), *Design Events – On Explorations of a Non-anthropocentric Framework in Design*, PhD dissertation, The Royal Danish Academy of Fine Arts, Schools of Architecture, Design and Conservation, Copenhagen.

Jönsson, L. and Lenskjold, T. (2014), 'A Foray into Not-quite Companion Species: Design Experiments with Urban Animals as Significant Others', *Artifact*, 3 (2): 7.1–7.13.

Jönsson, L. and Lenskjold, T. (2015), 'Stakes at the Edge of Participation: Where Words and Things Are the Entirely Serious Title of a Problem', Proceedings for the Nordic Design Conference *Nordes* 6.

Kohn, E. (2013), *How Forests Think: Toward an Anthropology Beyond the Human*, Oakland, CA: University of California Press.

Kohn, E. (2014), 'What an Ontological Anthropology Might Mean', Fieldsights – Theorizing the Contemporary, *Cultural Anthropology Online*, http://www.culanth.org/fieldsights/463-what-an-ontological-anthropology-might-mean (accessed 5 January 2016).

Koskinen, I., Zimmerman, J., Binder, T., Redström, J. and Wensveen, S. (2011), *Design Research Through Practice: From the Lab, Field, and Showroom*, Waltham, MA: Morgan Kaufmann/Elsevier.

Latour, B. (2005), *Reassembling the Social – An Introduction to Actor-Network-Theory*, Oxford: Oxford University Press.

Latour, B. (1990), 'The Forces and Reason of Experiment', in H. E. Le Grand (ed.), *Experimental Inquiries: Historical, Philosophical and Social Studies of Experimentation in Science*, 49–80, Dordrecht: Kluwer Academic Publishers.

Lenskjold, T. (2015), *Objects of Entanglement and Allure*, PhD dissertation, The Royal Danish Academy of Fine Arts, Schools of Architecture, Design and Conservation, Copenhagen.

Lenskjold, T., Olander, S. and Halse, J. (2015), 'Minor Design Activism: Prompting Change from Within', *Design Issues*, 31 (4): 67–78.

Lindström, K. and Ståhl, Å. (2014), *Patchworking Publics-in-the-Making: Design, Media and Public Engagement*, PhD dissertation, Malmö University.

Murphy, K. M. and Marcus, G. E. (2013), 'Epilogue: Ethnography and Design, Ethnography in Design … Ethnography by Design', in W. Gunn, T. Otto and R. C. Smith (eds.), *Design Anthropology: Theory and Practice*, 251–68, London and New York: Bloomsbury.

Otto, T. and Smith, R. C. (2013), 'Design Anthropology: A Distinct Style of Knowing', in W. Gunn, T. Otto and R. C. Smith (eds.), *Design Anthropology: Theory and Practice*, 1–29, London and New York: Bloomsbury.

Pedersen, M. A. (2012), 'Common Nonsense: A Review of Certain Recent Reviews of the "Ontological Turn"', *Anthropology of This Century* (5), http://aotcpress.com/articles/common_nonsense/ (accessed 5 January 2016).

Provinelli, E. A. (2014), 'Geontologies of the Otherwise', Fieldsights – Theorizing the Contemporary, *Cultural Anthropology Online*, http://www.culanth.org/fieldsights/465-geontologies-of-the-otherwise (accessed 5 January 2016).

Rheinberger, H.-J. (1997), *Toward a History of Epistemic Things: Synthesizing Proteins in the Test Tube*, Stanford, CA: Stanford University Press.

17 The Things We Do: Encountering the Possible

THOMAS BINDER

There are certain moments that have become particularly important for me in my work with what my colleagues and I call the design laboratory. A colleague once captured one of these moments by saying, 'Now it is as if the lid has come off and everything is possible.' In moments like this, we encounter the possible as a path to pursue, a landscape to venture into: a path that does not break away from the present, but on the contrary opens a way from the well-known everyday of the collaborators towards the world of the 'what if' of virtuality, instrumented and mediated by the collaborative encounter. These moments grow out of the collaborative encounter, which in my view sits at the very heart of the design anthropological project, but the encounter is not in any way confined to the here-and-now of such moments. It spans, temporally and spatially, both studio and field; and, just as encountering the possible seamlessly connects to and yet also expands what is already there, such an encounter also invokes a landscape of time and space that extends both back towards the past and forward beyond the horizon of the present.

In this chapter I will explore the things we do as they unfold in these moments of becoming, in the light of the bodily-material engagements that make up the design anthropological encounter.

Transformations in Design and Anthropology

The last two decades have brought professional design practices into contact with new venues of social change and innovation (Thackara 2006). This has resulted in a certain vagueness as to what constitutes design. What kind of bodily-material engagements with 'the design situation' coming out of the classical studio tradition can still be seen as hallmarks of professional design practices? To what extent are these engagements turning collaborative, as clients and other stakeholders participate in 'design thinking' and escape the confines of the studio? And what is the efficacy in time and space of the outcomes of these engagements? Are they solidified imprints of negotiated intent, to be implemented or 'rolled out' in a larger context of 'use'? Or are they evocative *things* that live only as traces of collaborative engagement? In mainstream design, these issues are largely dealt with through adherence to the inertia of genres and styles of traditional design professionalism;

but they are more pressing in the new cluster of emerging design fields showcased in this volume, all of which have at their core the coming together of designerly proposals and anthropological explorations. This is true of my own field, co-design, as well as social design, speculative design and design activism. To locate oneself in these emerging fields with a commitment to the genealogies of design and design research (as well as the discourse of design anthropology) raises questions about modes of engagement and outcomes that echo those taken up in this volume from the perspective of anthropology.

Marcus (this volume) argues that anthropology today is 'pushed back' towards fieldwork as richer and more collaborative modes of engagement are bringing prototypical concepts into circulation in the field. At the same time he maintains that it is through the ethnography that anthropology reaches a larger audience and he discusses how to balance the emphasis of fieldwork and ethnography. This immediately resonates with discussions within collaborative design on how to relate practices of design participation to the production of design artefacts. In the field of co-design, too, we can see collaborative encounters fuelled by design prototypes that experimentally and conceptually explore the everyday in ways that point towards design accomplishments going beyond the here-and-now of the encounter; and in design, too, we are prone to commit to our professional constituency by ensuring that these accomplishments are compatible with the legacy of the design field. In Marcus's argument, the ethnography provides the platform for the anthropologist to contribute to the genealogy of anthropology. Though he argues strongly for evocative methodologies of fieldwork (inspired by design and artistic practices) that can enhance the anthropological richness of the collaborative encounter, the encounter remains from this perspective somewhat instrumental in relation to what is accomplished through the ethnography. Here a parallel can be drawn with the traditions of speculative and critical design, in which design objects stemming from engagements with controversies are prepared for display at conventional design venues (as in the work of Dunne and Raby, see Dunne and Raby 2013).

Ingold (2008; Gatt and Ingold 2013) takes a different stance on how anthropology may be reinvigorated through leaning on practices of design. For Ingold, it is not the ethnography, but the participant observation of the anthropologist that forms the base of anthropological engagement. Through the collaborative encounter, a correspondence is established between the anthropologist and his or her collaborators, and it is through that encounter that possible worlds come into being. Rather than being represented through ethnography, that encounter, according to Ingold, must be made to unfold through collaboratively *making* things that can draw upon practices of design. Ingold's position also resonates with perspectives from design and design research, which see design engagements as the staging and enactment of design things. Drawing on the German etymology of the word 'thing' and following Heidegger, this is taken to denote an assembly of people and artefacts constituting a matter of concern (Telier et al. 2011). Here the collaborative encounter, in Ingold's terminology, becomes the thing that comes to life through what it draws together;

and the bodily-material presence of this thing can only be transported from the here-and-now of its engagement through re-invoking the traces that engagement leaves behind.

Taken together, the contributions of Marcus and Ingold define a design anthropology in which the collaborative encounter takes centre stage, as a third space of becoming. This third space draws upon and informs anthropological discourse, yet cannot be reduced either to the prototypes that flow into it or to the accounts it invokes. Both Marcus and Ingold remind us that the encounter is fuelled by the differences and frictions between those who are coming together, but they are relatively vague on what this coming together entails. To get to a parallel conceptualization of design anthropology that unpacks the objects and practices of design in this encounter, we will need to get to grips with the bodily-material engagements through which the correspondences between these differences are performed. Within a discourse of design and design research, design is ambiguous and enchanting in Bennett's words (cited in Khan 2009) through 'affective effects in excess of its intention'. From a design perspective, the design anthropological encounter must, in my view, be grasped through an embrace of this enchantment, as it emanates from the moments of becoming that I briefly touched upon at the opening of this chapter.

But before getting closer to these moments of becoming and the experiential qualities of the bodily-material engagements of the encounter, let me briefly introduce the collaborative encounters of the design-research practice that we call the design laboratory.

From Participatory Third Space to Design Laboratory

The participatory design tradition in which my colleagues and I have conducted our work provides a rich repertoire of tools and techniques for staging collaborative encounters between otherwise disparate communities (Brandt, Binder and Sanders 2013). From very early on, those encounters have been foregrounded as a space of mutual learning (Lanzara 1991), a coming together of language games (Ehn 1988), or a third space (Muller and Druin 2007), which, whatever the specific conceptualization, is seen as much more than a negotiation of interests between different stakeholders. Unlike for example Bødker, Kensing and Simonsen (2004), who brought participatory approaches to systems design, or Björgvinsson, Ehn and Hillgren (2010), who explored the role of things or infrastructures in participatory community development, we have not committed to a particular genre of design or a specific topical field. The centrepiece in our research has been the staging of collaborative encounters and the formation of third spaces in which everyday experiences are reconstructed through design interventions. We call this research practice *design laboratories,* making dual reference both to the Deweyan approach to open-ended experimentation (which we appropriated mainly through the work of Donald Schön 1987) and to the work of STS scholars such as Callon (2004) and Latour (2005), who have convincingly shown how the power of the scientific laboratory is inherently associated with its porosity in networked relationships between people and things. Rather than being confined to a particular place or a particular event, we see the design laboratory as a social space, a landscape of agency, unfolding through a series of collaborative engagements. When we started to talk about the design laboratory, it was often staged through a number of linked workshops in which people came together to explore overlapping issues through repeated cycles of staging, evoking and enacting what we called possible futures (Binder 2007). Later, we extended and expanded our repertoire of engagements in time and space. We staged design laboratories to unfold both in compressed formats like the one-day fieldshop (Halse in Halse et al. 2010) and in long-term collaborations resembling living labs (Brandt et al. 2012). In so doing we went further, embracing perspectives of emergence and performativity of network agency, as we conceptually and practically loosened our emphasis on discrete events and sought rather to accommodate the frictions of collaboration (Tsing 2005) between networks that only partly overlapped (Binder et al. 2011).

What to us makes the design laboratory coherent as a design-research practice is a particular set of strategies and instrumentations that, with reference to Rheinberger (1994), create an experimental system that is capable of producing difference without deteriorating (for an elaboration of the perspective of Rheinberger in relation to the design laboratory, see Olander 2014). In Halse et al. (2010), we name these strategies *exploratory enquiry*, *generative prototyping* and *sustained participation*. This means that we bring together a network of collaborators with whom we simultaneously research and prototypically intervene in the everyday practices that they (and we) bring to the collaboration. We commit to this collaboration of the laboratory as an on-going rehearsal of possible futures. The implicit references to the world of theatre and performance studies become even more pronounced in the instrumentation of the laboratory, where from an early stage the tradition of forum theatre was a formative influence (Brandt and Grunnet 2000). Alternating between estrangement and familiarization, we intermingle the re-enactment of everyday practices with a probing for glitches and breaches, through engagements with evocative props. The formats and media we employ range from video documentary to puppet theatre and concept design games (Brandt, Messeter and Binder 2008); and though *we* here can in a narrow sense be seen as the design-research group providing these formats and media, the *we* of the design laboratory always emerges through the collaborative encounter between researchers and the people who choose to join them in the lab. In Rheinberger's terms the difference produced in the laboratory is the enactment of a different everyday made actual through its bodily-material manifestations, yet deliberately performed or shown within the confines of the laboratory (and in this way separating it from, for example, action research). These are of course only coarse pointers to a particular research practice, but perhaps sufficient to indicate both the genealogy of our approach and my concern for coming to terms with the laboratory encounter also as encompassing moments of transformation.

Enacting a Different (Every-)Day at the Plant

I will start by revisiting a very specific encounter with a group of industrial process-operators with whom my colleagues and I worked some years ago. As a research group we were interested in approaches to process control and instrumentation that let process-operators configure their view of, and interactions with, operating process installations in ways that augmented their skilful practices of keeping the plant running (Nilsson et al. 2000). We also had a wider interest in expanding the interaction design for ubiquitous computing so as to encompass devices that transcended the separation between tools and automated systems. With this interest we negotiated a collaboration with a group of process-operators at a local waste-water plant who agreed to team up with us for a number of visits and workshops. On the first visit I teamed up with Rolf, a middle-aged process-operator who received me with some reluctance towards the project I wanted to involve him in. We had agreed to be together for half a day, and I persuaded him to have my video camera turned on throughout my visit. At first he showed me the plant control room and his office, and I did not have much to ask. The plant environment and what he told me about his work was overwhelming, and I had not come to learn about his background, the central control-room installation or the community life in the office corridor. Eventually he started his daily round, and something started to happen. He touched pumps, he listened to the flow of tubes, he noted the smell of the waste-water basins, and quite often he was on the intercom to discuss or exchange information with his fellow operators. My questions started to come more fluently, and with the directed camera as a very visible indication of my interests, Rolf began to tell stories about what he did, stories that presented him as the competent process-operator, with whom I wanted to get acquainted. Sometimes I was distracted, sometimes he was impatient, and through these imperfections we found a mode of conversation that ran smoothly onto my video recorder. After the visit, my colleagues, who had followed other process-operators, and I edited our video material into condensed accounts of our visits, which we brought back for discussion and confirmation. The tone of our collaboration loosened up, and while Rolf maintained his authoritative voice when the camera was running, he also started to joke and tell stories about what else process-operator work is about, when the camera was turned off.

The next stage was for us as researchers to bring in our ideas for a different kind of portable process control. At an afternoon workshop we brought very coarse cardboard mock-ups of small, medium and large screens and devices that we suggested using to 'dress up' the plant. We introduced the mock-ups by showing more closely edited videos from the earlier visits, highlighting what we saw as salient aspects of the operator work, and we ended our presentation by asking what uses they could think of for our cardboard devices. There was very little discussion. The atmosphere was friendly, but also somehow loaded with a sense that the researchers were undergoing a test, which the process-operators had not yet decided if they had passed. I asked if Rolf would be willing to take us on a tour where he could show us what the devices could do; when he agreed, I had very little idea where he would take us. We started walking to some of the places he had taken me before, and as we walked, we started talking again, as on the first visit. The camera was on, and as we went along Rolf pointed out where he might put the various screens and how he might use the device. There was no script, but a probing and groping into what the cardboard mock-ups could do that was improvised as we took clues from the environment. We ended the day by agreeing that I would come back a few days later to shoot a video story of the cardboard in use.

The day of the shooting became another of those moments when 'the lid came off'. I came with a colleague and a student, and very soon the student was taken on the same tour I had had on my first visit. Rolf moved around with the cardboard mock-ups and willingly explained to the student how he was leaving messages for fellow operators, adjusting a faulty meter, setting up a monitoring unit for a part of the plant that was malfunctioning. Rolf had his authoritative voice, which I already knew, and had no hesitation in detailing the operation of the fictitious devices or elaborating on an imagined collaboration with his colleagues. We later found out that Rolf had had quite lengthy discussions with his colleagues of how to use our cardboard products, but in the situation there was nothing that seemed scripted or make-believe, apart from a slight flush in Rolf's face or a sudden change of voice as he turned to us at the end of the walk and asked, 'Was it okay?'

For us as researchers, it was more than okay. The baton had been passed on, and we had just witnessed Rolf enacting a story of distributed plant control that we had only vaguely envisioned. When the video of this tour was later screened for the whole group of process-operators, we felt that they too were looking into a slightly altered world of process control which we would be able to enter over and over again. I still know very little about Rolf. I never interviewed him or followed up on the leads he gave me about how the work of process-operators often means long and boring hours in front of a computer screen where not much is happening. But for many years I have shown the video of Rolf to students, process-operators and fellow researchers, and still today, more than fifteen years later, it seems to convey a world of working with computing in industry that is both a vision and a very present realm of the possible into which the spectator can step.

When writing up this anecdotal account of my work with Rolf and his and my colleagues I am taken through a recollection of previous accounts and conceptu-alizations that I have performed on these and similar episodes. In some of my first writings on this I emphasized the role of the video camera in setting a stage for improvisation and reflection on an everyday in transition (Binder 1999; Buur, Binder and Brandt 2000). The going back and forth between producing video footage and screening edited videos created, in my view, a reflective dialogue with the situation much in line with Schön's conceptualization of design as a dialogue with the materials of a design situation (Schön 1987). Along with these writings I also wrote other texts that discussed the concepts of tools and skills in the light of the way Rolf performed his imagined practice with our cardboard mock-ups (Binder 2002). In the following years we got more acquainted with performance studies and particularly the work of Victor Turner and Richard Schechner. With Turner (1982) we started to see what was invoked in the collaboration as a liminoid space not ritualized yet betwixt and between, that could be playfully explored. Schechner (2011) gave us a vocabulary from the theatre that made us see Rolf as part of a kind of everyday theatre, in which exercises and rehearsals could eventually be turned into performances. What stands out for me in this recollection as I relate it to the account of this text is the absence of the collaborative encounter. Schechner insists that a performance has an audience and that it has a beginning and end. He would also say that what Rolf performs is a showing of what could be done rather than a doing of a different practice. Schechner's and Turner's perspectives are still productive for understanding how the subjunctive 'what if' is actualized in Rolf's performance. In this account I have however deliberately sought the open-endedness of the anecdote suggested by Michael (in Lury and Wakeford 2012) to acknowledge that the moment of becoming implicates a very particular entanglement of bodily-material participation that encompasses both me, Rolf, camcorder, process plant, cardboard etc. As I see it, the anecdote hints at a kind of fieldwork in which successive attempts to converse and correspond intermingle with the making of prototypical concepts and devices in such a way that both agency (like Rolf leaving imaginary messages to his colleagues) and things (like 'dressed up' plants, configurable screens and video scenarios) grow out of the encounter. What emerges as an object of design is a different plant operator and his companion researcher as they are enacted in the here-and-now of the video recording. This object of design is constituted by the things we do in the encounter, and it can only be re-invoked as these things open up towards new encounters.

Playing Around in the Office

What are then the practices of design that flow into the collaborative encounter and how does the issue of collaboration shape the encountering of the possible? Collaboration is, as Marcus also points out elsewhere in this volume, a precondition of fieldwork and not what forms the particularity of the encounter. While in the previous example I brought an anecdote that points towards design as a sort of event (for an elaboration of design as events see Jönsson 2015), in the following I will write up an anecdote that positions the moments of becoming separate from the immediate engagements with collaboration.

Some years ago we were commissioned with some colleagues to propose a methodology for employee involvement in office design (Binder and Lundsgaard 2014). As a case study, we had the opportunity to work with employees and management in one of the offices of a particular municipality. Our research group had already visited the office several times, and we had met most of the office staff at an introductory meeting. We had prepared postcard-size photos of the office taken on our first walk-through, and we prompted our first encounter with the office by asking people at the introductory meeting to collect any postcards they found interesting and to discuss why they thought the researchers had taken those particular photos. This started off the collaboration well, and by the time of the occasion I describe below we were all well acquainted. This time, it was not in a direct encounter in the office, but back in our research quarters that my colleague Christina and I experienced an opening into a world of the possible. We had been processing a number of workbooks filled out by the office staff in pairs so as to give us a visualization of how they moved about following particular paths and rhythms over the day, the week and the year. In the workbooks there were also little portraits of one another drawn by the pairs using photos of typical places and typical activities supplemented with drawings and handwritten text. As we went through the material, we were struck by the abundance of stories prompted by the photos. We could see how the office formed different landscapes, from the calm back office of local officials working for the politicians, to the intensity of preparing major sports events of the almost call-centre-like group of office workers in direct contact with members of the public.

But the episode I want to get to is further down the line. We were preparing design games for playing at the next workshop. One was called the landscape game. It offered a small selection of game-boards, marked with various abstract

Figure 17.1 Dreaming up different offices. Office workers are exploring their 'dream office' by playing design games with images from the well-known everyday at work. The dream office could be like this, but it could also be like this; and it is hard to tell whether what was emerging on the game-boards was how it was, or how we would like it to be © Christina Lundsgaard

topological patterns (a series of circles, parallel lines, overlapping elliptical patterns) for the workshop participants to choose between as they explored their 'dream office'. On the game-board, the participants were encouraged to take turns, placing and naming photos of locations and activities as they envisioned them best accommodated in the office. As in previous projects, Christina and I tried out the landscape game ourselves, to see if we could get it to work for us. We certainly could. We played for hours, becoming less and less role-players simulating the imagined role-play of our collaborators; less and less researchers and game designers trying out the mechanics of our game. We became adventurers of the game universe, which presented itself to us as increasingly real. The dream office could be like this, but it could also be like this; and in the fluidity of game moves and repeated replay, it was as if a mastery of the workspace was being played out, in a way that made it hard to tell whether what was emerging on the game-boards was how it was, or how we would like it to be. As with the process-operators and researchers in my first example, we were in the design game inhabiting *emergent landscapes of design*. The experience of a process-operator acting out a possible reality on a scale of 1:1 and of office workers and researchers moving indexical photos from a work context around on a game-board may seem very different; but across these differences, I can again see the possible standing out, not as choices between options, nor yet as agency to be exercised or not exercised, but as contingent landscapes, to be travelled and traversed with grace and ease.

I have deliberately edited this account without reference to what was accomplished through the design game. In the project that the anecdote stems from we were asked to provide tools that facilitate a dialogue between architects and office workers, and there was also in our own thinking a concern for how to mediate between the professional competencies of spatial planning of the architects and the (similarly professional) work practices of the office. In earlier writings on similar projects we have emphasized the collaboration across these differences and the role of design artefacts in providing boundary objects that connect and translate across these differences (Johansson et al. 2002). What, in my view, becomes particularly pronounced as we see these kinds of engagements as correspondences emanating from the encounters is, however, the coherence of situated practices of improvisation that do not exhaust or complete the inquiry. Instead they rather extend and enchant the realm of the present. As I have attempted to portray in the anecdotes, such improvisations are not residing exclusively with either design researchers or their collaborators, but are performances of a design practice that can only be brought to life through the encounter.

It is All Already Here!

My last anecdote comes from a series of encounters my colleagues and I had with a loose network of senior citizens and local municipal officials concerned with how the municipality could support community-building around mundane everyday activities like shopping and outdoor workouts. At the time, our research group was increasingly concerned with how to conceive of the interplay between our research agenda and our contributions to a wider community of design researchers on the one hand, and on the other hand our involvement in, and contribution to, changing local welfare policies, such as in the project I will report from in the following (see Binder et al. 2011). We asked ourselves if we could fuse the two different languages of involvement and accountability (one of research and one of the particular encounter) and how in doing so we could maintain the difference between ourselves and our collaborators that fuelled our encounters. One of the leads that became productive in our grappling with these questions was, again, the performance studies literature and particularly the writings of Barba, Fallesen and Larsen (1994). Barba et al. are interested in the pre-expressive qualities of theatrical acting and, though he shares with Schechner a broad definition of performances that also may accommodate design rehearsals such as those we have been involved with, his main focus is not, as with Schechner, on completion but rather on openings and attunement. In the anecdote that follows I have particularly been concerned with Barba et al.'s advice to the actor, that he must always be at two places at once: on the moon (of the stage) and in his hometown (of his mind).

Our research group was introduced to various community centres in which many seniors were active. Here we met Ketty and the women she met with once a week to knit sweaters for deprived children in Belarus. Part of our job in the project was to propose redesigns of social-media and mobile technologies which would make them relevant and appealing to seniors as a way of getting together with old or new acquaintances (Foverskov and Binder 2011). To recruit people for the project workshops, we had prepared a visual dialogue tool which invited miniature accounts of what we termed 'a good day', and also exposed and invited commentary on our initial design ideas. Ketty and a number of her friends accepted our invitation to take part in three workshops, though she persistently made it clear to us that 'mobile phones were not her thing'. In the workshops, we worked once again with the staging and enactment of fictitious stories of how seniors can come together, built implicitly or explicitly on collected stories of the 'good days'. In mixed groups of researchers, seniors and local officials, we produced doll scenarios about getting together. The scenarios were immediately video-recorded and screened for all the participants towards the end of the workshop. Between the workshops, the research group visited some of the participating seniors to pursue ideas or contexts raised within the workshops, and we also invited Ketty and her friends to visit us at the design school, both to take part in a project seminar and to meet our colleagues in the knitting department.

In the second workshop, the researchers had prepared new doll scenarios elaborating on what had been produced at the previous session; but they now brought in props that hinted at generic communication tools such as *the messenger*, *the seeker* and *the display*, which allowed the seniors to address several distinct networks of friends of which they saw themselves as a member. Again, the scenarios were

Figure 17.2 Reaching into a different everyday. Ketty seized the messenger, a large cardboard tube, and started to call her friend across the table to suggest an imaginary trip to the shopping centre. But she was still sceptical about mobile phones: 'My children say I should get one, but I really don't want to' © Maria Foverskov

commented on, and tentatively reworked. Ketty was still sceptical about mobile phones: 'My children say I should get one, but I really don't want to.' Despite this, she seized the prop called the messenger, a large cardboard tube, and started to call her friend across the table to suggest an imaginary trip to the shopping centre.

For the last workshop, we in the research group decided that we and the municipal officials had to put ourselves more explicitly on stage. Instead of asking the seniors to prepare stories and scenarios, we collected footage and rehearsed scenarios that re-enacted what the seniors had already presented to us, but in the voice of our role as designers and researchers. We prepared a 1:1 enactment of the polished scenarios, this time acted out in a forum-theatre format by the research group and the local officials, with the seniors as the audience. In the scenario presented to Ketty and her friends, we envisioned a group of seniors invited to a workout session with a fitness instructor in a local park. In the scenario, a lot of attention was paid to how the various individuals contacted each other to discuss whether they wanted to participate, and along the way the scenario brought up additional interactions in the network, including giving advice on outfits to buy at an autumn sale. Communication was supported by a mix of media, ranging from the physical noticeboard at the local senior-citizen activity centre to a smartphone communication on a particular social-media platform envisioned by the researchers. We had cautiously included topics and perspectives previously discussed with the seniors, including dialogue taken almost literally from the participants' earlier suggestions. To take advantage of the forum-theatre format, the scenario was played through once, then divided up into shorter episodes on which the audience could comment and propose changes. There were several comments and suggestions and the episodes were reworked a number of times until actors and audience felt satisfied. The moment of becoming that I want to address however came almost as an after-thought when Ketty, after the final applause, commented to all of us, with a mood of satisfaction, that 'it is all already here'.

Such a comment could mean that nothing was accomplished, or that Ketty had seen it all before, but as I sat with Ketty in this aftermath of more than three months of engagements I felt that a *we* had been formed that could now transgress the boundaries of workshops and visits. Ketty and I had both 'entered the moon' as we acted out and witnessed a virtual community of work-out seniors in public parks, but we had also both remained in our respective 'home towns' though, through the encounter, these had come closer together. In the year that followed, researchers, seniors and municipal officials met every second Friday for a work-out in the park and we learned that design collaborations can continue to be experiments.

Towards Hope in an Experimental Practice of Design Anthropology

The moments I have tried to present in this paper are not moments that we can plan or control. They grow from the design anthropological encounter as an experience of simultaneously becoming knowledgeable and taking possession of agency to enter emerging landscapes (Telier et al. 2011). This experience is not, as suggested by, for example, Bødker (2011), a breakdown in the flow of the everyday that separates us from acting in the world. Neither is it a moment of starting on a journey towards accomplishing a goal (though this may very well come later). Rather, I see these moments as *actuals* in Schechner's terms – the outcome of staged encounters in which the subjunctive 'what if' touches upon the real. Actuals perform the possible as a potentiality that becomes almost tangibly present. In the design laboratory, it is this actualization of the movement of the present that is both exposed and held back as an experience of difference. It is not action as either a cause or an effect of networks, but a moment of *becoming* which, paradoxically, is at the same time both imagined and real.

In my view, these moments of actualization, staged as I have attempted to portray them here through a varied set of formative practices, come about through the things we do as design enchants the here-and-now of the encounter. The prototype of the process plant as one large control interface, accessible and configurable to the process-operator through a range of imagined devices made present as rough cardboard mock-ups, becomes 'real' as it is acted out by Rolf in his own environment in front of a camera that presents him and me on video to his colleagues. My colleague Christina and I become absorbed in improvisations within various municipal office practices as we play our way through collages of visual fieldwork notes, bricolaged on top of game-boards that hinge onto topologies of generic office layouts so as to emphasize variations in temporal rhythm. Ketty and her companions experience themselves as on the brink of entering a different world of working out in a public park, as assistive technologies become props for an authorized presence as fellow citizens. This is design radicalized as an experiment in the here-and-now; it points to there-and-then only in the moments of its becoming. No ethnography is needed to account for this experiment. One may be produced that can build on the intermediaries that emanate from this encounter, and such an ethnography may very well contribute to new contraptions or conceptual prototypes that can re-enter the zone of experimentation; but this is largely external to the design anthropological encounter. What is accomplished and completed in terms of design similarly challenges the traditional status of the design object. Design is propositional, but in the moments of actualization presented here as the accomplishment of design experiments, the care and diligence through which design enchants the here-and-now cannot be separated from this accomplishment. The design proposal becomes a thing around which to gather, a thing that is not detached from what it invokes. As discussed by Miyazaki (2006), a proposal that encompasses both the past and the future may open up towards the present through a method of hope that makes the moment of becoming one that can be attended to through potential agency. To achieve such openness, we may think of such design things as invoking performances that are genuinely experimental (Binder et al. 2015). But following Miyazaki these design experiments must address hope methodologically as an inventive coming together of aspirations and genealogies of which one cannot re-present the other. Schechner argues that we experience and perform the actual not as *me,* not as *not-me,* but as *not-not-me.* It is precisely when we chance upon this extended presence between several here-and-nows that something is produced in the design laboratory.

References

Barba, E., Fallesen, A. and Larsen, N. (1994), 'En Kano af Papir', Gråsten: Forlaget Drama.

Binder, T. (1999), 'Setting the Stage for Improvised Video Scenarios', in *Proceedings of the CHI'99 Extended Abstracts on Human Factors in Computing Systems*, New York: ACM Press.

Binder, T. (2002), 'Intent, Form, and Materiality in the Design of Interaction Technology', in Y. Dietrich (ed.), *Social Thinking-Software Practice*, 451–68, Cambridge, MA: MIT Press.

Binder, T. (2007), 'Why Design: Labs', in *Proceedings of the Nordic Design Research Conference* (2).

Binder, T., Brandt, E., Halse, J., Foverskov, M., Olander, S. and Yndigegn, S. (2011), 'Living the (Co-Design) Lab', in *Proceedings of the Nordic Design Research Conference* (4).

Binder, T., Brandt, E., Ehn, P. and Halse, J. (2015), 'Democratic Design Experiments: Between Parliament and Laboratory', *CoDesign*, 11 (3–4): 152–65.

Binder, T. and Lundsgaard, C. (2014), 'Designdialoger om Rum og Arbejde', *Tidskrift for Arbejdsliv*, 16 (2): 30–45.

Björgvinsson, E., Ehn, P. and Hillgren, P.-A. (2010), 'Participatory Design and "Democratizing Innovation"', in *Proceedings of the Biennial Participatory Design Conference*, 41–50, New York: ACM.

Brandt, E., Binder, T. and Sanders, E. (2013), 'Tools and Techniques: Ways of Engaging Telling, Making and Enacting', in J. Simonsen and T. Robertson (eds.), *Routledge International Handbook of Participatory Design*, New York: Routledge.

Brandt, E. and Grunnet, C. (2000), 'Evoking the Future: Drama and Props in User-Centred Design', in *Proceedings of Participatory Design Conference*, 11–20, New York: ACM Press.

Brandt, E., Messeter, J. and Binder, T. (2008), 'Formatting Design Dialogues – Games and Participation', *CoDesign – International Journal of CoCreation in Design and the Arts*, 4 (1): 51–64.

Brandt, E., Mortensen, P. F., Malmborg, L., Binder, T. and Sokoler, T. (eds.) (2012), *SeniorInteraktion: Innovation gennem Dialog,* Copenhagen: Royal Danish Academy of Fine Arts, Schools of Architecture, Design and Conservation.

Buur, J., Binder, T. and Brandt, E. (2000), 'Taking Video beyond "Hard Data" in User-centred Design', in *Proceedings of Participatory Design Conference*, 21–9, New York: ACM Press.

Bødker, K., Kensing, F. and Simonsen, J. (2004), *Participatory IT Design: Designing for Business and Workplace Realities*, Cambridge, MA: MIT Press.

Bødker, S. (2011), 'Use is Everywhere and Changing: Analysis and Design with the Human-Artifact Model', in *Proceedings of the European Conference on Cognitive Ergonomics*, 3–10, New York: ACM Press.

Callon, M. (2004), 'The Role of Hybrid Communities and Socio-Technical Arrangements in the Participatory Design', *Journal of the Centre for Information Studies*, 5 (3): 3–10.

Dunne, A. and Raby, F. (2013), *Speculative Everything: Design, Fiction, and Social Dreaming*, Cambridge, MA: MIT Press.

Ehn, P. (1988), *Work-Oriented Design of Computer Artifacts*, Stockholm: Arbetslivscentrum.

Foverskov, M. and Binder, T. (2011), 'SUPER DOTS: Making Social Media Tangible for Senior Citizens', in *Proceedings of the DPPI Conference*, Milan, http://dl.acm.org/citation.cfm?id=2347575&CFID=587119898&CFTOKEN=33782816 (accessed 28 February 2016).

Gatt, C. and Ingold, T. (2013), 'From Description to Correspondence: Anthropology in Real Time', in W. Gunn, T. Otto and R. C. Smith (eds.), *Design Anthropology: Theory and Practice*, 139–58, London and New York: Bloomsbury.

Halse, J., Brandt, E., Clark, B. and Binder, T. (eds.) (2010), *Rehearsing the Future*, Copenhagen: Danish Design School Press.

Ingold, T. (2008), 'Anthropology is *Not* Ethnography', in *Proceedings of the British Academy*, 154: 69–92.

Johansson, M., Fröst, P., Brandt, E., Binder, T. and Messeter, J. (2002), 'Partner Engaged Design: New Challenges For Workplace Design', in *Proceedings of Participatory Design Conference*, 162–72.

Jönsson, L. (2015), *Design Events: On Explorations of a Non-anthropocentric Framework in Design*, PhD dissertation, Copenhagen: Royal Danish Academy of Fine Arts, Schools of Architecture, Design and Conservation.

Khan, G. (2009), 'Agency, Nature and Emergent Properties: An Interview with Jane Bennett', *Contemporary Political Theory*, 8 (1): 90–105.

Lanzara, G. F. (1991), 'Shifting Stories: Learning from a Reflective Experiment in a Design Process', in D. Schön (ed.), *The Reflective Turn – Case Studies in and on Educational Practice*, 285–320, New York: Teachers College Press.

Latour, B. (2005), *Reassembling the Social – An Introduction to Actor-Network-Theory*, Oxford: Oxford University Press.

Lury, C. and Wakeford, N. (eds.) (2012), *Inventive Methods: The Happening of the Social*, Oxford: Routledge.

Miyazaki, H. (2006). *The Method of Hope: Anthropology, Philosophy, and Fijian Knowledge*, Palo Alto, CA: Stanford University Press.

Muller, M. J. and Druin, A. (2007), 'Participatory Design: The Third Space in HCI (revised)', in J. Jacko and A. Sears (eds.), *Handbook of HCI*, 2nd edn, Mahwah, NJ: Lawrence Erlbaum Associates.

Nilsson, J., Sokoler, T., Binder, T. and Wetcke, N. (2000), 'Beyond the Control Room: Mobile Devices for Spatially Distributed Interaction', *Handheld and Ubiquitous Computing*, 30–45.

Olander, S. (2014), *The Network Lab: A Proposal for Design-Anthropological Experimental Set-ups in Cultural Work and Social Research*, PhD dissertation, Copenhagen: Royal Danish Academy of Fine Arts, Schools of Architecture, Design and Conservation.

Rheinberger, H. J. (1994), 'Experimental Systems: Historiality, Narration, and Deconstruction', *Science in Context*, 7 (1): 65–81.

Schechner, R. (2011), *Between Theatre and Anthropology*, Philadelphia, PA: University of Pennsylvania Press.

Schön, D. A. (1987), *Educating the Reflective Practitioner*, San Francisco: Jossey-Bass.

Telier, A., Binder, T., De Michelis, G., Ehn, P., Jacucci, G. and Wagner, I. (2011), *Design Things*, Cambridge, MA: MIT Press.

Thackara, J. (2006), *In the Bubble: Designing in a Complex World*, Cambridge, MA: MIT Press.

Tsing, A. L. (2005), *Friction: An Ethnography of Global Connection*, Princeton, NJ: Princeton University Press.

Turner, V. W. (1982), *From Ritual to Theatre: The Human Seriousness of Play*, Cambridge, MA: MIT Press.

Index